Visual Basic® 6: Design, Specification, and Objects

ISBN 0-13-085084-5

90000

9 780130 850843

PRENTICE HALL°SERIES ON MICROSOFT® TECHNOLOGIES

PRENTICE HALL SERIES ON MICROSOFT® TECHNOLOGIES

BILLY S. HOLLIS

Visual Basic® 6: Design, Specification, and Objects

Prentice Hall PTR, Upper Saddle River, NJ 07458
http://www.phptr.com

Editorial/Production Supervision: Nicholas Radhuber
Acquisitions Editor: Mike Meehan
Cover Design Director: Jerry Votta
Cover Designer: Anthony Gemmellaro
Manufacturing Manager: Pat Brown
Series Design: Gail Cocker-Bogusz
Marketing Manager: Bryan Gambrel

Prentice Hall books are widely used by corporations and government agencies for
training, marketing, and resale. The publisher offers discounts on this book when
ordered in bulk quantities. For more information, contact:

Corporate Sales Department,
Prentice Hall PTR
One Lake Street
Upper Saddle River, NJ 07458
Phone: 800-382-3419; FAX: 201-236-7141
E-mail (Internet): corpsales@prenhall.com

Printed in the United States of America

10   9   8   7   6   5   4   3   2   1

ISBN 0-13-085084-5

Prentice-Hall International (UK) Limited, *London*
Prentice-Hall of Australia Pty. Limited, *Sydney*
Prentice-Hall Canada Inc., *Toronto*
Prentice-Hall Hispanoamericana, S.A., *Mexico*
Prentice-Hall of India Private Limited, *New Delhi*
Prentice-Hall of Japan, Inc., *Tokyo*
Prentice-Hall (Singapore) Pte. Ltd., *Singapore*
Editora Prentice-Hall do Brasil, Ltda., *Rio de Janeiro*

CONTENTS

FOURTEEN   A Detailed Objects Example —
Selecting Records   171

ABOUT THE AUTHOR

Billy Hollis has been developing software for over twenty years, and has been using Visual Basic® since version 1. He has written for many technical publications, including the Visual Basic Programmers Journal, UniSphere, AS/400 Magazine, and Computer User Magazine. He is a frequent speaker at conferences, including the Visual Basic Insiders Technical Summit (VBITS), often on the topics of software design and specification, and object-based development in Visual Basic.

Mr. Hollis is General Manager of the Nashville branch of Oakwood Systems Group, a consulting firm based in St. Louis which specializes in software development with Microsoft technologies. He is also MSDN Regional Director of Developer Relations in Tennessee for Microsoft.

ACKNOWLEDGMENTS

I now understand quite well why many technical books have multiple authors. Certainly this book would not have been possible without a lot of help.

Thanks first to Mike Meehan of Prentice Hall PTR Press for insisting that I do this book. He convinced me that there was a void in the area of specification and design for Visual Basic developers, and then just kept at me until I gave in and did the book. He has also been very patient with the inevitable mistakes of a first-time author.

Truly Donovan did a magnificent job of editing the book, and challenged many of my ideas in the process. Responding to those challenges definitely made this a better book.

Many have volunteered to do technical reviewing for me, including Gary Bailey, Rick Lassan, Bill Locke, Tom Weathington, David Hanna, Bryan Hunter, Mark Wisniewski, and John Alexander. Their insights have been most helpful. Thanks also to David Woolbright and Fredrick Campbell for furnishing excellent suggestions for technical resources.

George Clark provided the first opportunity to teach the class that lead to this book, and I am most appreciative. I also offer sincere thanks to Kevin Thompson and Robyn Feigenbaum for their continuous support while the book was being written. I do not believe the book could have been written without it.

But the most important thanks go to my spouse, Cindy Dennis, who not only handled many routine editing chores, but also helped me find the time to actually get the work done. I couldn't have made it without her, and I especially appreciate those mornings I got to sleep late after staying up late writing. My sons, Ansel and Dyson, also deserve appreciation. I believe I have a large backlog of bedtime stories to make up to them.

I'd also like to thank those who have helped me gain some understanding of what software development is really like. The list starts with Dan Hillis, who taught me my first computer language, and Steve Weatherford, who got me started in this business. I'd especially like to thank Elaine Kush for giving me my first shot at developing a really big project.

This book contains many opinions, which are the result of years of work. No doubt some of them are wrong — many of them have changed over the years, and they'll no doubt change again. But I hope they are of benefit to the readers of this book. If I can help some folks avoid some of the huge blunders I've made, the book will certainly have been worthwhile.

This book is dedicated to the memory of Eric Martin, the finest software developer I have ever known. He's probably rewriting heaven's reservation system right now. I hope he includes a back door routine to make sure his friends get in.

Introduction

Our industry has a dirty little secret. More software development efforts fail than succeed. In fact, according to a survey by Microsoft, only 19% of Windows software development projects are unqualified successes.

What about the rest? About 30% of development projects are abandoned before completion. While a few projects are cancelled because of changing requirements, most abandoned projects would have to be considered *complete and total failures*!

That leaves about 50% of projects which are considered partial failures or projects which failed to meet expectations in some significant way.

Why are the odds this bad? There are two main reasons:

- Lack of technical capability
- Poor specification and design of software

Our industry pays a lot of attention to the first area. Books, seminars, conferences, and training programs of all types are devoted to increasing technical skill. And there's no denying that without enough technical capability, software will not get developed.

And yet, I am completely convinced that poor specification and design leads to more development disasters than lack of technical capability. This is especially true in the Microsoft world, where technology rules. There is a severe imbalance, with the technology side getting almost all of the attention, and the "soft" skill of system definition and design getting little or none at all.

Changing the Balance

This book attempts to help Visual Basic developers gain a better balance. It starts with the assumption that the best programmers in the world cannot produce an effective software system if the purposes of the system are unclear, or the overall design is seriously flawed. It offers concrete recommendations on specification and design, oriented specifically toward developers using Visual Basic and related tools.

Why is that important to you? I believe that doing design and specification properly is *the* most effective way for a good developer to add value to the development process. Even the best coders add value only to their own code. A good designer adds value throughout the development process.

This book is for the ambitious Visual Basic developer who wants to be more than just a coder. It's for those who want to solve real-world problems and increase their value to their organizations and customers. It's for those who want to be in the 19% of successful development projects.

How the Book Began

This book is based on a course I have taught for two years. The course was created to give relatively inexperienced software developers the tools to do good design and specification. Several of the students have said that the course completely changed how they view software development and that they now feel much more likely to succeed at their development projects.

I believe this book can lead Visual Basic developers through a process which will help them understand:

- The importance of good analysis and design
- How a good development process works
- Why an object-based approach is necessary
- How to implement an object-based approach, from analysis and design through development and testing

The book presents many techniques which are useful for the whole software development process. The goal is to help you become a *developer*, not just a *programmer*.

Intended Audience

All levels of Visual Basic developers can benefit from this book:

INTERMEDIATE DEVELOPERS • are the ideal target. They can use this book to advance their overall capabilities. By learning to do a better job throughout the development process, an intermediate developer can become more valuable and move to an advanced status more quickly.

BEGINNING DEVELOPERS • with some experience can use this book to form good practices, and to learn about objects. But even beginners should have some Visual Basic experience. At least six months of hands-on experience with Visual Basic is recommended. This book is definitely *not* a tutorial in Visual Basic. The only syntax elements covered are those related to creation and manipulation of objects.

ADVANCED DEVELOPERS • can also benefit, especially if they have not previously concentrated on skills relating to design and specification.

Understanding Objects

This book will also benefit any developer who needs to understand objects and object-based software development. Even though object capabilities have been in Visual Basic since 1995, only a small percentage of Visual Basic developers use such capabilities to their full extent. As Microsoft technologies become more and more dependent on objects, many Visual Basic developers risk being left behind for the most exciting projects if they do not comprehend and use objects.

Existing books which attempt to explain objects to Visual Basic developers typically use an academic approach. They start by defining inheritance, polymorphism, encapsulation, and so forth. While many of them are very good, this approach sometimes fails because, at the beginning, the reader has no conceptual structure on which to hang these concepts.

This book uses a different approach which is much more hands-on and pragmatic. It starts with concepts familiar to Visual Basic developers and gradually adds object concepts one at a time. Many real-world examples are used for illustration of these concepts. This approach seems to have a higher success rate than academic approaches.

As a side benefit, many of the examples of objects can be immediately applied in your own projects. All of them were inspired by real-world development efforts.

Using the 80/20 Rule

The Pareto Principle, also called the 80/20 rule, applies to most disciplines. It says that roughly 80% of the benefit comes from about 20% of techniques in the discipline. I believe this applies to software design and development.

This book attempts to cover the 20% of the tools and techniques which provide 80% of the value. This allows the reader to get a huge payback for time invested, because you get to put the techniques learned to immediate, beneficial use.

Of course, developers need to be aware of the other 80% of techniques, which are important but not used as often. For that reason, many chapters will refer the reader to additional books and materials which cover the chapter's subject in more detail.

You Can Actually Read the Whole Book

You probably have a lot of thick technical books on your shelf. Many of them are probably in excess of a thousand pages. You haven't read them all the way through — you just picked out the parts you needed the most. In today's fast-and-furious development projects, it's almost impossible to find enough time to read a thousand pages of dense technical material.

With the 80/20 Rule, this book can be much shorter and still offer a great deal of value. Because the material is concentrated, I would recommend that you read the whole book. I have tried to cover subjects as concisely as possible to make that practical. I've also tried to make the writing interesting enough that it won't put you to sleep.

Major Parts of the Book

The foundation of this book is analysis, specification, and design. Roughly half the book is devoted to these topics. However, this material is split into two parts. Part I of the book is on analysis, which includes functional specification. Part III is on design, which typically includes technical specification.

In between these parts is Part II, which is devoted to understanding objects in Visual Basic. Such an understanding is crucial to effective software design using modern tools.

The order of the material is very important. It is suggested that you go through most of the chapters in order. Each chapter packs the basics into a concise presentation, following the 80/20 rule to present the most important concepts and techniques.

If you are well-versed in objects, you can skim Part II or even skip it. But I would recommend that you take a look at the examples. You might find them useful for your own projects.

Analysis, Specification, and Design

Part I covers the complete analysis phase of development. It contains chapters on the subphases of requirements, functional specifications, estimating, and so forth.

Part III contains chapters on data and object design, prototyping, and related activities.

The analysis and design parts give you enough detail to go through your first formal specification and design process.

Other useful chapters discuss details on design-related subjects such as:

- An introduction to development methodologies, including the Microsoft Solutions Framework
- User interface design and usability testing

Much of the information in these chapters would be applicable to development in any language, but there is emphasis on areas that Visual Basic developers typically overlook.

Objects in Visual Basic

As mentioned earlier, Part II is devoted to helping Visual Basic developers understand and use objects. Modern technical design is just about impossible without object techniques. And you can't design something you don't understand. This part is aimed squarely at Visual Basic developers. All of the examples are done in VB, and there is complete coverage of the syntax and procedures for doing objects in VB.

There are, of course, many books that talk about objects in Visual Basic, but the approach in this book is different from the others, and complementary to those books in some respects. The approach in this book is more hands on, using real-world examples. (You won't see Dog objects with a Bark method.) The approach is also specially designed to build on what Visual Basic developers already know.

After the part on objects, there is a chapter specifically on doing object design. This chapter includes a short introduction to Universal Modeling Language (UML), which is becoming a standard tool for designing objects.

A Distillation from Many Resources

I mentioned earlier that this book is derived from a class on design, specification, and objects. But many other sources were also used to provide ideas, techniques, and concepts, including:

- Many years of work on software development projects involving Microsoft technologies, particularly Visual Basic
- The best ideas from over two dozen books on analysis, specification, design, and objects
- Suggestions from many professional developers

I believe this book can do a lot to increase the probability of success in Visual Basic projects. Of course, with a subject this complex, there is a lot of room for differences of opinion. You may not agree with every single thing you read. That's okay — circumstances vary, and there are many ways to do software development. Keep an open mind, and use the ideas and concepts you find worthwhile. Just one idea from this book might help you save a project from failure.

Naming and Typographic Conventions

Lines of code in this book are printed in a style which looks like this:

```
frmMain.Caption = "Report Definition"
```

Some lines have the Visual Basic line continuation character, which is an underscore.

For naming conventions, the code in this book will follow a slight modification of the standards presented in Appendix B of the *Visual Basic Programmer's Guide* for Visual Basic 5. As specified in that appendix, three-letter prefixes are used in most variable and object names, such as "frm" for form. The letter "g" before the prefix indicates a global (public) variable, and the letter "m" before the prefix indicates a module-level variable. If you are unfamiliar with these standards, you may want to review them before reading Part II of this book.

The only significant difference from these standards is the use of single-letter prefixes for very common data types. These include:

Data type	Prefix
String	s
Long integer	n
Boolean	b

This is Just the Beginning...

As with other development skills, instruction on design, objects, and related concepts only provides you with a starting point, and you will learn much during your real-world experience. But this book should be enough to dramatically increase the odds of success for your development projects. And your successful projects can be the springboard to a far more enjoyable and profitable career for you in software development.

Why Do Analysis and Design?

It seems odd that we have to justify design of software before we create it. No other technical or engineering discipline would question the value of defining and analyzing a problem before attempting to solve it.

And our mainframe brethren are way ahead of us in this area. We may quibble with the techniques they use — I don't care much for having programmers work solely from specs, for example. But at least they know that the design process is important.

So why is analysis and design so neglected in the Visual Basic world?

The Siren Song — "With VB, Who Needs Specs?"

Visual Basic's greatest strength is also its greatest weakness. Those wonderful capabilities for drawing beautiful screens on the fly seduce developers into bad habits.

In the typical VB project, requirements gathering usually comes down to a meeting of an hour or two, followed by some scribbled notes or perhaps a typed-up page or two. Then the developer begins drawing screens, and after getting something sufficiently pretty, shows it to the end users. Then the cycle begins.

The users like this part, but don't like that part. Oh, yes, and they forgot to tell you about this other thing the system needs to do. You hear those infamous words "It's not any trouble to add that, is it?" The developer goes back to redrawing screens and changing code.

The above paragraph may be repeated literally dozens of times. The process is sometimes called "protocycling." Eventually it leads to one of three possible outcomes:

1. The system is finally hacked into some semblance of what the user wants. The code is ugly and not very maintainable, but at least the system works.

2. The user gives up (or runs out of money), and puts an incomplete system into production. The project becomes a never-ending nightmare of bug fixes for the programmer.

3. The user gives up (or runs out of money), and decides to abandon the whole thing.

Notice that none of these is an unqualified success. The best you can hope for is a marginal success.

Also notice that the point of failure has *nothing to do with the programmer's ability to write code or manipulate Visual Basic.*

This protocycling approach will work (more or less) if the development project is simple enough. But it breaks down rapidly with complex projects. If a project is going to have more than one developer, the process described above is almost guaranteed to lead to a development disaster.

Confusing the User Interface with the Design

The biggest conceptual flaw in the above process is the assumption that designing screens is the same thing as designing a software system. It's not!

As we will see in the chapters on requirements gathering and specification, the screen design is only a part of a system design, and it should almost never be the first part. The most beautiful screens in the world are worthless if they don't accomplish what the user needs, or if the rest of the system is unable to carry out what the user wants to do.

This confusion is rampant. As best as I can tell, less than one-third of Visual Basic projects have any formal specification process. No wonder we see a success rate on development projects of only 19%.

What if the User Doesn't Have a Clue?

One of the reasons (or excuses) offered for protocycling is the complaint that users don't really know what they want. The theory is that users must have something tangible and visible to react to before they can give enough details to complete the design.

I believe this is a cop-out. That information is in the user's head somewhere, and there are better ways of getting it than protocycling. It is up to the developer to learn the skills needed. They include listening and interviewing skills, writing skills, and analytical skills. None of these are as difficult to learn as the average developer thinks.

The biggest challenge is to get users to take the up-front process seriously. Typical users have full-time responsibilities, so getting chunks of their time for a real design process is tough. But you can tell them honestly that:

- It will not take any more total time from them to do it right in the beginning
- The project is much more likely to succeed if proper design is done

"But We're in a Hurry! We Don't Have Time for Specs!"

I actually had a senior manager at a very large company say this to me. You have probably heard variations.

In a complex, time-critical project, you don't have time *not* to do specs. Specifications will reduce the time and expense required to produce software, sometimes dramatically.

Lack of specifications leads to two huge time-wasters — code that has to be changed later and code that is simply thrown away.

Coming back to code after it was originally written means taking the time to completely understand the original intent of the code. This is hard enough if it's your code. It can be very time-consuming if it is was written by someone else. It's much more time-efficient to write the code right the first time, and that requires a complete understanding of its purpose.

And of course, in a typical ad hoc project, much code is written which later proves to be redundant or completely unnecessary. Hitting the delete key and throwing away that code also throws away the time some developer spent writing it.

How the Cost of Fixing Errors Rises Over Time

Every development project generates errors which need to be fixed. But the point at which an error is discovered has a dramatic impact on the cost to fix it.

A study entitled Software Defect Removal (Dunn, 1984) evaluated this impact. The results were presented as a multiplication factor. Assuming the cost of fixing the error was one unit during the analysis phase, the cost rises during successive phases according to the following table:

Phase detected	Cost factor
Analysis (requirement gathering, function specification)	1
Design (technical specification)	2
Passive tests (testing at the module level)	5
Structural tests (testing at the program level)	15
Functional tests (alpha/beta testing)	25

The results show how investing more time in analysis and design has a big payoff in later phases. Catching errors in those phases saves lots of time in later phases.

Other Benefits of a Good Design Process

Doing specification and design appropriately also leads to many other benefits, including:

- **Better stability** — Well-designed systems have less unnecessary and redundant code, less hacked code, less changed code, and better communications among program modules. All of these result in dramatically fewer bugs.

- **Higher payback with systems more suitable to their purpose** — A well-designed system does what it is supposed to do efficiently and effectively, leading to more return on the development investment.

- **Greater maintainability** — All the factors above concerning stability also result in better maintainability. It is much easier to reliably change and maintain clean, well-thought-out code.

- **More reuse of software technology** — A properly designed module often has flexibility built in, which makes it useful over a much larger domain.

- **Better decision-making for development projects** — A good design process will halt ill-advised development projects much sooner. The costs of development are understood earlier in the process with much greater precision. It is not necessary to waste a year in haphazard development to discover that a system is not practical or useful.

- **Discovery of future bottlenecks** — Good specification will help pinpoint future bottlenecks in time to do something about them. Knowing what's coming helps managers and developers prepare.

- **Easier to add resources during development** — Specifications are a huge help if resources need to be added to a project. Without proper specs, a new developer on a project spends a month or so just getting familiar enough with the project to know what to do. With specs, the new developer gets a good overall conception of the goals and design of the system in the first day or two.

- **More fun (or enjoyable) for the developers** — Developers enjoy the development process more, especially the construction phase, because a good structured design means it is easy to understand the system, easy to see the big picture and easier to envision the end product. A chaotic development process that lacks a firm plan usually causes lots more stress than a good process.

Reduction of Risk

Perhaps the single biggest reason to invest the time needed for a good definition process is reduction of risk. Good definition increases the odds of success. This is good for everyone involved in the project, and business managers are especially happy to see anything that reduces risk.

How Does Analysis and Design Fit into the Development Process?

There are many descriptions of the software development process, but a typical description with traditional terms would include the following stages:

1. Requirements gathering
2. Functional specifications
3. Technical specifications and interface design
4. Validation and prototyping
5. Development
6. Testing and quality assurance
7. Post-production documentation

The first two stages we will call the "analysis phase." Discussion of the analysis phase begins in the next chapter.

Stages 3 and 4 are grouped together to form the "design phase." Part III of the book covers this phase in detail, and also includes some information on stage 7 (post-production documentation).

Since this book concentrates on analysis and design, the development stage and the testing stage are not discussed in detail. Some information on these stages is included in Chapter 24, "Methodologies and Best Practices."

Getting the Religion

If I sound passionate about doing analysis and design properly, well, I am. I hate waste. I hate to see development dollars flushed down the toilet. I hate to see grumpy, dissatisfied developers hacking away at code no one will ever use.

You probably hate those things too. But do you hate them enough to do something about it? Learning to properly define and design software will require you to learn a lot of new skills. They include:

- How to listen effectively
- How to write effectively
- How to apply analytical methods
- How to apply object-oriented technologies and methodologies
- How to enjoy (or at least tolerate) activities besides coding
- How to be less defensive about misunderstandings and mistakes
- How to tell managers above you when they are going astray

and a number of others.

You'll need to invest a lot of time and effort, not just in this book, but also in other books that this one leads you to. But the rewards, both financial and psychological, can be tremendous.

So let's get started...

The Analysis Phase

The Analysis Phase

This part of the book covers the analysis phase of software development. It offers concrete suggestions and ideas for Visual Basic developers to use in their projects, but most of the ideas presented are applicable to development done with any language.

Remember that we are following the 80/20 rule in this book. This presentation of ideas for analysis is definitely not intended to be exhaustive. The goal is to give you a good understanding of fundamentals, and to communicate some of the most valuable techniques.

It is also important to understand that not all suggestions are appropriate for all situations. Consider each suggestion in light of your particular circumstances. Don't dismiss ideas out of hand, but do reject ideas that are obviously not a fit for your project.

What vs. How — The Difference Between Analysis and Design

The central idea of the analysis phase is to discover *what* the software system is supposed to do. That includes areas such as:

- Why the software is needed (often called the business need)
- Information on expected users and their needs

- The capabilities the software must have to meet the needs of the users and the business need

- Enough explanation of the capabilities so that technical developers can design the system

This sounds straightforward, but the devil is in the details. It takes time and patience to do an analysis phase successfully.

The analysis phase is sometimes called the definition phase. This emphasizes that the primary purpose of this phase is to define what a system is supposed to do.

In contrast, after the analysis phase comes the design and development phases. These phases are concerned with *how* the software will accomplish its tasks. By the time these phases are reached, a good understanding of what the software is supposed to do should have already been accomplished.

This guiding principle can help you decide what belongs in the analysis phase. If you're trying to decide when to deal with some aspect of development, see if that aspect is concerned with what the system should do, or how the system should do something. A "what" answer points to analysis and a "how" answer points to design and development.

The Subphases of Analysis

Most analysis phases have two subphases — requirements gathering and functional specifications. Depending on your understanding of the business background, these may be preceded by a phase in which you gain additional understanding of the business situation being addressed.

The following chapters cover the analysis phase in detail, but here is a quick overview of the subphases.

Understanding the Business Concepts

Technology is not an end. It's a means to an end. It's always important not to let technological enthusiasm blind you to the real business need. And the first step in understanding a business need is understanding a certain amount about the business. This may require you to study background business concepts.

For example, if you are writing an order processing system for a clothing company, you need to understand some of the business background of the clothing industry. The system you create may not look very much like an order processing system for auto parts.

This informal phase is not necessary for all development efforts, but it can be very important for a developer coming into a new business area. You may not produce any documents from this phase. Its purpose is to gain a good background to understand the future requirements. It should help you understand the underlying business and understand why the users need this particular software system.

Some developers don't understand why they need to do this. Someone who thinks of herself as "just a programmer" may regard understanding the business as someone else's responsibility. But understanding the underlying business is a critical success factor, so it is the responsibility of everyone involved in the development.

In some cases, the whole development effort may be reconsidered during this subphase. If the business need for a system has never been explored, it may become apparent when that exploration is done that the need just isn't very important. That is, of course, for the users or sponsors to decide, but you may be the one to raise the issues that cause them to reconsider.

During this phase, the emphasis is on research into the business in general. This may involve observing normal production, checking out competitors on the Internet, and other typical research activities.

One activity that often occurs in this phase is simply following users around, observing them in their normal work environments. Doing this for a few hours can yield wonderful insight into their needs and challenges.

We will not cover this phase in any more detail. But the phases below will have their detailed chapters.

Requirements Gathering

Formal analysis starts by gathering information about the system during interviews and meetings with users and other people affected by the system. This information is distilled into a comprehensive listing of the capabilities the software must have, which is called a requirements document.

Many requirements can be listed laundry-list style. Additional organization can be done at the functional specification stage.

The requirements document can have some requirements which later prove to be superfluous. Wish lists, for example, are desirable and may be included. Based on later analysis, some requirements in the document may be removed.

Functional Specifications

Functional specifications begin as organized requirements. Writing this document demands that the requirements be checked for:

- Completeness (Are all of the necessary details known for a requirement?)
- Consistency (Do any requirements contradict other requirements?)

The functional specification also translates "requirements" into "functions" (hence the name). The main difference is that functions are more detailed, and result from in-depth analysis of the requirements. Chapter 5, "Functional Specifications," begins with a short example illustrating the difference between the requirements document and the functional specification.

Another important aspect of functional specifications is deciding which requirements will stay and which will be cut. This decision typically depends on estimates of the resources needed for development.

Finishing a functional specification is a major milestone in the development process. The finished functional specification should be viewed as a "contract" between the development team and the sponsors of the development project.

Combining Requirements Gathering and Functional Specifications

There are cases where these subphases can be combined. For example, if the development project is very simple and expected to be brief, the requirements list may be pretty short, and a combined document may be more time-efficient.

A "clone" of an existing system may also have a short requirements phase. You may be able to proceed straight to a functional specification based on the capabilities of the system to be cloned.

But these are the exceptions. For just about any typical development project, a robust analysis phase, with solid efforts at both requirements gathering and functional analysis, will shorten overall development times and result in better quality.

For example, consider the "clone" situation. Suppose you are cloning a mainframe system for managing telecommunications. The original system may have been designed from the point of view of the clerks in the telecommunications department. Simply cloning that system may miss huge opportunities to produce a system which meets the needs of all the users in the organization. Only a detailed analysis phase will uncover those needs.

Who Writes the Analysis Documents?

There are many opinions concerning who should write the requirements and functional specification documents for a development project. Should it be someone in marketing? How about the principle system sponsor? Or perhaps the lead developer? Should the two documents be written by different authors?

I believe the principal author of both analysis documents should be on the actual development team, and the lead developer is the most likely candidate. There are several reasons why I think this works well:

- Developers have the most to gain from developing a complete understanding of the system.
- Developers have fewer axes to grind concerning what the system is supposed to do than the sponsors or users of the system.
- Developers understand the level of detail they need to do the actual software construction.

There are drawbacks to having a developer in this role. Many developers are terrible writers (or at least think they are), and most would rather visit the dentist than write a long document. But developers can learn to write effectively with practice, and the pain of writing a long document is far less than the pain of a disastrous software development project.

High-level requirements can often be written by a non-technical author such as a user or a marketing person. This may be necessary because a development team has not been formed yet. Such requirements should be subject to revision and extension by the development team.

A technical marketing person is sometimes effective as the author of the functional specifications, if that person is a full-fledged member of the development team and understands enough about software development. Such individuals are rare.

I have *never* seen a non-technical marketing person produce a useful functional specification. (I suppose it could happen, but I've never seen it.) The author needs a certain level of technical sophistication to understand what the development team has to know and to do the analytical work to figure everything out.

The system sponsor is usually not a good candidate to be the author, regardless of technical or writing capabilities. The sponsor is usually too familiar with the requirements, and so leaves out many hidden assumptions. Even more critical, the sponsor seldom has the time to do the job properly.

Some highly structured development staffs have dedicated analysts who specialize in producing specifications. Such a person is supposed to step in, do the analysis, pass the result on to real programmers, and then step out of the way. This is contrary to good team-based software development methodologies, and I discourage it. For more discussion on this issue, see the chapter on development methodologies in the last part of the book.

This book will proceed with the assumption that a lead member of the development staff is the principal author of the analysis documents. In the last chapter of this part, we will discuss an extension to this — team-based authoring.

Requirements Gathering

It would be nice if there were a cookbook-style procedure you could use to do requirements for a software development project. But we can't do requirements from a cookbook any more than we can write code that way. Circumstances vary, and there is a creative component to the process.

But we can discuss some general guidelines for gathering requirements. These are certain phases that most requirements-gathering processes go through, and a typical order for these processes. There are many suggestions and techniques that can help you do it your first time. And there are several common mistakes which are discussed so that you can avoid them.

Defining the System Vision

I suggest that the first thing to do in gathering requirements is to get an understanding of the overall purpose of the system. I call this the "vision" of the system.

This should be only a few paragraphs. It should include the business need to be addressed by the system. It may be helpful to think of it in terms of writing a draft of a marketing brochure that will describe the new system.

The system vision should identify the main benefits of the system, expressed in non-technical terms. In fact, it should be as free of technical terms as you can make it. Even a high-level manager should be able to gain a quick understanding of the system from the vision.

You may know enough after the first phone call or informal discussion to write the system vision. If not, a short discussion with the sponsor of the system should be enough.

Remember, keep it short — one page, maximum.

Once you have written the vision, submit it to the sponsor or sponsors of the system to make sure you have the basics in place. They should be able to read it right then and there, and tell you at once if you have captured the essence of the system to be developed.

Don't get bogged down in details. If you have been told more than should be presented in the system vision, you can write that down for later use in a different document.

The system vision is typically the first item in a requirements document, and also the first section in the executive summary of a functional specification. It sets the stage for everything else that is used to describe the system.

Defining the Application Domain

Every software system interacts with some part of the real world. This piece of the real world is sometimes referred to as the "application domain" or "problem domain."

Either concurrently with developing the system vision, or just after getting it verified, you should clarify the application domain. This sets the stage for detailed definition of the problem.

For example, if our system is a system for internal processing, then our application domain might be the internal departments affected. If, however, some of those people are interacting with customers while using the system, then those customers are part of the problem domain as well.

Drawing a clear boundary around the application domain ensures that:

- Every role or aspect of the problem that needs to be examined is examined

- The problem definition does not wander off into areas that are of no consequence

As with the system vision, the application domain can often be specified during initial conversations with the principal sponsors of the project, perhaps in conjunction with defining the vision for the project. However, sometimes it must expanded or contracted later (usually expanded) when more detail comes up.

A good way to get a handle on the application domain is to ask the question, "Who are all the people directly affected by this system?" That's not just users, but anybody who is directly involved in the process when the system is being used. It also helps to ask, "What material objects (buildings, machines, vehicles, etc.) are directly affected by this system?"

Exercise 4.1..................

Think about your last project (or your current project). Attempt to specify the project vision and the application domain.

If there is someone involved with the project (preferably non-technical) who can critique your effort, have them do so. You may be surprised by some of the feedback you get.

Why is the Application Domain Important?

The success of a software system cannot be determined by looking at the system itself. It can only be determined by looking at the effect the system has on the real world.

For example, the success of a commercial package can never be determined by how pretty the screens are, or how elegant the database structure is. The success can only be determined by whether or not the package sells well, which presumably is connected to how well the package serves the needs of its users.

Similarly, the success of a system to track customer complaints can only be determined by whether it helps increase customer satisfaction.

As software developers, we often forget this. We are more comfortable focusing on the internals of the system. One of the great benefits of a well-done definition phase is that it helps focus developers on what really counts — how the system works in the real world.

Getting to the Details — Use Cases

Once you have an understanding of the basic purpose of the system (the vision) and the part of the real world affected (the application domain), it is time to start gathering detailed requirements.

There are many ways to gather the details for requirements, but a method that is becoming very popular is based on what are called "use cases." A use case is a typical user interacting with the system in a typical way, specified in detail.

For example, if the system is to support order entry, here are some examples of possible appropriate use cases:

An operator entering a new order

An operator changing an existing order

An operator cancelling an order

A manager inquiring about the status of an order

A user inquiring about the status of an order

An operator reordering from an existing order

And there could be many more for this system.

Note that use cases typically *do not refer to specific features or operations of the software.* Use cases are the real-world steps that are taken to accomplish a particular purpose. The use case of "an operator entering a new order," for example, might be briefly summarized like this:

1. A customer calls to order some merchandise.
2. The operator takes the call.
3. The operator asks the customer for their customer number.
4. If the customer number is available, the operator puts it into the system to look up the customer's name, address, etc. If the number is not available, the operator gets this information (name, address, etc.) from the customer.
5. The operator gets the credit card number from the customer.
6. The customer specifies the items they wish to purchase.
7. For each item, the operator makes sure the item is in stock, and tells the customer the price.
8. When the customer has no more items to order, the operator asks how the merchandise is to be shipped. That information is then entered into the ordering system.
9. The operator tells the customer the total (including shipping), thanks the customer for the order, and hangs up.

Note the lack of references to system features. Step 4 says to put the customer number, or their name and address, into the system, but doesn't say anything like "go to the new order screen and press F2."

Use cases are particularly useful whenever an existing manual or semi-manual process is to be automated. Careful examination of the existing manual system is essential to gather requirements for the new automated system. Use cases also work well when an older automated system is being replaced or substantially rewritten.

There are two alternative ways to write out use cases. The narrative technique above is one way. Another is to separate the steps taken by the user or operator, and the steps taken by the system. These are usually placed in separate columns. Here is the example above, rewritten to use the second format:

1. A customer calls an operator to order some merchandise

2. The operator takes the call.

3. The operator asks the customer for their customer number.

4a. If the customer number is available, the operator puts it into the system.

    5a. The system looks up the customer's name, address, etc. and displays them for the operator.

4b. If the customer number is not available, the operator gets the customer information and puts it into the system

    5b. The system accepts the customer information and assigns a customer number.

6. The operator gets the credit card number from the customer.

    7. The system accepts the credit card number and verifies that it is valid.

8. The customer specifies the items they wish to purchase to the operator.

9. For each item, the operator puts the item into the system.

    10. The system looks up the item and displays whether the item is in stock and the item's price.

11. The operator tells the customer if the item is in stock, and if so, the price.

12. When the customer has no more items to order, the operator asks how the merchandise is to be shipped. The operator enters that information into the ordering system.

    13. The system calculates the shipping fee, and adds up the total for the order. It then displays this to the operator.

14. The operator tells the user the total (including shipping), thanks the customer for the order, and hangs up.

The second technique has the advantage of making the flow of information more explicit, but has the disadvantage of assuming more about how the system to be developed will work.

The Terminology of Use Cases

Many books on use cases refer to "actors" and "roles." An actor is basically some type of user. Users are typically grouped in such categories as operators, supervisors, upper managers, and so forth.

A single actor may take on more than one role. An operator may have the "order entry" role on one call, and the "cancel order" role on another call.

This is oversimplified, but it will get you started. Check the suggested reading section for books which go into more detail on use cases.

Developing a List of Use Cases

The first step in use case analysis is to find out what use cases need to be documented. You may know some of them from initial discussions, but you will rarely know them all until you talk to a representative sample of users.

As you interview users (which we will discuss in detail below), you should ask them questions to find out what use cases are appropriate to document in detail. Here are some good questions to get started:

What are the typical tasks you carry out on a daily basis?

What tasks do you have to do that are less frequent? How important are these tasks?

What kinds of information do you need to get into the system? How do you gather that information?

What situations require you to access information in the system? How do you use the information? How do you need it presented?

Are there parts of your job that take up a lot more time than you think they should? Can you think of ways the performance of those tasks could be improved?

What are all the ways you interact with customers (or employees, or patients, or whatever)?

Keep An Open Mind

Some authors discuss use cases solely in terms of a "user" interacting with a "system." This is fine, but can be taken too far. In particular, make sure you don't assume too much about what the system is supposed to do. After all, that is what we're trying to find out at this stage. This means you need to be open-minded about what constitutes a use case. The questions above can help you do that.

For example, I once gathered requirements for a medical staff that wanted a new system for their clinical information management. There was an existing system in place, and it handled most of the information, but was hard to use.

Obviously the new system needed to handle all the functions of the existing system, hopefully doing them better. During requirements gathering for the new system, we needed to find out what all of those functions were. We asked the users questions about those functions, assuming the user knew something about what the "system" was supposed to do. This worked fine to document the detailed requirements for those functions.

But we did not stop there. For each user, we discussed *all* the typical tasks they performed that concerned patient information. This turned up routine tasks that the system currently did not handle, and that were not part of the original vision for the new system. In particular, we turned up a task which was a source of considerable frustration, wasted time, and patient dissatisfaction — handling phone calls from patients to clinical personnel.

The current method, using phone message slips, was utterly inadequate. A minor enhancement to the system requirements allowed phone calls to be handled *within the new system*, with considerable savings in time and frustration.

If we had focused on the current system too much, we would probably have assumed that patient call-ins were not relevant. Gathering broader requirements prevented that mistake.

The last two suggested questions in the list above are particularly good at making sure you don't overlook important use cases.

Remember, you can always document a use case, and then decide later that it does not need to be included in the final requirements or functional spec. Better to write some up and throw them away than to leave some out that were important.

Types of Use Cases

Since we are being open-minded about use cases, we need to spend some time understanding their relative importance. Later in the analysis process, we will begin sorting out system functionality into "must have," "important," and "nice to have" categories. It is helpful to start thinking about that as use cases are constructed. Use cases can be sorted into the same categories. Craig Larman, in *Applying UML and Patterns*, calls these primary, secondary, and optional use cases.

PRIMARY USE CASES

Some of the operations of the system will be essential to its success. That is, the system cannot be considered fully functional unless those operations are supported. The use cases used to describe these operations can be considered primary use cases.

In our list above, "An operator entering a new order" would be in this category.

SECONDARY USE CASES

Operations which are less frequent, but still important, generate secondary use cases. Supporting these operations in the system is important, but you may spend less time refining these processes because there is less benefit (fewer users or less frequent occasions to use the operation).

An example from our list above might be "A manager inquiring about the status of an order."

OPTIONAL USE CASES

Operations which would be nice to have, but are not essential, generate optional use cases. It is important that everyone involved understands that these use cases may or may not be incorporated into the final system. That decision will occur later and will depend on the benefits of the operation vs. the costs to include it in the system.

The only use case in our list above which might be of this type is "An operator reordering from an existing order." Depending on the details of the system, the sponsors might decide that old orders cannot be used as the basis for new orders.

Limitations of Use Cases

Use cases should *not* be the only mechanism for gathering requirements. It's too easy to let unspoken assumptions about how the system should work creep in.

In her book *Doing Objects in Visual Basic 5*, Deborah Kurata discusses how this can happen. She calls the problem "the dishwasher effect." If you were designing a mechanical dishwasher (and had never seen one), you might start by doing a use case on a person washing dishes. This would result in a long series of steps in which dishes are transferred among different sinks. Designing a dishwasher to imitate these steps would be disastrous.

It's more important to concentrate on the desired *end results*. Use cases may help you discover what these are, but they are just a starting point. Allowing use cases to dictate all the details of how a system is supposed to operate may result in a system which is impractical or uneconomical.

Some developers discover use cases and then base their entire requirements gathering effort on them. Be careful not to get carried away in this fashion. Use cases are just another tool to use to accomplish your mission, which is to develop good software.

Gathering Detailed Requirements

How do we gather the information for use cases and other requirements? The most common techniques are interviews and facilitated meetings. Both have pros and cons.

Interviews

The most common way to gather use cases or other requirements is to have interviews with people who are involved with the process to be automated. I prefer one-on-one interviews, but occasionally it is appropriate to interview two or three people at once.

Typical targets for interviews are people who have specific needs the system is supposed to meet. As discussed above, we can call such a person an "actor." For an internal client/server system, for example, a set of actors might be:

Power user (someone who uses the system all the time for heavy-duty work)

Casual user (someone who has an occasional needs to use the system, but whose primary job is doing something else)

Management user (someone who need to get management information out of the system, but again does not use the system constantly)

A complete set of interviews should cover all the roles. If there is a large group of people in one role, it is usually good to interview more than one person in that role.

One interview might generate several use cases, if an actor has several ways of interacting with the system (several "roles").

If the number of people gets past three, the interview format is not usually best. Then it's time to switch to a facilitated meeting (see below).

The Interview Process

Even though you probably have done interviews to gather requirements, there are probably several ways to improve your interview techniques. We will go through the typical sequence of steps in doing an interview, and then offer some general suggestions. Here are the typical steps to take:

DECIDE WHO TO INTERVIEW

Interviewing too few users is a common mistake in requirements gathering. You should interview the principal sponsors and representatives of all types of users. If you are doing commercial software development, you may also need to interview marketing and support personnel from within the software company.

PREPARE PROPERLY

You should prepare for each interview by writing down as many questions as you can think of, based on what you learned doing the vision and application domain. The questions will usually vary depending on the person being interviewed and the type of "actor" they are.

Some questions should be for gathering specific information, and they typically have short answers. But make sure some of your questions are "open-ended." These questions should encourage the person being interviewed to give detailed answers. Questions like "What are all the ways a customer can change an order?" and "How does a patient get signed up for a test?" are examples of open-ended questions.

If you intend to exploit use cases, you should have some idea of the ones you will be discussing for a particular user. But your list will rarely be complete. You will typically discover more use cases during the actual interview.

Schedule the time you need from the interviewee. Decide how much time is appropriate for the interviewees, and ask them to commit that time with no interruptions. I find that typical interviews take sixty to ninety minutes.

Arrange for a place to do the interview away from the interviewee's desk. It is helpful to have a white board or flip-chart handy.

CONDUCT THE INTERVIEW

During the interview, go through your questions in a logical order. Some answers will cause you to ask additional questions.

It is your responsibility to capture everything the person says in the interview that is relevant. Scribbled notes are not good enough. You need to capture it all.

The only way I have found that works is to record the interview with a micro-cassette recorder, and then listen to the interview later. This allows the written notes from the interview to be supplemented and fleshed out. I usually limit notes during the interview to key concepts and pictorial information (pictures, graphs, and such). That allows me to listen more closely to what the person is saying.

Take on each use case separately. You will confuse yourself and the user if you start combining discussion of use cases. For each one, go through the detailed steps in the use case. You typically lead the user through use cases by asking "What do you do first?," followed by a series of "What happens after that?" questions.

Go through each use case at least twice. When you think you have gone through the steps, summarize them for the user and ask if the steps are correct.

FINISHING THE INTERVIEW

Finish up with a general question along the lines of "Is there anything I have not covered about how you expect to interact with the system?" or "Is there anything we have not discussed which you think I ought to know?"

The very last thing to do in the interview is thank them for their time, and ask one additional favor. Ask them to *please* take the time to read and critique the write-up which you will be sending them later. Stress the importance of this and explain that validation of your documents is absolutely key to the success of the development effort.

DOCUMENT YOUR FINDINGS

Document your findings as soon as possible after the interview, preferably the same day. Otherwise you are certain to forget some of what you were told.

Use the tapes you recorded earlier to help you as you write. Word-for-word transcriptions are not necessary, but you should make sure all the key ideas and details from the tape are captured. Many recorders have a high-speed playback option which can save you time during this process.

For use cases, employ one of the suggested formats discussed above. Be sure to number the steps in the use case. If a use case is sufficiently complicated (with lots of decision points), you may want to draw a flowchart for it.

ASK FOLLOW-UP QUESTIONS IF NECESSARY

Typically, during your writing, you will think of new questions or notice some items that need clarification. Most of the new questions will have brief answers. Contact the interviewee and get those clarifications and additions. Then add them to the document.

HAVE THE INTERVIEWEE VALIDATE YOUR DOCUMENT

As soon as practical, have the person you interviewed read your document. They may catch incorrect details, or recall additional information which is important.

This is a very important stage. Recall that during the interview, you should stress the importance of the document review, which sets the stage for the user to take the validation seriously. Remember that these people are busy. You may have to take extraordinary effort to get enough of their time to do validation properly. This problem gets more acute the deeper you get into definition. We will discuss it in more detail in Chapter 5, "Functional Specifications."

No doubt all of this sounds like a lot of work. It is. But the investment of this effort will have a huge payback later on in the project.

General Suggestions For Interviews

Here are some additional suggestions for making interviews effective:

STAY ON TRACK

Don't let a requirements interview deteriorate into a discussion of exactly how the system is going to work, and how long it is going to take to do it. Developers make this mistake all the time. They talk to a system sponsor for an hour or two, and then start discussing system architecture and time estimates.

This blurring of definition and design can lead to several bad outcomes. Bad estimates are so damaging and pervasive that they get their own chapter later. Other fallout includes:

- Failure to gather enough detail before designing, which can lead to a poor design
- Focusing too heavily on what this sponsor thinks the system should be like, and ignoring the other users or sponsors

How do you keep on track? The number-one thing to keep in mind is that you are there to *listen*, not to *talk*. Keep asking questions. Think up more questions as you hear details. Write them down so that you don't forget to ask them.

You should dig into the details so that you really understand what the person is saying — don't just decide that you'll figure it out later.

Keep the questions centered on *what* the system is supposed to do, not *how* it is supposed to do it.

If the person being interviewed starts asking you questions ("How long will this take? What will the screen for that look like?"), gently tell them that it's not possible to answer those questions this early in the definition. Resist the temptation to tell them what they want to hear. If you do that, you are just storing up trouble for yourself in the future.

LISTEN, LISTEN, LISTEN

If you are like me, as soon as you hear a problem posed, part of your brain goes to work on solving it. That's part of what makes a good software developer.

It is also a liability during requirements interviews. While we work out the solution to what they said a few minutes ago, they are still talking. We sit there, pretending to listen, but not really hearing anything they are saying.

Listening is a skill that can be learned, even for software developers, but you must consciously work on it. If you absolutely must write down some great idea you just had while listening to your interviewee, ask them to pause for a moment while you write it down. Then put it out of your mind, and go back to listening to them. (Don't discuss it with them! That will throw you off track as we discussed above.)

AVOID LEADING QUESTIONS

Don't ask questions that assume their own answers. For example, this question would not be a good one:

> "I understand that taking orders from new customers is just like taking orders from existing customers except that you have to get the name and address for a new customer. Is that correct?"

It would be much better to ask:

> "What are the differences between taking orders from new customers and taking orders from existing customers?"

Even if you think you know the answer, ask the question as if you did not. Most of the time you will get the answer you expect. But occasionally you will find that you have a mistaken assumption somewhere, or have received incorrect information from someone else.

TALK ABOUT CAPABILITIES, NOT FEATURES

Address your questions to capabilities of the software. Don't ask "What features do you want the system to have?" Instead, ask "What do you want the system to do?"

This helps keep the person being interviewed focused on the business purpose of the software instead of bells and whistles.

Facilitated Meetings

Sometimes requirements are gathered in a meeting in which the people who have some understanding of the needs of the system attempt to communicate those needs to the people who will do the development.

Here are the people who should typically be involved in such a meeting:

Facilitator

This is the person who runs the discussion. It may be one of the developers, or a development project manager. The key is to have someone who will control the discussion, but not dominate it. Technical savvy is helpful, but not essential. This person should definitely *not* be one of the typical users of the system.

If no one on the development team feels comfortable doing this, a professional facilitator can be brought in. They are expensive, but not nearly as expensive as having a project go off course because no one can gather requirements properly.

The main objectives for the facilitator are:

- Involve everyone in the discussion
- Keep the discussion going
- Keep the discussion from wandering off track
- Ask questions to explore when requirements are not sufficiently detailed
- Ensure that everything discussed is documented adequately

It is helpful if a facilitator is prepared to diagram processes, etc., based on input from the group. But a facilitator must be careful not to interject too much personal input into such efforts.

Documentor (Sometimes Called Scribe)

This person actually writes down all the ideas discussed. The writing should be done on some medium that can be carried out of the meeting. This person can participate in the discussion, but their participation is typically less than that of other meeting attendees.

This person must also strive to avoid imposing personal biases onto the transcribed material. Often, this role is filled by someone on the development staff (see below).

Common User(s)

These attendees represent the most typical users of the system. Their needs are given high priority in design.

There should be several representatives of the group. But there should be no more than three or four for typical requirements gathering.

Power User(s)

These attendees are there to make sure the system does everything it needs to do. They often supply details on detailed processes and obscure requirements.

It is especially important not to let these attendees dominate the discussion at the expense of typical users.

Managerial User(s)

I try to discourage these folks from coming to the meeting at all. I find that other participants are a lot more forthcoming if their managers are not there. But sometimes it is not possible to exclude them.

As with power users, it is important that representatives of this group do not dominate the discussion. It is often helpful to assure them beforehand that you will meet with them separately after the group meeting, and to stress that this meeting is for the users to provide their input.

Development Staff

This group includes programmers, analysts, documentation writers, and testers who will be working on the project. These attendees should be mostly silent, but may provide some guidance on the scale of proposed capabilities. That is, if a given request is obviously going to have a dramatic impact of development costs and timelines, the development staff may want to bring this point up.

The development staff should always be ready to ask for more clarification on any requested items that they do not understand.

While attendance of this group is not absolutely necessary, having them involved will typically save time in the end because eventually they have to understand everything discussed. (Involvement of the development team in requirements gathering is discussed in detail in Chapter 24, "Methodologies and Best Practices.")

Ground Rules for the Meeting

At the start of the meeting, make sure you discuss the "ground rules." These include:

- The discussion will be centered on what the system is supposed to do, not how the system will work in detail
- Users should feel free to express "wish list" capabilities
- Not all capabilities discussed will necessarily make it into the final product
- There will be no discussion of the user interface at this stage (stress that the users will be involved in UI design, but that it will take place later)

Take a few minutes to prepare your ground rules before going into the meeting. Making them clear to the participants at the outset can avoid a lot of problems later on.

General Suggestions

Keep the total number of people in the group down to ten or twelve. Eight to ten is an ideal number, but this may not be practical if there is a large development staff involved.

Provide sufficient whiteboard or flipchart space to document lots of input. If flipcharts are used, have masking tape to hang up pages which are written on as fresh pages are needed. Tape up the pages sequentially around the room.

If it is obvious that the system is too big to do all the requirements gathering at one sitting, try to break the discussion along one or more natural lines. Then have separate meetings for each line.

Don't meet all day. About four or five hours per day is all the productive time you can get.

Remember that one of the objectives is to brainstorm. Don't dismiss any ideas out of hand, no matter how silly they sound or how impractical they sound. Encourage wish lists. Don't let the discussion wander into too much detail. In particular do not let the discussion get too far into technical details that will be dealt with later in the process. This meeting is to establish what the software will do, not how it will do it.

It is extremely important not to let the discussion wander off into design of the user interface. This is the area most likely to generate conflict. It is also completely impossible to define an appropriate and complete user interface until the capabilities of the software are pinned down.

This type of requirements gathering is especially appropriate for building commercial products. There, new ideas can make a dramatic difference in competitiveness of the product. However, even typical corporate development can benefit from this type of meeting.

I like to combine the interview (use case) method with the facilitated meeting. They offer different views of the requirements.

Documenting a Facilitated Meeting

The meeting should result in a document which encapsulates the content. The materials created by the scribe serve as a starting point, and not a lot should be added to them. But enough should be included so that each point is clear.

The document should be sent to all of the meeting participants with an invitation to submit changes, additions, or corrections.

Constructing a Requirements Document

Once the interview and meeting documents are complete and verified, it is time to construct a comprehensive requirements document.

It should start with the system vision and application domain definition. How it goes from there depends a lot on the nature of the system being defined.

All use cases that are relevant to the system should be included. They should generally be classified into related categories. For example, there could be categories of "common tasks," "infrequent tasks," and "management tasks." Or you can use the "primary, secondary, and optional" classification.

Use cases can be presented in diagrammatic form, using one of the diagram types from Universal Modeling Language (UML). A short introduction to UML is included in Chapter 22, "Designing Objects," and the "Suggestions for

Further Reading" section at the end of this chapter points out a book which goes into more detail on documenting and diagramming use cases.

Then the use cases and all the rest of the information gathered should be analyzed for general system requirements. Usually, these requirements should just be presented "laundry list" style. Requirements may be in logical groups, if such a grouping exists.

Each requirement should have some indication of its importance. This can be as simple as assigning a status of "must have," "important, but not essential," or "would be nice to have."

Remember to concentrate on the desired end results. Don't spend all your attention looking at processes. They are important, but often the desired end results are even more important.

Using a Template Document for Requirements

A requirements document does not have to be highly structured. But you may get a jump-start by using a template or outline.

The enclosed CD contains a template for Word 97 (/Templates/requirements.dot). It contains some suggested sections of the document (with some comments on completing the sections). It also contains suggested styles to use, and automatically generates a table of contents if the styles are used appropriately. Some of the books in the suggested reading section of this chapter contain other outlines you may want to consider.

Do not let a template or outline be a straightjacket. If you think some sections are unnecessary, cut them. If you need to add your own sections, do so.

Include the System Vision and Application Domain

The first section of the document is typically your statement of the system vision and the application domain. Even though these should have been previously reviewed and validated, they should be included again for readers who didn't do such reviews. These statements set the stage for the rest of the document.

Trimming Requirements During Future Stages

Not all the requirements documented in the requirements document will necessarily make it into the final version. The functional specification (next chapter) is the appropriate place to make first-cut decisions about what stays and what goes.

Requirements should have some "wish lists" because some of the items on such a list may be very helpful to users while being extremely easy to implement. But some wish list items will prove to have development costs exceeding their benefits. These can be cut as soon as that is discovered. This is usually during functional specification. In some cases, precise development cost estimates may not be done until technical specification, so decisions to drop functions or features may occur at that point.

However, to make this strategy work, expectations must be set at the front end. Everyone involved should understand that items listed in the requirements document are provisionary, and subject to later removal if circumstances so dictate.

Unanswered Questions

If you are the writer of a requirements document (or indeed any specification document), please keep one thing firmly in mind. The purpose of the document is to improve the software development process. The purpose is *not* to make you look like you know everything.

I mention this because many writers of requirements documents write as if they *do* know everything. The entire requirements document sounds like the writer is totally confident that it's all correct.

That's never the case. The writer will be reasonably sure of many items, more unsure of others, and downright confused by a few. *This uncertainty and confusion should be captured in early drafts of requirements documents.*

That means writing down unanswered questions, and including comments on items about which you are unsure. In fact, I strongly suggest highlighting those questions in some way so that reviewers of the document can't possibly miss them. I use a special style in Microsoft Word which indents the question, places a border around it, changes the font, and uses a shaded background. (The template for requirements on the enclosed CD has such a style, named "Question.") Even if reviewers don't pay close attention, they can't possibly miss the items I am most uncertain about.

Unanswered questions should also be used in the next stage (functional specifications) and the chapter on functional specs contains an extract from a real document to serve as an example.

Success Measurements

You should consider a section of the requirements document which lays out the criteria for judging the system's success. This is rarely done, but can be very helpful in clarifying the real purpose of the system, and how it relates to the real world. It helps the developers stay focused on the most important requirements of the system.

The criteria should be as measurable as possible. For example, a success measurement standard might read, "Overall, the system should reduce average time for resolving a customer complaint to under two hours." Saying something generic like "The system should increase customer satisfaction" is meaningless unless you have a tangible way to measure customer satisfaction.

Other Sections Which May Be Needed

Depending on circumstances, a requirements document many need a number of additional sections. Here are some examples you may wish to consider:

INFRASTRUCTURE DETAILS

If there are certain platforms on which the software system will definitely be expected to run, this information should be listed in the requirements document. For example, if the system is browser-based, but must work with both Netscape and Microsoft web browsers, this should be in the requirements. Or if a client-based software package must run on several versions of Windows, they should be listed.

INTEGRATION WITH EXISTING SYSTEMS

If there are existing systems with which this system must integrate, high-level requirements for this integration should be included. For example, there may be an existing customer database which a new system must use. If so, where is this database? What format is it in? These are important considerations for the new system.

DOCUMENT HISTORY

In a good requirements development process, the requirements document will go through several versions. It can be helpful to know what the previous versions were, and the major changes that were made for each version. This is primarily helpful for very complex projects.

Verifying Requirements Documents

Each draft of the requirements should be reviewed and verified by all necessary actors. If requirements are not verified as correct, they have limited usefulness as design documents.

As we've discussed, this is not easy, because many of the people involved will not have the time to properly review. We'll discuss this in more detail in the following chapter on functional specifications.

The Importance of Ignoring the User
Interface During Requirements Gathering

As a Visual Basic developer, you are probably especially interested in user interface issues. As we have previously discussed, the ease of drawing screens in VB causes most developers to get to that stage too early.

I strongly urge you to resist the temptation to start working on the user interface during the requirements gathering phase. It's another case of "what" vs. "how." The requirements phase is to discover *what* the system is going to do. The user interface is part of *how* the system will accomplish its functions.

Resisting this temptation will not be easy. It's not just your own inclination you have to worry about. Windows-literate users often think they know all about user interface design (they're usually wrong), and many are very visual thinkers. Sometimes, they will push you toward screen design too early if you let them. We'll discuss more about that in the chapter on user interface design.

I have a flat rule in my projects — no screen shots or layouts in requirements documents or functional specifications. It is sometimes hard to enforce. People will get up during a requirements gathering meeting and start drawing screens on a white board, for example. It takes patient and persistent explanation that the user interface design must wait until later.

One of my typical stratagems is to ask the person to please think out the user interface and put it down on paper. Or use VB to draw a sample screen if they know how. Anything to get them to do it outside the meeting.

It's not that their opinions on user interface don't matter, or that the user interface is not important. It is of paramount importance. But until you know what the system is to accomplish, I maintain that it is impossible to design a user interface to do the job. How can you possibly design a user interface to something you have not yet realized is necessary?

What Else You Should Usually
Leave Out of a Requirements Document

- Detailed data flow diagrams
- Database formats (if an existing database, refer to the formats, but don't list them)
- Detailed algorithms — they go in the functional spec

Danger Signs

Here are some danger signs that the requirements process is too short, not being taken seriously enough, or just being mishandled:

- It takes well under ten percent of the projected development time
- Programmers start coding the system before the requirements are established
- No one concerned with the system is bothering to validate the written requirements. The users never seem to have the time to read the documents produced by the development team
- The requirements document has ballooned to a such a size that no one will bother to read it
- The requirements document is being completely rewritten with each version (indicates poor information gathering, poor writing or both)

Some of these will, of course, be beyond your control. But it is your professional responsibility to make the development process go smoothly and effectively, so do your best to get the problems addressed. Or start looking for another development project to work on, since this one is probably destined for failure.

Suggestions for Further Reading

For both requirements gathering and functional specification, *Software Requirements and Specification: A Lexicon of Practice, Principles and Prejudices* by Michael Jackson offers a wealth of good ideas. It is not oriented around a particular methodology. It is not language specific, and offers practical advice for many different aspects of software definition.

For some more ideas about doing use cases, check out *Applying Use Cases: A Practical Guide* by Geri Schneider and Jason P. Winters. It gives more detailed use case examples, including UML diagrams, which we will discuss in Chapter 22, "Designing Objects."

Functional Specifications

The functional specification is the keystone on which the rest of the development process rests. Gathering requirements sets the stage by determining in general terms what the system is supposed to accomplish. Drawing up functional specifications is the process which sets down in detail what the software system is supposed to do. This involves sifting through the requirements, classifying them, and responding to them in enough detail that technical design can be done in the next phase of development. Functional specifications present the actual "functions" which will accomplish the requirements.

For example, suppose a requirements document included the following requirement:

> The system must track and manage an arbitrary number of tests for a patient. Some tests can be done at any time. Some tests are dependent on other tests which must be completed beforehand. Users need to see a list of all the tests for a patient and the status of those tests (complete or incomplete), and users should be able to change the status of a test at any time.

This information was presumably gathered during interviews with the users or sponsors. But more detail is required before doing technical design to implement this requirement. Is the set of possible tests fixed, or should users be able to add brand-new tests on-the-fly? How exactly are tests "dependent" on other tests? Are there situations where such a dependency can be bypassed?

The requirements implied that a test could have a status of either complete or incomplete. But the functional specification needs to go deeper. In the real world example from which the above statement is taken, we ended up with *six* status states. "Incomplete" was broken down into "Available" (meaning the patient is ready to take the test), and "Pending" (meaning that the test has not been taken, but cannot be taken right now because another test must be taken first). We had a status for cancelled tests, and tests which were postponed until a different visit. A good functional specification for this example should contain a comprehensive list of all the possible status states for a test, going beyond the generalities of the requirements document.

Why aren't these things pinned down during requirements? Because they require analysis and thought. Until the requirement stated above is compared to all the other requirements, and analyzed for completeness and consistency, some of the details to fulfill the requirement cannot come out.

Functional specifications are seldom taken seriously in Visual Basic projects. In many cases, they are completely ignored. In others, a half-hearted attempt is made, based on the fact that lots of books (including this one) say it's the right thing to do.

Writing good functional specifications is one of the toughest things to do in the development process. That's why it is so seldom done well.

But the rewards are well worth it. Creating a useful, complete set of functional specifications adds more value to the development process than any other single task. Done well, functional specifications can do a lot to decrease the number of errors, reduce development time, and increase the quality of the final product.

The Functional Spec — A Detailed Response to Requirements

Once requirements are finished and validated, the next step in the development process is to turn them into functional specifications. This process may actually begin before final validation of the requirements document.

In a sense, functional specifications contain the requirements previously gathered. But as the example above illustrated, these requirements must be systematized, classified, and analyzed for completeness and consistency.

In addition, decisions must be made concerning what functions and features will actually be included in the development effort. There may be many "nice-to-have" items in the requirements document that a detailed analysis reveals will be too expensive to include. These can be dropped from the functional spec, or there may be a section that summarizes these dropped items. Occasionally, even an item in the "important, but not essential" category must be dropped because of high resource requirements to implement it.

Constructing the Functional Spec

Here are general suggestions for the process of constructing the functional specification:

Use a Template

As with requirements, you can use a template for functional specs, but don't feel bound to the template. Broaden the document as necessary to capture the requirements of the system, and trim out any parts of the template which clearly do not apply to the current project.

As with requirements, there is a template on the enclosed CD which can be used to start your functional spec document. It is for Microsoft Word 97 and is called FunctionalSpec.doc.

Start with an Executive Summary

A good functional specification should always include an introductory explanation of the system to be developed. This overview section should be understandable by anyone involved in the development process, so it should be light on technical terminology.

I always call this section the Executive Summary, emphasizing that it should be understandable to even non-technical managers. It could also be called Introduction, or Overview.

The system vision and application domain statements (done during requirements gathering) are the starting points for the executive summary. It is usually appropriate to expand and refine this material. However, remember that this is a summary, so don't expand it too far. The executive summary should normally be three pages or less.

The goal of the executive summary is to give the first-time reader a high-level introduction to the system and its purposes. While you are writing it, it may help to pretend that the reader is someone who is not on the project team and has never heard of the project or system.

Organize the Main Body of the Document Along Functional Lines

While it's okay for requirements documents to be loosely organized laundry lists, functional specifications need more structure. Usually the best structure is based on the functionality of the system. Some functions naturally relate to one another, and they should be discussed together.

For example, if your system supports both financial transactions and non-financial database management, the functionality for these would be covered in separate sections. There may be some cross referencing.

Functional areas can then be decomposed into finer functional areas. There might be five types of financial transaction, for example, and each would get a subsection within the financial transactions sections. The subsection for a type of transaction would contain all of the functional requirements that are specific to that particular type.

Another subsection would be used to discuss the functional requirements that are shared by all transaction types. This section would usually come before the individual transaction types.

Let's summarize these suggestions with a hypothetical outline:

FUNCTIONAL SPECIFICATIONS FOR SYSTEM X
    Executive Summary
    Financial Transactions
        Functional requirements common to all transactions
        Transaction type A
            When the transaction is appropriate
            Information needed to complete the transaction
            Actions of the transaction
(Repeat above for each transaction type)
        .

        .

        .

    Database Management
    (break down into its own subsections)
    (other functional areas follow)
        .

        .

        .

    Dropped Requirements
    Possible Enhancements for Future Versions
    Summary and Conclusion

Include Summarized Use Cases

Use cases will be helpful for developers doing technical design, so they should be included.

But not all use cases that were in the requirements document will necessarily need to be in the functional specification. Some use cases may turn out to be very loosely related to this particular system. These should be left out.

You may want to have one section which contains all of the use cases, but I usually prefer placing use cases in the appropriate functional section. For example, use cases related to transactions can have a subsection in the transactions section of the document. Use cases related to database maintenance would similarly be in the database maintenance section.

Some spec writers prefer to leave use cases out of the functional spec completely. If the use case exposes a process or algorithm, then such spec writers will often translate the use case into the process or algorithm, and include that in the functional spec.

An Iterative Process

Developing a functional spec is an iterative process, even more so than doing requirements. It is literally impossible (except with the very simplest of projects) to get everything correct and complete in the first version.

Early drafts should contain many questions and unresolved issues. Just as with the requirements document, these issues and questions should be highlighted in a fashion that makes them impossible to ignore. Remember, the objective is not for the authors to show how smart they are. The objective is to get a complete definition of the program or system.

Here is a short excerpt adapted from a real functional specification which illustrates the inclusion of unanswered questions and other "sideline" discussion. Note the use of initials to identify the author of the sideline comments and questions.

"As an alternative to inputting numbers for each age/gender group, the user must have the option to enter a total population and select a statistical distribution to used to divide the total population into age groups automatically. The distributions to be available should minimally include a 'US Population Distribution' and a 'Typical Workforce Distribution.'

"Is this correct? What other distributions are mandatory? Which are optional and under what circumstances? BSH

"Ideally, these population 'sets' should be saved for future use. A set of populations could then be recalled by selecting the set name. This would be an enhancement over the current system.

"Will the population entered for input pop need to be displayed on the report headers? DLC

"I know they do that now — could we make it an option? If I were the user, I don't think I would want to see it on the report. RRP"

Review and Validation of the Functional Specification

Here's what you would like to happen:

1. You complete a fresh version of the functional spec.
2. You take it to key participants and leave it with them.
3. They review it in a timely fashion, and return it to you with corrections and additions.

Fat chance. Here's what will probably actually happen:

1. You complete a fresh version of the functional spec.
2. You take it to key participants and leave it with them.
3. A week later you ask them about it. They reply that "they'll get to it soon."
4. Another week goes by with no results. You ask again. They again say they'll get around to it real soon now.
5. You repeat step 4 as many times as you can stand, and finally give up and go ahead without their feedback.

It's not really their fault. They probably feel that they have done enough by reviewing the requirements document. They may also have moved onto another task and lost focus on this particular project.

But you still must head off this outcome. One way to do that is to get up-front commitment from your reviewers. Tell them from the first interview or meeting that their involvement is critical, and ask them to commit the time and effort needed.

Even then, it's hard to get them to follow through. Sometimes you have to literally place the document in their hand and stand there until they review it.

Whatever you do, don't skip the validation of the document by the system sponsors. We will talk later about the functional spec being like a contract between the sponsors and development team, and that means it must be confirmed by the sponsors.

Place the Most Important Material Early in the Document

One way you can promote the most effective reviews of the document is to put the most important material toward the front. This ensures that the time spent by the reviewer is put to good use.

It also helps them stay awake. If you put lengthy, unimportant material first, the reviewer can easily get bogged down in it, and never get to the good stuff.

Validation Meetings

Another option for validation is to get the key participants together and go through the document line-by-line. If you can get everyone together, and get enough of their time, and keep the meeting from turning into a boxing match, this can work well.

If you are going to have such a meeting, plan it and give notice of the meeting when the specification is delivered for review. You can include a cover letter with the specification that a specific time and place for the meeting, and its expected length. If you expect some of the participants to do preparation for the meeting, highlight that in the cover letter. Since the cover letter goes to everyone, the participants who need to do preparation will take it more seriously.

Make sure you know how conflicts in opinion are to be resolved before the meeting. Also reserve the right to declare a particular topic "unresolved" and work through other channels for resolution outside the meeting. You cannot let the meeting get completely hung up on one contentious point. These "ground rules" can be in your cover letter announcing the meeting.

Don't underestimate the amount of time that such meetings can take. For a decent size project, you could easily be looking at two or three days of meetings.

Completeness

One of the main differences between a requirements document and a functional specification is that the functional spec must be analyzed much more closely for completeness. Each functional area should have a description which is sufficiently complete that it can used as the basis for technical design.

How can you do this? You must step outside your role. You must look at the document from the eyes of someone who has not been through the definition process up to this point.

You should ask yourself, "Do the developers have enough to go on? What am I leaving out that they need to know?"

For example, it is not enough to say that a system should support five types of transactions, and then name the transactions. You have to go further. For each transaction, a developer would need to know:

When is the transaction allowed? What conditions must exist for the transaction to be possible?

Who is allowed to carry out the transaction?

What are all the pieces of information needed for the transaction?

What actions will the transaction carry out?

What happens if the transaction fails?

This helps explain why it's good for the author of the functional spec to be a developer. Such an author understands the level of detail a developer needs, where a non-technical person might not.

Even if you include all this information, there is another pitfall. You must resist the temptation to express these in terms which are highly technical. You must use terms which are easy for all readers of the document to understand.

For example, the pieces of information needed for a checking account transaction might be expressed as

"the account owner, the destination of the funds transfer, the amount, and the date"

Here is an inappropriate way to express the same thing:

"a long integer field for the account id, a foreign key to the destination table, a currency variable holding the amount, and a date field holding today's date"

Here's one which is even worse:

"ACCT_ID field, FUND_DEST field, AMT_TRANS field, and TRANS_DATE"

What's wrong with these descriptions? They assume too much. At this point, the functional specification should just say that such a transaction should be supported, not exactly how it is carried out. Trying to pin down data types and such should be done during technical design.

Remember that non-technical folks have to understand and validate the functional specifications. It should be written in terms they can easily grasp.

Of course, you may have to interface to existing data which is already structured. It is fine to reference that information, but do so with both English terms and the technical terms, like this:

Transaction inputs

Information	Field name	Source of information
Account owner	ACCT_ID	ACCOUNTS table
Destination of funds transfer	FUND_DEST	EXTERNAL_ACCOUNTS table
Amount of transaction	AMT_TRANS	user supplied
Date of transaction	TRANS_DATE	system date

Checking for Consistency

Here's a common occurrence during software coding. The programmer realizes that requirement X and requirement Y cannot both be implemented. They are contradictory, at least in some cases. The programmer has to get up, go find the person who knows how it's all supposed to work, spend time explaining the contradiction, and then wait while that person figures out the answer. It's pretty easy to see that this is a time-wasting process.

You can keep such incidents to a minimum by analyzing for consistency during functional specification. And requirements which have any relationship whatever should be checked to see that they are compatible for all combinations of circumstances.

This sounds difficult because it is. The number of combinations of circumstances can get out of hand easily. But you still need to try, so you should consider as many combinations as practical. Catching such problems now is much more cost-effective than catching them during coding, or (even worse) during beta testing.

Relationship Grids

One good format for checking both consistency and completeness is a grid or table which has one set of possible options along the side, and another set along the top. This allows you to check all possible combinations of these options.

For example, suppose we have five types of transactions and three classes of users. The grid can tell you what transactions are possible for each user and vice versa. It might look like this:

Transaction type	User class 1	User class 2	User class 3
Type A	OK	OK	Not possible
Type B	Not possible	Only available for customer type X	OK
Type C	OK	OK	?? — still to be determined
Type D	OK	Not possible	Available only during the last week of the month
Type E	Only available if security clearance is above level 7	Requires override from manager	OK

You can make sure you have covered all the combinations by making sure each cell in the grid is filled in and verified.

If the options being analyzed represent user interface elements, this information is also very useful for the interface designer. When the designer decides what kind of controls to use to select the option, the grid specifies the logic needed to enable and disable the controls, as necessary.

Exercise 5.1

Suppose you are writing software that will control a home's audio-visual equipment. You have four classes of such equipment: VCRs, TVs, stereos, and cable boxes. There are two types of inputs (sound and video), and two types of output (sound and video again).

Write a relationship grid like the one above analyzing the possible combinations.

A sample of a completed answer is at the end of this chapter.

The Functional Spec as a Contract

The members of the development team should feel that the functional specification is a sort of "contract" that sets out what they are to deliver. That contract cuts both ways. The development team commits to delivering that functionality, and the users and sponsors of the system commit to the functional spec as a complete understanding of what they want. This avoids the typical "scope creep" that kills so many development efforts.

If a functional spec is done well, one end result should be a reasonably reliable estimate of the time required to deliver the functionality. Depending on the size of the project, this estimate may have to wait until technical design is complete. But at least a preliminary estimate can usually be rendered upon completion of the functional spec. (See Chapter 6, "Estimating," for more discussion about estimates.)

If a user or sponsor tries to add more functionality, or radically change the system's definition, the development team can point out that such additions and changes are not reflected in the original plan or estimate. That doesn't mean additions or changes are not considered (in fact, at least some small ones are inevitable), but that adjustments in estimates and timelines *must* be made in response.

Of course, the sponsors may then decide that the change or addition is necessary, and that they will bear the additional development time and cost. In that case, you should revise the functional spec to reflect the changes or additions necessary. Then it becomes the new contract, and it becomes your new commitment.

▶ Spinal implants

Just having a functional spec helps control sponsors who can't make their minds up about what they want. If it's down on paper, they are a lot more likely to stick to it. If they insist on a change, and it is pointed out that the change will definitely affect timelines, a sponsor will often make a better judgement about whether the change is really needed.

However, this only works if you make it work. Sponsors will always push for more functionality and want you to bear the consequences. The functional spec can help you make your case for adjustments in estimates.

But the functional spec does not automatically give you a spinal implant. You must have the backbone to stick to your guns. You have committed to your part — delivering the functionality in the spec. The sponsors should live up to their side of the bargain — telling you what they want up front and sticking to it, or bearing the consequences of changing the deal.

If a sponsor pressures you to change the functionality without adjusting the project timelines, you must resist that pressure. You are not doing yourself or your sponsor any favors by rolling over in that situation. If you do roll over, you just create unrealistic expectations, and then you look bad when you can't meet them. Far better to deal with the problem now than to store up trouble for the future.

Thinking about the functional spec as a contract can help you do a better job of writing it. If you know that you will be held to what is in the document, you will work harder to be complete and to avoid ambiguity.

Other Sections That May Be Needed

There's no way to list all the possible sections you might want to have in a functional spec. If there is any information the developers will need to know concerning what the system is supposed to do, it should be in there someplace.

Here are some sections that might be appropriate, depending on circumstances:

DATA SOURCES • Information on existing data sources the system will need to work with.

DISTRIBUTION AND SUPPORT REQUIREMENTS • Information relating to how the software will be distributed into the field, and special considerations for supporting it. For example, the functional requirements for an installation program might go here. An example of a support requirement could be an event logging capability.

HARDWARE/SOFTWARE COMPATIBILITY REQUIREMENTS • This information should have been part of the requirements document, and should definitely be in the functional spec.

FEATURES FOR FUTURE VERSIONS • This can contain those desirable capabilities that it was not practical to include in this version. Knowing about these now can help the development team design hooks for use in the future.

SUCCESS MEASUREMENTS • These should also have been gathered for the requirements document.

COMPETITIVE PACKAGES • If you are developing a commercial software package, the functional specification may wish to refer to the packages that will be competitors. The development staff may want to check out the competition for good ideas to use for inspiration.

This is far from an exhaustive list. Use it as a springboard to generate ideas for your own circumstances.

Documenting Algorithms in Functional Specifications

If your software system has complex processes that must be carried out, the functional specification must furnish enough information for the developers to design and code modules to carry out the processes. The generic logic for carrying out such a process is often called an algorithm.

If an explanation of an algorithm is already available from another source (a reference book, or previous specification), then a reference to that source may be sufficient. Otherwise, you should describe the algorithm in detail in the functional spec.

This can be done is several styles — narrative, flowcharts, and pseudocode are some of the possibilities. Choose the one that seems to make the most sense for the particular algorithm in question. For example, the narrative style works well for highly sequential algorithms, but does not work well for algorithms with many branch points.

Using Diagrams and Visuals

Requirements documents are often mostly text. Functional specifications should usually include more graphical material. Such additions to the document help clarify the content, and reviewers will find documents with visuals easier to review.

Here are some examples of visual elements which can be included in the functional specification:

- Flowcharts for algorithms
- Tables and grids of organized, related information
- Use-case diagrams (typically done in UML)
- Existing system architectures (often done with a diagramming tool such as Visio™)
- Maps, pictures, floor layouts, or other graphical material which will help explain the requirements and functions of the system

Look for opportunities to add graphical material to your specification. It can be time-consuming to produce, but can dramatically raise the quality of the spec.

Why There's (Still) No User Interface Design at this Stage

All the reasons to leave user interface design out of the requirements document apply just as strongly to the functional spec. We are still dealing with the "what" at this stage, and user interface is part of the "how."

However, the functional specification may have some general requirements for the user interface. It may specify the platforms which are supported, which imposes limitations. The functional spec may also require the look and feel of a system to match that of another system which the users already have. It would be fine for example, for a functional spec to say "The system should have a general look and feel similar to Microsoft Office."

But user interface *design* should be done in the *design* phase. The design phase may overlap the analysis phase, but it should not begin until the functional spec is well along.

We'll be talking a lot more about the design phase later in the book.

What Else to Leave Out

Detailed Database Designs

Normally, this is done in the technical design phase. The functional spec may list all the pieces of information that may be stored, but it is usually premature at this stage to start talking about data types and so forth.

There are exceptions. Existing database structures that will be used by the system should be either included or referenced in the functional spec (preferably referenced). Or a detailed algorithm may require certain data types which must be specified. But, in general, leave as much data design as possible to later stages. That kind of material puts reviewers to sleep, and most are not equipped to tell if a detailed data design is good or not.

Reference Material and Other Filler

Some writers of functional specifications apparently think the objective is to make the document as long as possible. They want to maximize the "thud factor" of the document, which is how big a thud the document makes when it is dropped on the table. Consultants seem especially susceptible to this problem.

Such writers will include incredibly long tables of reference material, and add other kinds of filler. The result is very hard to review. It is also hard for developers to use because they can't tell what's important and what's not in all the bulk.

Keep filler material out of the document. If necessary information is in another book or document, and does not really need validating, then just place a reference to it in the functional spec. The people who need that information can then go to the external source, and the people who don't need to look at it don't have to.

If reference material simply must be included, put it in appendices instead of smack dab in the middle of functional descriptions. Then place references to the appendix in the document as necessary.

Danger Signs

You should watch for the same danger signs as with the requirements phase, with the two most common being (1) participants not taking the process seriously enough, and (2) programmers starting to write production code too early.

Answer to Previous Exercise

Here's a sample of a relationship grid that would meet the requirements of the exercise:

Type of equipment	Audio input	Audio output	Video input	Video output
VCR	Yes	Yes (2)	Yes	Both standard and cable pass-through
TV	?? (TVs we examined did not have any — are there exceptions?)	Yes	Yes	Yes
Stereo	Yes (several)	Yes (powered and unpowered)	No	No
Cable box	No	No	Yes	Yes

Suggestions for Further Reading

As mentioned in the previous chapter (Chapter 4, "Requirements Gathering"), *Software Requirements and Specification: A Lexicon of Practice, Principles and Prejudices* by Michael Jackson is a great source of ideas for the whole analysis phase, and includes many topics specific to functional specification.

Estimating

Developers tend to cringe when the subject of estimation comes up. Every experienced developer has horror stories to tell of estimates done poorly and deadlines missed by wide margins.

Estimation is a bit of a black art even when done well, and it is seldom done well.

Upper Management Directives

In fact, in many projects, genuine estimating is not done at all. I am continually shocked at the number of development shops where deadlines are set completely externally to the development effort. Some upper manager says "The project has to be done by June 1," and that's that. Often the requirements for the system have not even been done when such a deadline is imposed.

I recently gave a presentation on specification to a crowd of about six hundred developers. I asked how many of them had been involved in projects where the estimate was set by upper management directive with little or no involvement from developers. Almost every single person in the room raised their hand.

"I Can't Change the Laws of Physics, Captain"

Such silly pronouncements by upper management remind me of a scene from Star Trek™. You may recall one of those episodes where the Captain is demanding that Scotty get the engines back on line, and Scotty responds, "I can't change the laws of physics, Captain. I've got to have thirty minutes!"

Development efforts are also constrained by the laws of reality. If a development effort absolutely requires six months to finish, it is counterproductive to set a deadline of three months. It guarantees missed deadlines. If done continually, it anesthetizes the developers to the point that they don't even feel anything when the deadline is missed. Deadlines become meaningless and lose any ability to motivate the development staff.

That does not mean that deadlines should never be aggressive. In fact, a deadline which is aggressive but still possible to meet can focus and motivate a development team. But there's a big difference between an aggressive deadline formed with the participation of the development team and an inflexible directive from a clueless manager.

How can you convince managers not to do this? I don't know. I have never found a foolproof argument. Some of these folks seem impervious to logic. (It's no accident that Dilbert™ is such a huge success among software developers.)

But you have to try. Some managers will understand the logical disconnect involved when setting a deadline before even knowing details on the task. Living through a development disaster can give them perspective, too, so a good time to try to break that habit is on a new project right after a disastrous one.

The most common counter-argument you will hear from managers is that there are "strategic reasons" why the deadline has been set to a particular date. I do not find this argument very persuasive because the laws of reality still apply. If there really are such strategic reasons, then the manager needs to understand that (1) the only way to attempt to reach such deadlines is by adding whatever resources are necessary, which can be horrendously expensive, and (2) even if the money is committed, with the industry-wide shortage of competent developers, it may be impossible to find the resources needed.

Making the Case for Analysis and Estimation

Here's one argument that some managers respond to. Bypassing an estimation process means that no one has any idea how long a project will really take. So no one ever gets a chance to look at the costs and benefits of the project and make a "go/no go" decision. The project just stumbles along, and it can waste enormous sums of money before anyone gets a glimmering that the project never made economic sense to begin with.

Sometimes analogies work. The sidebar on a construction analogy is one example.

▶ The construction analogy

Consider the following hypothetical conversation between a home builder and a customer:

Customer: "I want you to build me a house. Here's a picture of how I want it to look on the outside. How much will it cost?"

Builder: "Well, we usually do blueprints before we talk about that."

Customer: "We don't have time for blueprints. You need to get started right away. I need it in six weeks."

Builder: "What about the interior layout?"

Customer: "Just go ahead and build it. I'll let you know if you've built it the way I want. If it's wrong, you can just rip out the walls and do it over."

Builder: "OK, I'll start the foundation tomorrow."

Placed in this context, the conversation is ludicrous. But let's rephrase it for a computer project:

Customer: "I want you to build me a software system. Here's a picture of how the screens need to look. How much will it cost?"

Developer: "Well, we usually do a system design before we talk about that."

Customer: "We don't have time for a design. You need to get started right away. I need it in six weeks."

Developer: "What about the detailed requirements?"

Customer: "Just go ahead and start coding. I'll let you know if you've built it the way I want. If it's wrong, you can just rip out the incorrect parts and do them over."

Developer: "OK, I'll start coding tomorrow."

Unfortunately, variations of this conversation are all too common in software development. Making the analogy to a construction effort helps some non-technical folks understand how silly it is to start building before analysis and design are done. They can grasp intuitively that tearing out walls and rearranging plumbing would be expensive and result in a lower quality end result. Tearing up code and rearranging it has exactly the same problems.

Is Good Estimation Possible?

Knowing that estimation is important does not mean it is easy. Jim McCarthy of Microsoft tells the story of a feature that his C++ development team originally estimated as taking three months. Then they estimated eight months.

He asked them to look at it again for a couple of days to see if there were any shortcuts they could take, since he really wanted the feature in the next release. After studying the problem for two days, they came back to talk to him. He asked "Well, how long is it going to take?" Their response? "Forget it, we already did it." As he put it, these are the best programmers in the world and they can't tell the difference between an eight-month project and a two-day project. His advice to managers is "You can't find somebody who knows how long it will take. You can only find somebody who lies."

In application software development, it's not quite that bad. I typically can estimate a project plus or minus twenty percent, and be within that range about eighty percent of the time. In other industries that would be considered laughable, but it's a goal to reach for in software development.

Foundations of a Decent Estimate

There are really three ingredients to good estimation:

EXPERIENCE • Until you have seen many projects over the years, you can't really estimate, because you haven't seen a large enough sample of the stuff that can go wrong. And, of course, doing something once means you have a better idea of how long it will take to do something similar.

DEFINITION INFORMATION • No one, and I mean no one, can do a good job of estimation before a complete set of functional specifications are done. Lots of folks try. Their seat-of-the-pants estimates may sometimes be correct by random chance. But it is impossible to consistently estimate by just glancing at a project.

A FEEL FOR RESOURCES • In a team-based project, it is essential to know how long a particular developer can take to get something done. You can make mistakes both ways. You can blindly assume a programmer can do something in a given amount of time that is ludicrously short by not understanding their capabilities. You can also allot too much time, which does not push a developer to an optimum level of performance.

Opposite Mistakes in Estimation

Some developers never become good at estimation. Some are blindly optimistic, even in the face of continual missed deadlines.

Other developers become so gun-shy that they are afraid to give a real estimate, preferring to estimate timelines that are so long that they are 99.9% sure that they can be met. These are the folks who want a week for a two-hour task.

Neither of these is satisfactory. For business managers to gauge the cost-effectiveness of a project, a decent estimate is essential. We owe it to those business managers to tender the best estimate we can. That doesn't mean we always give highly optimistic estimates on every project and then kill ourselves to meet them. It does mean that we give an honest estimate (that we have a decent chance of meeting), and that our estimate is not off so far that we cause a manager to make what, in retrospect, was an obviously bad decision.

"I Won't Hold You To It..."

People who want software done always want to know how much it is going to cost very early in the process. You are not doing them or yourself (certainly not yourself!) a favor if you give an estimate too early. Better to just estimate how long it will take to do a decent spec, and then revisit the entire estimate when the spec is done.

You will sometimes get incredible pressure to violate this practice. Stand firm. They may say, "I just want a general idea — I won't hold you to it." They may even mean it. But when a number, any number, is given, it assumes a concrete importance, and it can come back to haunt you.

The counter-offer of a definition process (analysis phase) should always be made at the first sign of pressure for an estimate. You still have to decide how long the definition will take, but that's a lot easier than coming up with an estimate for the whole project.

The counter-offer of an analysis phase has another benefit. If you emphasize that you will need the sponsor's help and commitment to make the analysis phase successful, you will sometimes find that the project is simply dropped. Some managers believe they should just sketch out a few generalities and see a fully developed system a few months later, with no involvement during the development. This often leads them to demanding a system which doesn't add much value. Once they are informed that their involvement is essential, they may decide that the system is not really so important after all. Or the analysis phase itself might conclude that the business need is not worth the expenditure of resources.

Two Different Types of Estimate

The estimation process should yield two different results. One is the amount of developer resource (person weeks or person months) that the project requires. This amount is used to estimate development costs, and to help decide when a project is economically not feasible. This is sometimes called the "resource estimate."

The second result is the deadline — the calendar date by which development on the system should be done. A moderately complex project may have several interim milestones, each with its own deadline.

The first result (the amount of resource required) is one of the primary factors leading to the second result. We will talk in detail first about getting that estimate on resources. Then we will discuss translating resources into deadlines.

When Should the Estimate Be Made?

In most projects, a general estimate of resources required can be made when functional specifications are finished. This estimate should be good enough to make a "go/no go" decision on the project, but it must be considered subject to revision unless the project is small (no more than a few person weeks).

A more precise estimate should usually be set in conjunction with the technical design phase. One of the earliest parts of technical design is to decompose the project into smaller pieces. That's a necessary part of producing a reliable estimate.

Decomposing into Tasks

As a general rule, the bigger a particular task is, the more uncertain the estimate for the time required. At two-day task is easier to hold in your mind than a two-week task, so you can do a better estimate for it.

That leads to a method for improving the quality of your estimates. If you can break down the development effort into small enough chunks, then you can do a fairly reliable estimate for the time needed to do each chunk. Then you can add together the time needed for the chunks to get a reasonably good estimate of the total time needed.

The process of breaking down the effort into smaller pieces is another example of decomposition.

Here are some general suggestions for using decomposition during estimation.

Initial Decomposition

In the first round of decomposition, you will break out the project into the major functional areas. Many of these functional areas will have their logic encapsulated as components, so one product of this stage of decomposition is a list of the major components needed.

The next stage is to estimate for each component, and that requires further decomposition. The component may consist of several related objects (class modules) and each of these class modules needs to be further decomposed. This involves identifying their properties and methods, and other major pieces of logic. See the chapter on object design for more detail on this process.

It's also important to list the significant tasks that do not involve the actual coding of the primary system. Here are some of the additional tasks that may need to be broken out at this stage:

- Installation program
- Help files
- Other documentation
- Integration of components
- Prototyping
- Usability testing
- Exploration of alternatives for key technology decisions

There may be a large number of such tasks for a complex development effort.

Let the Actual Developer Do the Estimate Whenever Possible

Whenever possible, place the responsibility for estimating a task or subtask on the person who is going to perform the task. If a particular developer is probably going to develop a certain component, that developer should do the decomposition and develop the initial estimate for the time required to do that component.

There are two big advantages to this approach. First, developers get a head start on understanding how the development of the component is going to proceed. Second, developers will usually work harder to meet their own estimates than they will to meet an estimate imposed by an outsider.

If developers are inexperienced or inept at estimation, then it may not be possible to give them complete responsibility for estimating a task or subtask. Even then, though, they should be involved. They have to learn, and their involvement will increase their commitment.

The "Three-Day" Rule for Decomposition

It's good practice to continue the decomposition process until the tasks you are estimating have an expected time of no more than three days, and most of them should be two days or under. This helps in both getting a more reliable estimate and in planning a strategy for carrying out the development.

Occasionally, there will be a task that is resistant to decomposition. This may happen, for example, because there is uncertainty about the technologies that will be used. For such cases, do the best you can. But if your decomposition contains many such tasks, you probably need to do additional investigation and technical design before getting serious about your estimate.

Getting the Final Estimate

Knowing the tasks required for the project, and the amount of time needed for each, the first cut at the final estimate of resources is simply a sum of the times needed for the individual tasks. However, unless you have superhuman capability to decompose and estimate tasks, you need to build in a fudge factor. We'll discuss fudge factors below.

Using Project Management Software

Depending on the scale of your project, you may find it helpful to use a project management package such as Microsoft Project to manage your lists of tasks. There are capabilities in such packages to help you specify dependencies among tasks ("task 12 must be done before task 19 can be started"). The package will also help assign tasks to individuals, track what tasks have been done, and accumulate estimates on subtasks to give an overall project estimate.

If a project is big enough to need such a tool, don't forget to budget in your own time for the work needed to define and manage tasks with the tool. This can take you several hours a week in a large-scale project.

For smaller projects, a manual task list will often be sufficient. A spreadsheet is a good tool to use for this simple form of project management.

Fudge Factors

Every good estimating process includes fudge factors, because none of us are smart enough to anticipate all contingencies. But fudging can be taken to extremes.

For example, there is the "next time unit" technique. This is a favorite of developers who have been burned by optimistic estimates before. In this technique, you decide how long you think a project will take, then double that time amount, and then change up to the next available time unit. Under this technique, if you think a task will take two weeks, you double the two to four, and change from weeks to months, giving as estimate of four months. Similarly, you would fudge a three-day task to six weeks.

All joking aside, it is tough to come up with any quantitative process for building in fudge factors. The amount of fudge that's appropriate depends on the scale of the project, the quality of the developers, the amount of new technology involved, and many other factors.

I find that my estimates of resources typically incorporate fudge factors of 25% to 50%. If the estimates for the initial tasks are reasonably good, this amount of fudge will cover most unforeseen tasks and delays.

Expressing Estimates as a Range

If your estimates seem to have a high fudge factor, or the task list has lots of fuzzy tasks, you may need to tender an estimate as a range. You might say the estimate is "six to nine months" rather than saying that it is precisely seven months or eight months. The very first estimates done for a project are the most likely ones to need such a fuzzy estimate.

There is one pitfall in using such estimates. Some managers will immediately seize on the low end of the range, and thus get unrealistic expectations. If you use a range in estimating, emphasize that you really don't know where in the range the final estimate will be. That will not be known until more detail is gathered or more design is done.

Handling Surprises

No matter how well you plan, your project can get delayed by obstacles or circumstances that were not anticipated. These may require you to revise your estimate, sometimes dramatically.

If such a change in the estimate becomes necessary, tell everyone who needs to know as soon as possible. It's easy to put this off because it is painful, but it will just be more painful later. It's better to make the revision and commit to the new deadline right away than to do it just before (or just after) the original deadline.

Adjusting Deadlines —
The "Time-Resource-Functionality Triangle"

In *The Dynamics of Software Development*, Jim McCarthy describes the elements in a software project as "resources (people and money), features (the product and its quality), and the schedule." He recommends visualizing these as a triangle to emphasize their connection to each other.

If a project begins to fall behind, any of these elements can be adjusted. You can add more people, reduce the feature set, or extend the schedule (or some combination). That's basically all the options you have.

Reducing the feature set or extending the schedule are the best-defined alternatives. Adding resources can be chancey. Can you find the right person soon enough to have an impact? How long will it take for them to ramp up?

Adding resources is also subject to the limitation best expressed by the analogy, "Just because one woman can make a baby in nine months does not mean nine women can make a baby in one month." Communications overhead, task dependencies, and other project management issues make adding resources an inexact way to deal with deadline slippage.

Finding a Balance

Deadlines should be important to a development team. Meaningless deadlines cause frustration and friction. Deadlines set after an appropriate amount of definition, and with the involvement of the development team, should serve as a realistic goal to strive for.

Yet there are situations in which deadlines must be adjusted. Unforeseen things do happen. They range from technological glitches to people leaving projects.

Finding a balance between these two facts is one of the biggest challenges faced by developers and their managers. But you must find that balance. Neither of the extremes — meaningless deadlines or those etched in stone — are acceptable.

General Suggestions for the Analysis Phase

We've now looked at the major parts of the analysis phase, with recommendations for working your way through each subphase. To wrap up recommendations for the analysis phase, here are some general suggestions and ideas.

Getting Your Documents Reviewed

Review and validation of the analysis documents is essential. No matter how smart you are, you can't possibly know everything the users know. You'll make mistakes, and the sooner they are uncovered the better.

There are a number of things you can do to promote effective review of the analysis documents. Let's discuss some of the most important ones.

Up-Front Commitment

We have previously touched on the problems in getting analysis documents reviewed properly. You can pre-empt some of those problems by emphasizing early and often how important the reviews are. You should explicitly ask for commitment of the necessary time at the beginning of the process.

One of the best times to do that is right at the conclusion of an interview done for requirements gathering. I usually say something like this:

"Thanks for giving me all this information. You've been a great help. I'd like to ask for your help in one more area. There will be documents that incorporate the information we just discussed. The most important thing you do from this point forward to help us have a successful project is to review those documents carefully. You will need to look at any sections that pertain to you, and tell us anything you find that is incorrect, incomplete, or unclear. Will you do that for me?"

This puts such participants in the right frame of mind to take the document reviews seriously.

Give Users a Deadline for Reviewing Documents

You can remind them of their commitment by attaching a note to the documents when you submit them for review that says something like this: "As we discussed earlier, I need you to carefully review the parts of this document that pertain to you. If possible, I would like to discuss your comments with you on {insert an appropriate date}. Thanks."

This re-emphasizes the importance and also sets a tentative deadline for them to do the review.

Press for Feedback

Remember that these people are busy. Their primary job is usually not to be part of the software development team. Their priorities may be elsewhere. If that's the case, you will have to press to get the feedback you need. Don't be surprised if documents and e-mails get lost. Be prepared to supply them again.

In extreme cases, you may need to hand-deliver a document and stand by their desk while they review it. If that's what it takes, do it. But you *must* get that feedback to do your job effectively.

Set an Example

In any moderately complex project, you probably write some documents and review others. You must set an example for other reviewers during your own reviewing responsibilities. That means being timely, of course, but it also means doing an effective job of review.

When you validate documents, constantly question what you are reading. Does this make sense? Are there hidden assumptions? For visible assumptions, are they correct? Is there any way of proving the assumptions wrong? Is anything left out of this description? Could this have more than one meaning?

Pay attention to the graphical elements. Trace through the diagrams and really understand and critique them. Try to be exhaustive in examination of tables, especially those that express relationships.

Michael Jackson, in *Software Requirements and Specifications*, calls this skill "critical reading." It doesn't just apply to documents created by others.

Before you send out a document for validation, do some critical reading of it yourself.

Use Non-Technical Language Whenever Possible

Users can't effectively review something they don't understand. And they usually cannot understand highly technical phraseology.

When doing your own review (before sending a document out to others), check it carefully for "geek-speak." If at all possible, eliminate it.

The requirements document should be almost completely free of geek-speak. The functional specification may need a little, but keep it to a minimum.

Strive for Clarity

Suppose I am defining a software system to manage patients who have to take a series of medical tests. Here is one requirement which might be included: "A patient can only take one test a time."

What does this mean? Does it reflect the fact that physically speaking, a patient can only be in one place at a time? But surely that does not rule out more than one test at a time. The patient might start a glucose tolerance test, which begins by giving the patient a dose of sugar. To get the results of the test, it is necessary to wait a while for the body to process the sugar. While that is happening, the patient could take an x-ray.

Is it a desire on the part of the facility staff? Perhaps they think it is too complicated to administer overlapping tests. But in that case, it is no longer an objective reality, like the fact that a person can only be in one place at a time. It is a subjective judgement, and therefore subject to interpretation and possible modification.

When you write and review analysis phase documents, try to make your writing as clear and unambiguous as possible. The requirement above might better be written as something like this: "When a patient is busy with a test, their status in the system should indicate that they are unavailable for other tests." In this case, the system might still have a capability to override the unavailable status and allow concurrent tests for rare circumstances.

The phrase "A patient can only take one test a time" looks fine at first glance, but it's actually quite vague. It's easy to write a vague analysis document, and they are common in Visual Basic projects. But vague documents don't accomplish the purpose, which is to discover errors before someone writes code around them.

It's much harder to make your requirements documents and functional specifications clear. But their value rises almost in direct proportion to their clarity.

Document Your Assumptions

Defining software is a process of abstraction, which always involves ignoring or simplifying difficult details. Abstraction requires the making of certain assumptions about how things are supposed to work, and what is important and unimportant.

For example, suppose you are gathering requirements for a system to do internal billing of telephone calls. You discover that each employee has an extension, and a bill is to be generated for each extension at the end of each month. Employees are assigned to departments, and a bill is also needed for each department at the end of the month. This bill is supposed to be a sum of the bills all the employees in the department.

This seemingly simple situation has several hidden assumptions. Let's look at just one of them. The bill for a department is a sum of the bills for all the employees in the department. Bills are only generated at the end of each month. But for both of these to be true, you need one of the following assumptions to be true:

1. Employees never change departments in the middle of the month.
2. Employees can change departments during the month, but the department they're in at the end the month gets their bill for the entire month.

Common sense would tell us that the second assumption is probably the appropriate one, and it would be acceptable in most companies. The fact that departments end up with a few calls on their bills that were made when an employee was in another department is probably an unimportant detail.

But there would be situations where the second assumption is not acceptable. Perhaps there is a business where one particular department has very high bills, and employees transfer out of that department a lot. A manager who gets one of these employees may not be willing for those high phone bills for a partial month to come out of his budget.

You don't want to find out that you have such a problem during beta testing. The time to find it out is during the analysis phase. So analyze your requirements and functional specifications for hidden assumptions. Then bring them out of hiding by writing them down. Allow them to be validated by your users and sponsors.

In the above case, you would probably want to take the second assumption on your initial draft, and allow users to validate it. If the assumption is found to be invalid, there are various ways the requirements could change in response. Some of them would require radically different data structures and programming logic to implement, and that's why it is important to find out those requirements up front.

Some specification outlines have a sub-section named "Assumptions." I have no objection to that, as long as it is used for general assumptions about the system. Specific assumptions, like the telephone billing example above, should be stated alongside the material that leads to the assumption.

How Long Should the Analysis Phase Take?

This is a very tough question, because the answer depends so much on specific circumstances. But a good rule of thumb is that the analysis phase should take around 15 to 25 percent of the total calendar time for the development process. (That does not necessarily mean 15 to 25 percent of the resources, because the actual development phase may have a larger active team.) These guidelines do not include technical specification and design — just the analysis phase.

The split between requirements and functional specifications is roughly even for most projects. That is, the amount of time for requirements should be roughly equal to the time for functional specs. Your mileage may vary.

Time estimates are complicated by the fact that construction of the functional spec may begin before final validation of the requirements document. And technical design and prototyping may begin before the final version of the functional spec.

How Long Should the Documents Be?

There's no exact answer for this question, but there are indicators when the documents are too long or too short.

The Right Level of Detail in Specification Documents

The Three Bears principle applies to requirements documents and functional specifications. They can be too sketchy, or they can contain too much detail, or they can be just right.

Most Visual Basic developers start out by being too sketchy. They don't include as much detail as they need. I've seen a functional spec for a three-month project that was only four pages. The problems this causes are obvious. No one has written down the details, so developers are back to guessing or asking somebody.

Less obvious are the problems of a document that is too long. There are two big ones:

- Those responsible for reviewing the document get bogged down in irrelevant details

- The development team cannot pick out the important information because there's too much fluff. They give up on using the document and (just as before) go back to guessing or asking somebody

There are no hard rules for the appropriate length. I had an eighteen person-month project that had a forty-page functional specification, and that seemed about right. Another project, which was about one person-month, had a twelve-page requirements document.

In general, if you are below twelve pages, or above fifty pages, reconsider your level of detail. Especially for documents that are too long, work on saying things more concisely. This is much, much tougher than it sounds. (Trust the author of a book to know!)

Here are some recommended lengths, depending on the scale of the project. If the main content of the functional spec (exclusive of lengthy technical appendices) comes in outside these limits, you should be looking at it closely to see if there is a good reason.

TABLE 7.1

Scale of project	Expected minimum length	Expected maximum length
Small (less than two person months of coding)	Ten pages	Thirty pages
Medium (two person months to ten person months)	Fifteen pages	Fifty pages
Large (over ten person months)	Twenty-five pages	One hundred pages

These numbers obviously depend on things like margins, font sizes, and such, so don't be dogmatic about them. Just use them as general guidelines. Also understand that they don't apply to "mega-projects" — large, multi-year, team-based efforts.

As you get up around one hundred pages, people will start to ignore the document because they can't assimilate it all.

If you start pushing these limits, look for places you can be more concise. Start looking for sections of the document that can be seriously cut back or outright dumped. And, as previously discussed, keep reference material in separate sources or appendices to keep the main body of the document tight.

The requirements document typically comes in smaller than the functional spec, but not a lot smaller. While the functional specification contains a lot more detail than the requirements document, some marginal material in the requirements document is not included in the functional spec.

Risk Analysis

To counteract the natural optimism of software developers, it's a good idea to do a risk analysis at some time during the analysis phase. It can be done during requirements gathering or functional specification or both.

The thought process in risk analysis starts with the following types of questions:

"What could go wrong with the project?"

"Are there major unknowns concerning the technology needed for the project?"

"What could the competition do that would detract from the project's value?"

"Are there people or other resources absolutely critical to the project? Are we at risk of losing them?"

"What if the system is wildly successful? What are the consequences of over-use?"

"Will the technology being implemented be sufficient for the expected life-span of the system?"

"Will the legacy systems that the system will interact with be on-line for the expected life-span of the system?"

You should be able to brainstorm many additional questions about risk. Budget some time during analysis to draw up these questions and answer them. This investment of time can significantly reduce the risk of a development project.

The risk analysis can be placed in the analysis documents (requirements and functional specification) so that users and sponsors can also render opinions and ideas concerning risk.

A typical list of risk factors may look something like this:

Not enough developers in the area to recruit for the project

Users may move to Windows 2000, causing technical incompatibilities

Our main competitor is probably working on a similar system. If the competitor reaches market first, the value of the system would decline significantly

The development team needs additional experience with browser-based interfaces

Only one person understands the tariff structure in detail. If this person becomes unavailable, development will be significantly impaired

The number of users could dramatically increase if the potential merger with Company X goes through

The list should be prioritized, with the highest risk factors first. If a risk factor is sufficiently important, contingency planning should be incorporated into the analysis phase.

Just Because a Document Says "Functional Spec"...

I have about twelve books on my shelf right now which talk about the importance of doing analysis documents. So lots of people who are involved with software development know it's the right thing to do. Unfortunately, not all of them understand how to do it.

That can lead to a half-hearted or misguided effort at analysis. The end result is often a document which says "Functional Specification" at the top, but which fails miserably at achieving the objectives of a functional spec. It may be too short, poorly structured, or padded with irrelevant material. The language may be vague. There may have been no analysis to uncover questionable or mistaken assumptions. In short, it may be close to useless.

If you have the bad luck to be handed one of these documents, you are in a very tough spot. Any action you take will have negative consequences. Basically, your responses fall into two categories:

1. You accept the document and try to do the best you can with it. The typical end result here is frustration on your part and poor-quality software. Missed deadlines are also common in this scenario. (It seems people who can't write specs also tend to be incurable optimists when it comes to estimating timelines.)

2. You refuse to accept the document. This makes the people who prepared it mad, and throws everybody's carefully prepared schedules into disarray.

If you find yourself in this situation, sit back and plan your strategy. If the principal sponsor is realistic enough, you may want to make your case for reworking the functional specification before beginning development. If that is not politically feasible, then you should consider a stealth effort at definition. Begin the process of writing a real functional spec under the guise of "clarifying details" in the worthless one.

I don't think it's ever a good idea to just accept the bogus spec and start coding. If you don't know what the software is supposed to do, you'll have a very tough time creating it.

Team-Based Approaches

Most of the discussion in this section has implied that one person (presumably you, the reader) is the author of the analysis documents. In fact, if the system is being developed by a team of programmers, I recommend a team-based approach to writing the documents as well.

Most members of the programming team can write parts of the analysis documents. This has several advantages:

- Paralleling of the work results in shorter calendar time for the documents to be produced

- The greater involvement of the programming team gives them better understanding of the system and a bigger psychological stake in the outcome

- Junior programming staff can be gradually introduced to the concept of design and specification. They can start by writing small pieces and increase their participation in later projects

That still leaves a need for a principal author — the one who puts all the parts together and determines the structure of the document. This is typically the most experienced writer in the group.

This suggestion may sound like lunacy to a traditional software development staff which is divided into analysts, designers, and programmers. But it fits well with more modern development methodologies, which are discussed in Chapter 24, "Methodologies and Best Practices."

"Gosh, this Sounds Like It's Going to Take a Long Time..."

When you propose to do an analysis phase as this book describes it, people in a typical Visual Basic shop will probably be skeptical. Because of Visual Basic's great capacities for screen design, and because most VB programmers started out doing small, user-interface-oriented programs, they lack an understanding of the importance of analysis and design.

A typical objection is that the analysis phase sounds good in practice, but it's just going to take too long. That's not true at all. The project will probably be shorter in total duration if an analysis phase is included. But this is not apparent to someone who has never done it that way.

You'll have more luck if you implement this kind of process in a smaller development project in which you have lots of control. A successful example is your best bet to convince skeptics.

Unfortunately, you may be confronted with individuals who simply will *not* participate in definition. You can often spot these folks when they say "I really just want to write code." If it becomes obvious that you can't change their minds, find the best role on the team that you can for them, and live with it. You may console yourself with the thought that they will never add as much value to the development process as you will, so your career prospects are far superior to theirs.

Occasionally, you will encounter management or marketing people in the software development process who similarly fail to understand how to do it right. They will insist on having non-technical folks writing (probably useless) specs, for example, and relegate developers to be mere coders.

Your strategy here is more clear cut. Get out. Find an organization that knows how to do it right. You will not further your own career working in a defective software development environment.

A Quick Overview of the Phases in Analysis

Here is an outline of the typical phases and tasks associated with analysis. You may not need all of them, but you can use this outline to make sure you have not skipped any.

> Business background research
> System vision
>> Articulate business need
>> Articulate major benefits
> Application domain
>> Find all users, direct and indirect
>> Determine what impact on the outside world will affect success
> Gather requirements
>> Make up preliminary questions
>> Find representative users
>> Contact users and schedule interviews and meetings
>> Carry out interviews and meetings

    Document results from interviews and meetings
    Have documentation validated by users
    Analyze documentation for requirements
  Prioritize requirements
  Check compatibility and infrastructure requirements
    Combine documents into complete requirements document
    Have final document validated
  Create functional specifications
    Group related requirements
    Derive functional areas
    Check requirements for completeness
    Check requirements for consistency
    Cull requirements, removing those not cost-justified
    Diagram as necessary
    Validate functional specifications
    Get sign-off (see "Functional Specification as a Contract")
  Do estimate
    Draw up tasks
    Decompose tasks
    Estimate individual tasks
    More decomposition if necessary
    Add up times for individual tasks to get total resources needed
    Go/no-go decision based on resources estimated
    Find task dependencies
    Allocate tasks and determine project schedule
  Do risk analysis
    Brainstorm questions concerning risk
    Enumerate and prioritize significant risks
    Develop contingency plans if necessary
  Move into design and development

A Checklist for the Analysis Phase

To help keep you from overlooking items during the analysis phase, you may want to go through this checklist of questions. This list is far from exhaustive. As you think of more questions, add them to the list for future projects.

PRELIMINARY

- Do you understand the business background?
- Do you understand the basic business need for the system (system vision)?
- Do you understand the application domain?

USERS

- Have you identified all of the users, even those who are not direct operators of the software system?
- Have you identified all of the use cases?
- Have the users verified the requirements you have gathered?

DEFINITION DOCUMENTS

- Are all the tasks the users need to accomplish specified?
- Does the description of each task discuss data requirements for the task?
- Are legacy systems which must be supported specified?
- Is the security structure specified?
- Are success measurements included?
- Do you understand the life span of the system and consequences of future evolution?
- Are unanswered questions included?
- If the system satisfies everything in the document, will the system be judged a success?
- Does the functional specification include gray areas? Are some parts impractical, but included anyway to keep a user or sponsor happy?
- Are the requirements written in non-technical language that users and sponsors can understand?
- Do any requirements have conflicts with other requirements? How are the conflicts to be handled?
- Do the requirements avoid discussion of design issues, particularly user interface design issues?
- Do the requirements in the functional specification have enough detail for a technical developer to understand?
- Can each requirement be tested? Does the functional specification contain enough information to generate a test plan?

Suggestions for Further Reading

There are more books on analysis and definition than you can shake a stick at. Unfortunately, most of them are written in an academic style and are tough to read.

We've already mentioned one exception, which is *Software Specifications and Requirements* by Michael Jackson. Rather than presenting a methodology or process, this book just talks about various elements of good software definition. The topics are actually listed alphabetically. It will give you a lot of good ideas and concepts without having to work so hard to read it.

Other books from the bibliography which are helpful include:

Applying UML and Patterns: An Introduction to Object-Oriented Analysis and Design by Craig Larman

Applying Use Cases by Geri Schneider and Jason P. Winters

Another checklist for requirements can be found in *Code Complete* by Steve McConnell, starting on page 33. While this book concentrates on the construction (development) phase, Chapter 3 discusses definition as a prerequisite for construction.

An Introduction to Objects in Visual Basic

In This Part

Introducing
Objects

This part of the book introduces the concept of objects, and how objects are constructed using Visual Basic.

If you are a developer who already uses objects in VB extensively, it is not necessary for you to read this part in detail. But I think that describes a small minority of VB developers.

If you are unsure whether you are using objects up to their potential, here's a rule of thumb. Look at your last large- or medium-size VB project. Add together the number of forms and BAS modules. Compare that to the number of class modules. If the number of class modules is much less than the number of forms plus the number of BAS modules, you are probably not using objects as extensively as you should be.

Why Don't Most VB Developers Use Objects?

Objects are not just useful in today's complex systems. They are essential. It is becoming impossible to construct large-scale, n-tier software systems in the Windows world without using an object approach. Yet only a small minority of VB developers use a true object-based approach to designing and developing their systems.

VB developers typically understand how to use objects constructed by others. They don't get far using VB otherwise. The problem is bridging the gap between *using* objects and *creating* objects.

Crossing that bridge requires a major change in how you look at the whole software development process. The trendy business books call this a "paradigm shift." Whatever you call it, it is a huge adjustment.

There are, of course, existing books on objects, and many have benefited from them. My personal favorites are listed in the bibliography. But they don't work for everyone. Most books on objects use an academic approach. They start by defining all the object terminology — encapsulation, inheritance, polymorphism, and so forth. Their examples also tend to be abstract.

The explanation of objects in these books would work for most any language. There's not much there tailored to helping VB developers specifically make the object transition.

A Different Approach

To help developers who worked with me overcome these obstacles, I began teaching a class on objects. The approach used in the class (and in this book) starts with objects already familiar to Visual Basic developers — forms and controls. It builds from this foundation to an understanding of the fundamentals of objects.

The Need for Concentrated Effort

This approach has a fairly good success rate. But that does not mean you can learn objects by just sitting back in a chair and reading the following material. It will be necessary to concentrate on the material and really delve into the examples. Objects require a radical readjustment of your thinking, and it will not come easily.

It's a good idea to make sure you have a good basic understanding of each example before going to the next one. For those exercises which take you through construction step-by-step, you should definitely follow the steps and actually code the example in Visual Basic. If you just glance through the examples, it will be very difficult for you to get the nuances that allow you to make the dramatic adjustment you need.

Using the Enclosed CD

A few examples are discussed in the abstract. But most examples have code presented. These examples are available on the enclosed CD. If you run into trouble getting an example or exercise to work, you can get a working example from the CD. Also, some examples use the CD to provide a starting point for an exercise which will eliminate some tedious and routine Visual Basic programming. The CD has a Readme.doc file to get you started, and a file named license.txt which explains the terms for using the code.

▶ For those who already understand objects in VB

If you already understand objects in VB pretty well, you can still benefit from this section. The examples are from real software development projects. You may find that these objects (or objects derived from them) are useful in your projects.

All of the code examples are included on the CD that comes with the book. Feel free to use them in your projects. In legalistic terms, you are granted an unlimited license to use the code, which means you do anything you want with it (except keep others from using it). Read license.txt and Readme.doc on the CD for more information.

The examples on the enclosed CD are in the directories /Examples/VB5 and /Examples/VB6. All of the examples except the one in Chapter 16, "The Prisoner's Dilemma — An Exercise in Inheritance" are available in both versions of Visual Basic.

Do the Material in Order

It's important to do all the material in succession. Later examples build on earlier ones. It is recommended that you don't skip sections or exercises.

A Non-Traditional Approach

A traditional approach for explaining objects would start off with a definition of an object and then define encapsulation, polymorphism, inheritance, and so forth. If you prefer such an approach, there are several books listed in the "Suggestions for Further Reading" section at the end of this section.

This books offers an alternative which is specifically tailored to those experienced in Visual Basic. We will take an indirect path to objects by first looking at forms in VB and some of the things you can do with them. Don't worry — we'll get to all those polysyllabic terms later. But when we get to them, we will be able to point to concrete examples of them to explain what they mean.

The approach begins in the next chapter by looking at something every Visual Basic developer is familiar with — a form in Visual Basic.

Custom Properties and Methods for Forms

This chapter introduces the concept of objects. To make the process fairly painless, we begin with objects you've been using since the first day you started with Visual Basic — forms and controls.

A Review of Forms as Objects

In Visual Basic (even back to version 1), forms are objects. Objects are basically pieces of software that can be manipulated in a particular way, namely with methods and properties. (I can hear computer science professors howling about this definition of objects. Don't worry about that. We'll refine it later.)

What are Methods and Properties?

Properties are characteristics of forms and controls in Visual Basic. Some programmers might use the term *attributes*.

Properties generally represent data in some form. They identify what the object "knows" about itself. Property names are usually *nouns*.

Some of the properties of a form are its width and height, its background color, and whether or not it can currently be seen. These properties are named Width, Height, BackColor, and Visible, respectively. You should be familiar with these and many other built-in properties of forms.

Some properties specify how a form should act. For example, the KeyPreview property tells the form whether it should "peek" at keystrokes before they are processed by the currently active control. Such properties don't affect the visual appearance of the form, but they are still important for determining how the form works.

Controls also have properties. A text box, for example, has a Text property which lets you put text data into the editable area of the box, and to get out what has been entered into the box. Part of becoming an effective VB developer is to learn the properties of controls so that the full capability of the controls can be put to use.

METHODS

Methods are behaviors of forms, controls, and other objects. They identify what an object can do. Since they are an action, their name is usually a *verb*, or at least contains a verb. Typical methods of forms include showing the form to the screen (Show), printing a copy of the form to the printer (Print), and hiding the form from view (Hide).

Controls typically don't have a lot of methods, but most of them have a SetFocus method which brings the screen focus to the control (and away from whatever control had it before).

SYNTAX FOR USING METHODS AND PROPERTIES

You should be very familiar with the syntax for accessing methods and properties. Here are examples of code manipulating some of the methods and properties listed above. These should all be easy to understand if you have experience with any version of Visual Basic.

```
Load frmEmployee

If frmEmployee.Width < 3000 Then  ' If form too narrow, then
    frmEmployee.Width = 3000      ' set width to 3000 twips
End If

frmEmployee.Height = frmEmployee.Width   ' makes form square

' load employee ID
frmEmployee.txtEmployeeID.Text = "111-22-3333"

frmEmployee.Show                    ' show form to screen
```

If the syntax above does not make any sense to you, then you probably will not get much benefit from the rest of this section on objects.

Two Ways of Using Properties

Notice that properties can be used in two different ways. If a property is used on the *right* side of an equal sign (or in an expression for an If statement), then the property is being used like a function. That is, it returns a value. Here's are two examples:

```
sCaptionText = frmEmployee.Caption

if frmEmployee.txtEmployeeID.Text = "111-22-3333" Then
```

If the property is being used on the *left* side of an equal sign, then it is being used to set a value. This line of code illustrates this usage:

```
frmEmployee.Caption = "Customer Options"
```

The line of code above which makes the form square shows properties being used both ways. The Width property is being used like a function, and the Height property is getting set.

Custom Form Properties and Methods

Properties and methods for forms have been in VB since the beginning. However, starting with Visual Basic 4.0, something new was added. The developer gained the ability to add *customized* properties and methods to forms. That is, the developer of the form could specify a new property or method, and define how it worked.

Why would you want to do this? There will be many examples later, but here is a quick idea. With VB3 and earlier, if a form needed to pass information to another form a global variable was often used. Every good developer knows the problems global variables can cause.

A custom property is a far better alternative. Let's look at a typical example. Suppose you have a data entry form which handles employees. It needs a way for other modules to tell it which employee to work on. It also needs to be able to let other modules know what employee it is working on right now. The form could have an EmployeeID property to take care of both requirements.

This EmployeeID property has the following huge advantages over global variables:

Validation logic can be included with the property to make sure the EmployeeID is valid. For example, the property could check to see if number being passed is in the employee database.

Several forms can have their own EmployeeID properties without conflicting with one another.

If you construct such a property for a form, it is accessed with the same syntax as built-in properties. Here are examples of both:

Type of property	Example syntax	Effect
Built-in	`frmDataEntry.Width = 3000`	Sets the form's built-in Width property to the value 3000 and causes the form to become 3000 twips wide on the screen.
Custom	`frmDataEntry.EmployeeID = 3000`	Sets the form's customized EmployeeID property to 3000 and causes the form to bring up employee number 3000.

Custom Form Methods

Telling a form to carry out an action was very hard in VB3 and earlier. You could not use a public subroutine on a form — that was invalid syntax. A typical kludge was to use an invisible control and put the action logic in one of the control's events. (Don't do this! It's just an illustration of the ridiculous lengths you had to go to before custom methods were available.)

With a custom method, a form can now be told to carry out an action. And again, the syntax is the same as with built-in methods:

Type of method	Example syntax	Effect
Built-in	`frmDataEntry.Hide`	Tells the form to hide itself.
Custom	`frmDataEntry.Update`	Tells the form to update the database with the current information.

Constructing Custom Methods for Forms

The syntax examples above show how properties and methods are used from *outside* the form. Now let's see how to construct the code which makes the properties and methods work *inside* the form.

Custom methods are really just public subroutines in a form module (which is valid syntax in VB4 and later). They are inserted into a form module exactly as subroutines are inserted into a BAS module.

Even though custom methods are really subroutines, they can be accessed via the object-style syntax we saw above: frmFormName.Method-Name {argument list if any}. Here are two more examples:

EXAMPLE 1

```
frmSelectionList.Clear
```

For this to work from outside the form, the code module for frmSelectionList would need a subroutine with the declaration line:

```
Public Sub Clear()
```

What goes in the Clear subroutine? Anything you want. Typically, it would contain logic to clear out the information in the various controls on the form, preparing for a new record to be accessed. Here is some typical code which might go in a Clear method:

```
txtEmployeeID.Text = ""
txtEmployeeName.Text = ""

' employee status defaults to active
txtEmployeeStatus = empstatusActive
```

Additional lines could take care of other controls, placing them in whatever state was appropriate for a "cleared" condition.

EXAMPLE 2

Calling line:

```
frmDataEntry.AddField "Last used", gnFIELD_TYPE_DATE
```

In this case, frmDataEntry would need a subroutine with the declaration line:

```
Public Sub AddField(sFieldName as String, _
                nFieldType as Integer)
```

The calling line (which would typically be in code outside the form) is passing the string "Last Used" in for the field name, and a value in gnFIELD_TYPE_DATE for the field type.

The AddField subroutine could have logic to place a new control on the form, based on the information passed in by the arguments.

METHODS AS PUBLIC FUNCTIONS

Before we go on to properties, there is one more item to mention about methods. We talked above about a method being a public subroutine on a form. A method can also be a public function on a form if it needs to return a value. Examples of this are discussed at a later point. For the rest of this chapter, we will assume custom methods are always public subroutines in the form.

Constructing Custom Properties for Forms

Custom properties are a bit more complicated than custom methods, but not much. Each property has *two* routines associated with it — a Property Get and a Property Let. (There's a third type call Property Set which we will take up much later, in Chapter 15, "More About Objects.")

To place a property on a form, first bring up the form's code window. Then open the Tools menu in VB and select the Add Procedure option, just as you would to create a function or subroutine. The resulting dialog box is shown in Figure 9–1.

Select the option button for Type that says "Property" and leave the option for Scope set to "Public" (which is the default). Enter an appropriate name, and press OK. Shells of both the Property Let and Property Get routines will be inserted into the form's code. You have already seen shells inserted when you create a Function or Sub, and this works exactly the same except that *two* routines are inserted when creating *one* property.

If we named our property EmployeeID, the two inserted shell routines would look like this:

```
Public Property Get EmployeeID() As Variant

End Property

Public Property Let EmployeeID(ByVal vNewValue As Variant)

End Property
```

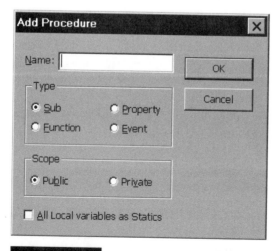

FIGURE 9–1   Add Procedure dialog box.

These are the starting points for you to construct your property. Now you can edit them just like any other code.

The first thing to do is to change the Variant type to whatever type the property needs to be. Just like functions, a Property can be any valid Visual Basic data type. Most properties will be of type String, Integer, Long, or Boolean. Our EmployeeID property might be a Long or a String, depending on how we stored our ID numbers in our employee database.

Property Get Procedures in Detail

Suppose a data entry form had a property named Complete which was used to tell other forms or modules if all the fields on the form were properly filled in. Another module might use the following line to check the Complete status:

```
If frmDataEntry.Complete then
    ' data entry is valid ...
```

In this case, the property is being used like a function. That is, the property is being used to *get* a value.

The Property Get is the routine that is executed when the property is used this way. Since the property is being used like a function, the routine looks a lot like a function.

For the above property named Complete, a Property Get routine (which is part of the form's code) might look like this:

```
Public Property Get Complete() As Boolean
' This property tells if data entry on this form is
' complete.

' The data entry is considered complete if all text boxes
' have something in them.

If txtName.Text <> "" And txtAddress.Text <> "" And _
    txtCity.Text <> "" And txtZip.Text <> "" Then

    Complete = True
Else
    Complete = False
End If

End Property
```

Notice that, just as with a function, there should be at least one line somewhere in the routine which assigns the value. In this case, there are two lines:

```
Complete = True
```

and

```
Complete = False
```

which correspond to the two possible states the property could have. The Property Get is not complete unless such an assignment line exists.

From the code, we can see that this property would check to see if all controls had some data in them, and return True if they did, or False if any one of them was blank.

Many properties are simpler than the Complete property. In the most common case, properties just hold values for reference either inside or outside the form (or both).

For example, suppose we are constructing a form that gets a password. We will call it frmPassword. It needs a property named MaxRetries which stores the maximum number of retries the user gets on the password before being locked out.

It is typical programming practice to store values for such properties as member variables of the form. That is, the variables are declared in the Declarations section at the top of the form's code, and they have form-level scope.

From outside the form, the MaxRetries property might be set with syntax like this:

```
frmPassword.MaxRetries = 4
```

The retries value could be stored inside the form module as a variable named mnMaxRetries. The Declarations section of the form would have a line that looked like this:

```
Private mnMaxRetries As Integer
```

The Property Get would look like this:

```
Public Property Get MaxRetries() As Integer

MaxRetries = mnMaxRetries

End Property
```

Property Let Procedures

Property Let is used to set a value for the property. It is more like a subroutine in construction. It does not have any lines which return a value. The Property Let for the MaxRetries property discussed above might look like this:

```
Public Property Let MaxRetries(ByVal nNewValue As Integer)

mnMaxRetries = nNewValue

End Property
```

This is a simple example. Below we will cover more complex examples for Property Let.

READ-ONLY PROPERTIES

Sometimes properties should not be set from outside the form. Our Complete property above is like that. It doesn't make any sense for a module outside the form to "command" the form to be complete. The value of the Complete property is dependent on the states of various controls, not on the value of a member variable.

Such properties are called read-only properties. For these properties, the Property Let routine can be left out. Or the Property Let can be included, and it can simply raise an error. For example, the Property Let for the Complete property could look like this:

```
Public Property Let Complete (bNewValue As Boolean)
Err.Raise 383   'this is the error for a read-only property
End Property
```

Making Sure All the Types Match Up

For a particular property, the Property Get and Property Let procedures should have their types match up. That is, the declared type of the property in the Property Get must be the same as the type of the argument in the Property Let.

As an example, our Property Get and Property Let declarations for MaxRetries are:

```
Public Property Get MaxRetries() As Integer

Public Property Let MaxRetries(ByVal nNewValue As Integer)
```

In this case, the declared type of the property in the Property Get is Integer, and the type of the argument (nNewValue) in the Property Let is Integer, so they match.

If they are different, you will get the error message shown in Figure 9–2.

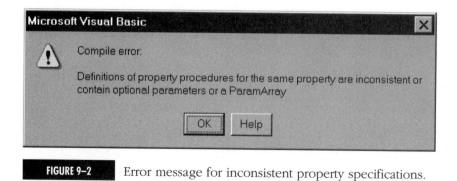

FIGURE 9–2 Error message for inconsistent property specifications.

Public Variables as Properties

It is actually not necessary to set up Property Let and Property Get procedures to have property values on forms. If a variable is declared Public or Global for a form, that variable is available using object property syntax. That is, if the form had the following line at the Declarations level:

```
Public MaxRetries As Integer
```

then it could be accessed as a MaxRetries property exactly as if the property procedures had been created, that is, with syntax like:

```
frmPassword.MaxRetries = 10
```

or

```
If nTries > frmFormName.MaxRetries Then …
```

So why do it with property procedures and incur extra work? Because property procedures are much more flexible. For example, if we wanted to limit the number of retries a form would allow to no more than twenty in all cases, we could have a Property Let procedure that looked like this:

```
Public Property Let MaxRetries(ByVal nNewValue As Integer)

If nNewValue <= 20 and nNewValue > 0 Then
    mnMaxRetries = nNewValue
Else
    Err.Raise 380      ' invalid property value
End If

End Property
```

This example "screens" the incoming value to see if it is OK to use it. If not, an error is raised. You can't do that with globals. This kind of control stops invalid information from getting into the form at a centralized point in the code. The ability to exert such control is one of the most powerful capabilities of custom form properties over alternative ways of getting information into and out of the form.

Some More Comprehensive Examples

Now that we've seen how to construct custom methods and properties for forms, let's see how they might be used to "package" a form for use in multiple projects.

Example 1 — A Splash Screen

Suppose I have several programs that need a splash screen, but the same graphic goes on all of them. The only thing that varies is the program name, program version, and copyright notice. In that case, we could create a splash screen called frmSplash that could be used in all the programs.

If we are using VB3-style techniques, we would probably set up label controls on the form to hold and display the information we need (program name, program version, and copyright notice). Our form might look like the one shown in Figure 9–3.

Various programs use the form, and each needs to load product and copyright information. The code which loads the splash screen sets the caption property for each label to the value it needs right now (see code below). This works, but it has some limitations, as we'll see.

FIGURE 9–3 Splash screen form using label controls.

In the object-oriented counterpart to this, frmSplash would have the string properties ProgramName, ProgramVersion, and CopyrightNotice. frmSplash could have labels to put these string values in. Alternatively, they could be printed directly on the form. The Property Let routines would handle putting the information on the splash screen using whatever technique we want. It would not matter to the code in the calling module how the information is displayed to the screen.

A fully developed example is available with the enclosed CD so that you can examine how property procedures in frmSplash might look.

Here's a comparison of the way some of the code in the calling module would look in each case:

VB3 STYLE

```
Load frmSplash
frmSplash.lblProgramName.Caption = "Buzzsaw"
frmSplash.lblProgramVersion.Caption = "Version 2.11"
frmSplash.lblCopyrightNotice.Caption = "Copyright (C) 1999"
...
frmSplash.Show
```

OBJECT-ORIENTED STYLE

```
Load frmSplash
frmSplash.ProgramName = "Buzzsaw"
frmSplash.ProgramVersion = "2.11"
frmSplash.CopyrightNotice = "Copyright (C) 1999"
...
frmSplash.Show
```

The first thing to note in this comparison is how much cleaner the code looks in the object-oriented style. But there are additional advantages.

With the object-oriented approach, the splash screen form could be changed right under the nose of other programs. If the splash screen originally had label controls, they could be discarded and information placed directly on the form with Print methods. Or the form could use Windows API calls to have the name and version displayed at an angle.

For the object-oriented case, such changes in frmSplash would not require the programs that use frmSplash to be changed in the slightest. For the traditional case, such changes would require the calling code in all programs which used frmSplash to change.

Example 2 — A Custom Database-Open Form

Suppose your application needs to give the user the option of opening a database by choosing from several which are available. However, only certain databases are valid for the functions you need, so you don't want them opening any .mdb file they happen to run across on disk. You want to restrict access to a particular directory, and you want to validate that the file is OK for use before they leave the database-open form.

Now, it's not hard to design such a form in VB3. Let's suppose you do that. How do you get the information into and out of it? You guessed it — global variables. (Actually, there's another choice — invisible controls. But we'll pass over that for the moment.)

Unfortunately, that makes reusing the form in other programs rather tough. It becomes subject to the Christmas-tree-light effect. That's what occurs when trying to extract one module from a program causes other modules to be pulled along whether you want them or not. (Think of trying to pull just one strand of Christmas tree lights out of a box. It always gets stuck and pulls others with it.)

But properties and methods allow such a form to be completely packaged. (The object-oriented term for this is *encapsulation.*) It could have properties of FileMask, DirName, and SelectedFile. It could have a Clear method in case the file list needs to be flushed and reloaded with new parameters. With such encapsulation, several projects (several EXEs) can share this form. It is identical in all of them. Each program sets the properties of the database selection form as needed.

It gets better. Suppose your user tells you during beta testing that the database-open function should remember the last database chosen. In that case, the form could be enhanced to automatically do that. (Typically, this would be implemented as a private method, with the information stored in the Windows Registry or a private INI file.) Note that there are again zero changes in the various modules which call the form.

Finally, let's presume that the user comes back again, and says that actually there are several directories the form should have access to, not just one. You can now add functionality to the form by indexing the DirName property. You can make the index parameter optional and default it to zero. Now the old modules still don't need any changes, but new modules which need multiple directories can add them.

This example shows some of possibilities of what we'll learn to call encapsulation.

Example 3 — A Login Form

Suppose I need to implement a standard log-in procedure at various points in my program. I want to use just one login form for the different log-ins. That is, the same form would be used whenever necessary to do a login.

There are several things that vary with each login. They include:

The type of login (what the user is getting access to)

The number of retries allowed

I also need to be able to find out from the form what the final result was (login approved, or user cancelled, or user tried to login too many times and was rejected).

▶ *Exercise 9.1*

Let's write such a login form. Start VB with a new project.

Step 1

Modify the blank form that comes up to look like Figure 9–4.

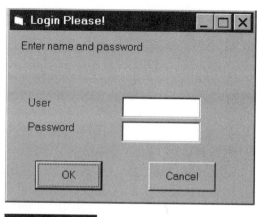

FIGURE 9–4   A simple log-in form.

To do that, place a text box for user and another text box for password. With typical naming conventions, these text boxes would be called txtUser and txtPassword, respectively. (If you want asterisks to come up for each password character typed, don't forget to set the PasswordChar property of txtPassword.)

Place a label at the top of the form for specifying what the login is for. Call it lblDescription.

Place two command buttons at the bottom — OK and Cancel. Call them cmdOK and cmdCancel.

Step 2

Create the following properties for the form. For each property, set its type and place code in the Property Get and Property Let routines to implement the property.

The code for each property is shown below. You may wish to attempt to write the code for the properties yourself, and then compare with the code below to see how you did.

Property	Usage
LoginType	an integer property restricted to one of the following: 1 — Any user is permitted, but the password must be "ABC" 2 — Any user is permitted, but the password must be "XYZ"
LoginDescription	A string property used to find out what to put in the label at the top of the form (this will be an informational string describing what the login is for).
MaxRetries	The maximum number of times the user can attempt a login (maximum number of times the user can press the OK button).
Action	A read-only integer property that specifies what happens when the form is finished. The possible values are: 1 — Login approved 2 — User cancelled 3 — Login denied — too many retries

Here's the code that goes in the form's declaration section to declare the variables we will need to hold the properties' values:

```
Private mnLoginType As Integer
Private msLoginDescription As String
Private mnMaxRetries As Integer
Private mnAction As Integer
```

Here's the code for the properties:

LoginType:

```
Public Property Get LoginType() As Integer

LoginType = mnLoginType

End Property

Public Property Let LoginType(ByVal nNewValue As Integer)

If nNewValue < 1 Or nNewValue > 2 Then
    Err.Raise 380    ' Invalid value for this property
Else
    mnLoginType = nNewValue
End If

End Property
```

LoginDescription:

```
Public Property Get LoginDescription() As String

LoginDescription = msLoginDescription

' We could also do it this way
'LoginDescription = lblDescription.Caption

End Property

Public Property Let LoginDescription(ByVal sNewValue _
                                        As String)

msLoginDescription = sNewValue
lblDescription.Caption = msLoginDescription

' We could also do it this way
'lblDescription.Caption = sNewValue

End Property
```

MaxRetries:

```
Public Property Get MaxRetries() As Integer

MaxRetries = mnMaxRetries

End Property

Public Property Let MaxRetries(ByVal nNewValue As Integer)

If nNewValue < 1 Or nNewValue > 10 Then
    Err.Raise 380        ' invalid value for property
Else
    mnMaxRetries = nNewValue
End If

End Property
```

Action:

```
Public Property Get Action() As Integer

Action = mnAction

End Property

Public Property Let Action(ByVal nNewValue As Integer)

Err.Raise 383        ' This property is read only

End Property
```

<u>Step 3</u>

Now write code for the OK and Cancel buttons. It should go in the Click event.

Do the Cancel button first. It is easy. Just set the Action property to show that the user cancelled and hide the form. Here is the code:

```
Private Sub cmdCancel_Click()

mnAction = 2
Me.Hide

End Sub
```

Now for the OK button. You will need a variable that tracks the number of times the user has attempted a login. Call this variable mnLoginsAttempted and make it a member variable. That means that this line should go in the form's declaration section.

```
Dim mnLoginsAttempted As Integer
```

In the OK button click event, first check to see if the login is correct. That means checking the password. The valid password depends on what the login type is.

If the password is valid, set the Action property to show that the login was approved, and hide the form.

If the password is not valid, display a message to that effect.

After checking the password, increment mnLoginsAttempted. See if it is now too large (more than the MaxRetries property). If it is, set the Action property to show too many retries, and hide the form. Otherwise, exit the click event.

Here is all of the code for the OK button's click event:

```
Private Sub cmdOK_Click()
Dim msValidPassword As String

Select Case mnLoginType
    Case 1
        msValidPassword = "ABC"
    Case 2
        msValidPassword = "XYZ"
End Select

If txtPassword.Text = msValidPassword Then
    mnAction = 1
    Me.Hide
    Exit Sub
Else
    MsgBox "Password is incorrect"
End If
```

```
mnLoginsAttempted = mnLoginsAttempted + 1
If mnLoginsAttempted >= mnMaxRetries Then
    mnAction = 3
    Me.Hide
End If

End Sub
```

Note that when the user cancels, or when a login is accepted, the form should be hidden (not unloaded). If the form were unloaded, the value in the Action property would no longer be available.

Step 4

Now we need to use the login form from a different routine. We will use Sub Main.

Create a BAS module in the project with any name. Insert a Sub Main procedure into the module. Then change the Project Properties to make Sub Main the start-up object for the project. (If you are not familiar with using a Sub Main to start a VB project, check out this capability in the VB documentation.)

Now write code in Sub Main which sets up the login form. This requires the login form to first be loaded, and then have its properties set. For our first exercise, set LoginType to 1, LoginDescription to "Enter User and Password," and MaxRetries to 3. Then show the form modally.

After the line which shows the login form, insert code to tell what the result was based on the Action property of the login form.

Here is sample code for Sub Main.

```
Public Sub Main()

Load frmLogin
frmLogin.LoginDescription = "Enter name and password"
frmLogin.LoginType = 1
frmLogin.MaxRetries = 3

frmLogin.Show vbModal

Select Case frmLogin.Action
    Case 1
        MsgBox "Login approved!"
    Case 2
        MsgBox "The user cancelled."
    Case 3
        MsgBox "Login denied - too many retries."
End Select

End Sub
```

Step 5

Try the login form to see it works properly. If you have trouble, you can compare your version with the version on the enclosed media, which contains a finished, working version of the completed exercise.

If it works, try different login types and numbers of retries to make sure the login form works with different values for its properties. One of the most important steps in creating an object is testing it with various values for its properties.

Additional Comments

If you are familiar with enumerated constants, you may wonder why we did not use them for the Login-Type and Action properties. We will discuss enumerated constants in Chapter 15, "More About Objects."

Notice that we did not show error messages in the code for properties, but instead raised errors so that the calling routine could handle the error. This makes our custom properties work just like a form's built-in properties. Errors in properties and methods are often handled this way.

This exercise was just for instructional purposes, and the example code was kept as simple as possible. You can probably think of several obvious improvements in the program, such as a property to return the user name which was entered.

Example 4 — A Generic Select-From-A-List Form

Now let's get really ambitious. Suppose we need a form which is used to pick items off a list. Unfortunately, the list might be constructed from any one of several tables or recordsets, using one or two fields in the recordset.

Typically, the form would be implemented with a multi-select list box. When used, it might look something like the one shown in Figure 9–5.

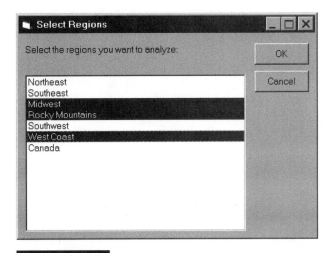

FIGURE 9–5   A multi-select list box.

The exact same form being used in a different situation might look like the one shown in Figure 9–6.

This form is going to need several properties:

Property	Purpose
Recordsource	A SQL statement that describes the recordset
CodeField	The first field used for constructing the list, presumably containing a code value
DescriptionField	The second field for constructing the list, presumably containing a description
Selection	Indexed property to return the items selected by the user. SelectedItem(1) is the first selected item, SelectedItem(2) is the second selected item, etc.
ItemCount	How many selected items there are
Action	Tells what the user's action was when the form was finished 1 = Ready to proceed, 2 = User cancelled
Description	something to put into a label to tell the user what he/she is choosing

We also need to set the form's caption, but we don't need to create a property for that — it's built in.

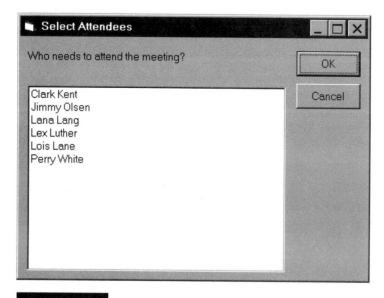

FIGURE 9–6   Another use of the multi-select list box

We'll also need some methods. Load and Reload come to mind to load up the list of items, although we can dispense with Load by having the form check internally to see if it has been loaded when it is accessed.

FINDING OUT THE SELECTED ITEMS

The SelectedItem and Count properties can be used from outside the form to find out what items were chosen. Typical syntax would look like this:

```
Dim nSelectedRegion As Integer
For nSelectedRegion = 1 To frmSelectionList.ItemCount
    Debug.Print frmSelectionList.SelectedItem(nSelectedRegion)
Next nSelectedRegion
```

Of course, there is an alternative way of getting the selected items. You could read them right out of the list box. The code to do that would look something like this:

```
Dim nRegion As Integer
For nRegion = 0 To frmSelectionList.lstItems.ItemCount - 1
    If frmSelectionList.lstItems.Selected(nRegion) Then
        Debug.Print
frmSelectionList.lstItems.ListItem(Region)
    End If
Next nRegion
```

▶ Recommended practice

In general, once you switch to object-oriented design, you should *never* reference a form's controls from anywhere outside the form. The controls should be considered private. If you need to get to information in a control, establish a form property for it, and have the Property Let and Property Get procedures manage the control's value.

The selection list example above shows why you should do this. Here's another example.

Suppose you have a form which uses five option buttons to get a piece of information. Setting up a property simplifies the initial work in getting the choice to the outside world (the calling code does not need to know how the option buttons are arranged, for example). But more importantly, suppose later you have to switch to a combo box holding the choices because they increase in number and start varying. If you have implemented communication without outside routines through properties, the changes to those outside routines are minimal or non-existent. If the outside routines are making direct calls to your option buttons, all that calling code would need to be changed to accommodate the new combo box.

Why wouldn't you want to do it that way? Suppose our sponsor comes back and says the list is too long, and users can't keep track of what's been selected. They want the form to look like the one shown in Figure 9–7 instead.

We have to go back and make extensive changes to the generic selection list form. We would change the form to have a source list and a selected list, with buttons to put items in the selected list and remove them as needed. But if we do this right, using form properties and methods, the calling routines will need *zero* changes.

If we do it with direct calls to controls, we're in trouble. We no longer have a single list box with selected items in it. So our code to call the list box directly doesn't work anymore. We would have to go track down every instance of such code and change it.

USING A SINGLE COPY OF THE SELECTION LIST FORM

To use the selection form above, we would typically use code something like this:

```
Load frmSelectionList
frmSelectionList.Table = "Parts"
frmSelectionList.CodeField = "PartNumber"
frmSelectionList.DescriptionField = "PartDescription"
frmSelectionList.ListDescription = _
                    "Select the parts you need"

frmSelectionList.Show vbModal
If frmSelectionList.UserAction = gnACCEPT_DATA Then
    For nPartIndex = 1 To frmSelectionList.ItemCount
        ' do something with
        ' frmSelectionList.SelectedItem(nPartIndex)
    Next nPartIndex
End If
```

(We don't really need to include the first line. The form will load automatically when the first reference is made to it. I've included it for comparison with another example later.)

Once frmSelectionList is loaded, it is accessible from anywhere in the VB project.

WHAT IF WE WANT MORE THAN ONE SELECTION LIST?

The beauty of creating such a generic selection form is that we can use multiple copies of it for different selection lists. And we might want to have more than one of those lists active at a time. That is, we might want to simultaneously have a selection form for parts and one for vendors, both loaded and active in our program.

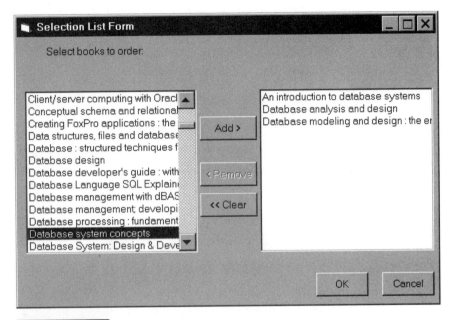

FIGURE 9–7 A selection list box with a different user interface.

In other words, we want to use our original frmSelectionList like a template. Some people like to think of it as a "cookie cutter." We need to make more than one "copy" of frmSelectionList and use the properties to make each copy individual.

Here's the code to do exactly that (assume the code above making the single copy was never run):

```
Dim frmPartSelectionList As Form
Set frmPartSelectionList = New frmSelectionList

frmPartSelectionList.Table = "Parts"
frmPartSelectionList.CodeField = "PartNumber"
frmPartSelectionList.DescriptionField = "PartDescription"
frmPartSelectionList.ListDescription = _
                        "Select the parts you need"

frmPartSelectionList.Show vbModal
If frmPartSelectionList.UserAction = gnACCEPT_DATA Then
    For nPartIndex = 1 To frmPartSelectionList.ItemCount
        ' access
        ' frmPartSelectionList.SelectedItem(nPartIndex)
    Next nPartIndex
End If
```

In this example, frmPartSelectionList is an *object variable*. It contains a reference to a form which of the type frmSelectionList. We can come up with as many such names as we want and create new templates of frmSelection-List for each of them. They will typically all have different properties. We could create one for vendors with code almost exactly like that above, just by changing "Part" to "Vendor" throughout the code sample.

A DETAILED SELECTION LIST EXAMPLE

The following chapter goes through a detailed process to construct a selection list form like the one described above. You can use the resulting form, or a version with your own enhancements, in your own projects.

THE SET STATEMENT

Notice the line above which says:

```
Set frmPartSelectionList = New frmSelectionList
```

We have not used a Set statement like this with forms in previous examples because it was not necessary. However, the Set statement is a very important piece of object syntax. It allows an object variable to be "hooked" to an object. We'll talk more about it later.

SOME OBJECT TERMINOLOGY

Now we are ready for some object terminology. Each form created this way is called an "instance" of the form object. The initial creation of an instance is called "instantiation." The code above is said to "instantiate" frmPartSelectionList as an object.

In this case, frmSelectionList is no longer playing the role of a form loaded into memory. It is now playing the role of a "template." It is the generic example of a selection list. We call such a generic template a "class." The class is used to create instances, with each instance being an individual object.

SCOPE OF THE OBJECT VARIABLE

There's another complication in all this. In the first example above, we just loaded frmSelectionList. This is probably the way you are accustomed to loading and using forms in Visual Basic.

When a form is loaded this way, an instance of it is created automatically with the same name as the generic form. Moreover, this instance is automatically available globally. That is, as soon as the form is loaded as frmSelectionList, we can immediately manipulate frmSelectionList from any code in our VB project. This is the way you are probably accustomed to using forms.

▶ The cookie cutter analogy

To visualize this idea of a "cookie cutter" being used to make copies of an object, picture the cookie cutter (the template) stamping out copies of the cookie from the dough. When they are first stamped out, they are effectively identical.

Then think about making each one individual. Some might have raisins on them, others might have chocolate chips.

Using object terminology, each time you stamp, you create an "instance" of the cookie. Then, for each instance you can set the "Topping" property to raisins or chocolate chips. The cookie cutter itself is referred to as a "class." We might have several "classes" (several cutters) that create differently shaped cookies.

However, if the form is instantiated via the second mechanism, *we have no such global reference.* The form can only be accessed with the object variable, and this variable follows the same scope rules as any other variable. That means the form can only be accessed in places that the variable is in scope.

This might seem like an inconvenience if you are accustomed to just referring to forms from anywhere you like. But it turns out not to be nearly as limiting in practice once you are accustomed to object techniques.

This selection list example illustrates the true power of objects. With functions and subroutines, there is never more than one copy available and active. That means we can't effectively use functions and subroutines to "wrap" data. But objects can hold their own data. Each copy of an object can have data elements with values different from every other copy, but they can all share the same logic.

We will construct this example in detail in the next chapter. It contains a step-by-step exercise for creating the selection list form, and a shell program to test it.

Example 5 — A List of Valid Drives

Now suppose we need a form which gives us a list of valid drives on a system. Perhaps we need to look on all valid drives to see if a certain directory exists. So we need to look at any floppy disks, hard disks, or network drives that the system has.

To do that, we could set up a form with a drive list box. You may recall that a drive list box automatically fills with a list of all valid drives when the form loads. Such a form with the drive list box opened might look like the one shown in Figure 9–8.

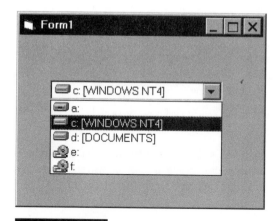

FIGURE 9-8 A form with a drive list box.

From our calling code (outside the form) we could just reference the drive list box to get the drives directly. However, that violates our guidelines that we will not refer to controls from outside the form. Besides, the drive list box passes back a string with the drive letter plus the volume name, and we might not want the volume name.

Instead, we can give the form the indexed property ValidDrive(n) to allow the form to expose the valid drives it found. Then we could get the first valid drive (from anywhere in our project) with code like this:

```
sDriveLetter = frmValidDrives.ValidDrive(1)
```

The code which implements the ValidDrive property would look something like this:

```
Public Property Get ValidDrive(nIndex As Integer) As String
' We assume our property is one-based
ValidDrive = Left$(cboValidDrives.List(nIndex - 1), 2)

End Property
```

▶ Indexed properties

Visual Basic has many built-in properties which are indexed. For example, the List property of a List-box is indexed. If you want item number 4, you would refer to "lstListBox.List(4)."

Custom properties for forms can also be indexed. The Property Get and Property Let for an indexed property must have an argument for passing the index. Otherwise, indexed properties are just like other properties. See the ValidDrives example for the code which implements an indexed property.

The form will also need a DriveCount property to tell us how many valid drives there are. (It would be nice to name this just Count. Unfortunately, forms already have a Count property — it refers to the number of controls on the form.)

With these properties, we can construct a loop from anywhere in our project to do something on each valid drive. That code might look something like this:

```
Load frmValidDrives
For nDriveIndex = 1 to frmValidDrives.DriveCount
    Debug.Print frmValidDrives.ValidDrive(nDriveIndex)
next nDriveIndex
```

This code assumes that the index for valid drives is one-based rather than zero-based. That's purely a matter of preference, and it could be done either way. The frmValidDrives example on the CD is one-based with some comments on code which would have to change to make it zero-based.

A Form We Don't Need to See

We have just created a form that we never want to look at! We're not actually interested in seeing the drive list box, so we never need to show this form to the screen. We just load the form (without showing it) and manipulate its ValidDrive and DriveCount properties.

This example further abstracts the idea of a form as an object. The visual manifestation fades into the background. In this case, the form is really just a container for information and the logic to manipulate the information.

In the next chapter, we'll do a detailed example of a form with custom properties and methods by actually implementing the selection list form from Example 4 above. Then, in the following chapter, (Chapter 11, "An Introduction to Class Modules") we'll revisit the frmValidDrive example, and see how this concept of a container for logic and data can be taken to the next level.

The Selection List Form — A Detailed Example

In the previous chapter, we looked at several examples of forms with custom properties and methods. Example 4 was for a generic selection list form. This form is a particularly good example to look at in detail for a couple of reasons:

- It can be useful in real-world situations (typically with some adaptation)
- It is an example of a form which might need to be instantiated several times in a project

The selection list form is completely configurable at runtime. The selection list can be constructed on the fly, given the database, the recordset, and the fields in the recordset to use for the list. We listed these properties that the form would need:

- Recordsource (the string name of the table or a SQL statement that describes the recordset)
- CodeField (the first field used for constructing the list, presumably containing a code value)
- DescriptionField (the second field for constructing the list, presumably containing a description)
- Selection or SelectedItems (could be an indexed property, or a delimited string, or a collection)

- ItemCount (how many selected items there are)
- Action (some code that indicates whether the user pressed Accept or Cancel)
- Description (something to put into a label to tell the user what is being chosen)

In this chapter, we will go through the details on constructing the selection list form. Going through this procedure should help you master the fundamentals of using forms as generic objects.

As with other examples in the book, the complete program is on the enclosed CD. Look in either \examples\VB5\SelectionList or \examples\VB6\SelectionList, depending on which version of Visual Basic you want to use.

Step 1 — Create the Form and Put the Controls On It

We will not spend a lot of time on this part because any experienced VB developer already knows how to do this. Create a form in a project and name it frmSelectionList.

We want the form to look like the one in Figure 10–1.

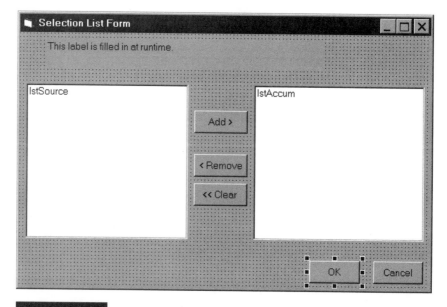

FIGURE 10–1   A selection list form.

To create this form, place the following controls on the form using the layout in Figure 10-1:

Control Type	Name	Special Properties
Label	lblDescription	Caption = "This label is filled in at runtime"
Listbox	lstSource	
Listbox	lstAccum	
Command Button	cmdAdd	Caption = "Add >"
Command Button	cmdRemove	Caption = "< Remove"
Command Button	cmdClear	Caption = "<< Clear"
Command Button	cmdOK	Caption = "OK", Default = True
Command Button	cmdCancel	Caption = "Cancel", Cancel = True

Step 2 — Add Logic to Support Moving Items Between List Boxes

To make the three buttons between the list boxes functional, place the following code in the click events for those buttons:

```
Private Sub cmdAdd_Click()

Dim sSelectedItem As String
Dim nAccumIndex As Integer, nSourceIndex As Integer

' This routine adds selected items in the
' lstSource list box to the accumulator
' list box (lstAccum). lstSource may have multiple items
' selected, so a loop through its entries
' is necessary to see which are selected.
' Any items which are added
' to lstAccum are removed from lstSource

' When an item is selected, it must be
' checked against all the items in lstAccum to
' see if it is already in there
' (in which case, it should not be added again).
' If a duplicate is found, the string to be added
' is changed to a carriage return, which serves
' as a flag that the item should not be added.

' Need to get all selected items in the source list box
' (have to go backwards because we are removing items,
' which affects the list index of items further down)
```

```
For nSourceIndex = lstSource.ListCount - 1 To 0 Step -1

  ' Check the item to see if it is selected
  If lstSource.Selected(nSourceIndex) Then
    sSelectedItem = lstSource.List(nSourceIndex)
    lstSource.Selected(nSourceIndex) = False

    ' Check for duplicate already in the accumulator box
    For nAccumIndex = 0 To lstAccum.ListCount - 1

      ' if it's a duplicate, mark it -
      ' using carriage return for marker
      If lstAccum.List(nAccumIndex) = sSelectedItem Then
        sSelectedItem = vbCr
        Exit For
      End If
    Next nAccumIndex

    ' If not a duplicate, add the item
    If sSelectedItem <> vbCr Then
      lstAccum.AddItem sSelectedItem
      lstSource.RemoveItem nSourceIndex
    End If
  End If
Next nSourceIndex

  ' Make sure the clear button is enabled,
  ' since the list is not empty after an addition
  cmdClear.Enabled = True

  ' Disable the add button, since all selected
  ' items were just added
  cmdAdd.Enabled = False

End Sub


Private Sub cmdClear_Click()
Dim nAccumIndex As Integer

' First stick the accumulated items back in lstSource
For nAccumIndex = 0 To lstAccum.ListCount - 1
  lstSource.AddItem lstAccum.List(nAccumIndex)
Next nAccumIndex

' Then clear the accumulated items,
' and fix the button states

lstAccum.Clear
```

```
cmdRemove.Enabled = False
cmdClear.Enabled = False

End Sub


Private Sub cmdRemove_Click()

Dim sSelectedItem As String
dim nSourceIndex As Integer, nAccumIndex As Integer

' This routine puts selected items in the lstAccum list box
' back in the lstSource list box.
' It works a lot like the code in cmdAdd, so we won't
' repeat all the comments.

For nAccumIndex = lstAccum.ListCount - 1 To 0 Step -1

  ' check the item to see if it is selected
  If lstAccum.Selected(nAccumIndex) Then
    sSelectedItem = lstAccum.List(nAccumIndex)
    lstAccum.Selected(nAccumIndex) = False

    ' check for duplicate already in the source box
    For nSourceIndex = 0 To lstSource.ListCount - 1
      ' if it's a duplicate, mark it -
      ' using carriage return for marker
      If lstSource.List(nSourceIndex) = sSelectedItem Then
        sSelectedItem = vbCr
        Exit For
      End If
    Next nSourceIndex

    ' If not a duplicate, add the item back to lstSource
    ' and remove it from lstAccum
    If sSelectedItem <> vbCr Then
      lstSource.AddItem sSelectedItem
      lstAccum.RemoveItem nAccumIndex
    End If
  End If
Next nAccumIndex

' Fix the button states.
' cmdRemove must be disabled because no item is selected.
cmdRemove.Enabled = False
If lstAccum.ListCount = 0 Then
  cmdClear.Enabled = False
End If

End Sub
```

We need some logic in list box events so that the list boxes can support double-clicking on an item, and to make sure buttons are enabled or disabled as necessary:

```
Private Sub lstAccum_Click()

cmdRemove.Enabled = True

End Sub

Private Sub lstAccum_DblClick()

cmdRemove_Click

End Sub


Private Sub lstSource_Click()

cmdAdd.Enabled = True

End Sub


Private Sub lstSource_DblClick()

    cmdAdd_Click
    cmdClear.Enabled = True

End Sub
```

A few lines in Form Load are also needed to set the initial states of the buttons:

```
Private Sub Form_Load()

cmdAdd.Enabled = False
cmdRemove.Enabled = False
cmdClear.Enabled = False

End Sub
```

Step 3 — Add the Properties and Methods

All the code above is standard Visual Basic logic. Now we are ready to add the code that relates to the object capabilities of the form.

Here are the properties we need to add to the form:

Property	Type	Purpose
Recordsource	String	A SQL statement that describes the recordset
CodeField	String	The first field used for constructing the list, presumably containing a code value
DescriptionField	String	The second field for constructing the list, presumably containing a description
Selection	String	Indexed property to return the items selected by the user. Selection(1) is the first selected item, Selection(2) is the second selected item, etc.
ItemCount	Integer	How many selected items there are
Action	Enumerated type	Tells what the user's action was when the form was finished: 1 = Ready to proceed, 2 = User cancelled
Description	String	something to put into a label to tell the user what he/she is choosing

The code to implement these properties follows. First are the lines that go in the declaration section to declare the member variables for the properties and define the enumerated type. (If you are unfamiliar with enumerated types, they will be discussed in some detail in Chapter 15, "More About Objects.")

```
Private msDatabaseName As String
Private msRecordSource As String
Private msCodeField As String
Private msDescriptionField As String

Public Enum enuAction
  actionOK = 1
  actionCancel = 2
End Enum

Private mnAction As enuAction
```

Next are the property procedures for all the properties except the Selection property (we'll cover it separately). Note that the Action and Item-Count properties are read-only.

```
Public Property Get Description() As String

Description = lblDescription.Caption

End Property

Public Property Let Description(ByVal sNewValue As String)

lblDescription.Caption = sNewValue

End Property

Public Property Get DatabaseName() As String

DatabaseName = msDatabaseName

End Property

Public Property Let DatabaseName(ByVal sNewValue As String)

' could place validation logic here to make sure file
' exists, is a valid database, etc.
msDatabaseName = sNewValue

End Property

Public Property Get Recordsource() As String

Recordsource = msRecordSource

End Property

Public Property Let Recordsource(sNewValue As String)

' could place validation logic here to make sure recordset
' can be opened, etc.
msRecordSource = sNewValue

End Property

Public Property Get CodeField() As String

CodeField = msCodeField

End Property

Public Property Let CodeField(ByVal sNewValue As String)

msCodeField = sNewValue
```

```
End Property

Public Property Get DescriptionField() As String

DescriptionField = msDescriptionField

End Property

Public Property Let DescriptionField(ByVal sNewValue _
                                As String)

msDescriptionField = sNewValue

End Property

Public Property Get ItemCount() As Integer

ItemCount = lstAccum.ListCount

End Property

Public Property Let ItemCount(ByVal nNewValue As Integer)

Err.Raise 383    ' Read-only property

End Property

Public Property Get Action() As enuAction

Action = mnAction

End Property

Public Property Let Action(ByVal nNewValue As enuAction)

Err.Raise 383    ' read-only property

End Property
```

The Selection property is an indexed property. That means that the property requires an argument, which is an integer, to tell which particular selected item you want. The integer argument can be anywhere from 1 to the number of selected items, which is found using the ListCount property.

Many Visual Basic controls have indexed properties that work this way. The List property of a Listbox is one example. In fact, the Selection property is basically a "wrapper" around the List property of the lstAccum Listbox.

To implement an indexed property, the index argument must be part of the property procedure declaration. Here is code for the Property Get procedure for Selection:

```
Public Property Get Selection(nIndex As Integer) As String

Dim sItem As String

If nIndex > lstAccum.ListCount Or nIndex < 1 Then
   Err.Raise 381    ' invalid property array index
   Exit Property
End If


' Have to subtract one from index to switch from zero-based
' list box to one-based property
sItem = lstAccum.List(nIndex - 1)

' Strip off the description field - the property
' should only pass back the code field.
Dim nTabPosition As Integer
nTabPosition = InStr(sItem, vbTab)
If nTabPosition = 0 Then
   Selection = sItem
Else
   Selection = Left$(sItem, nTabPosition - 1)
End If

End Property
```

Notice that each list item is constructed from a code field and a description field. (That's done in the LoadList method which we will cover below.) Our Selection property only returns the value of the code field, so we need to strip off the description field.

We don't require a Property Let for our initial version of the form because we are not allowing selected items to be determined from outside the form. But we will show the declaration for the Property Let, because this is a capability which might be desirable to add later.

```
Public Property Let Selection(nIndex As Integer, _
ByVal sNewValue As String)

' could insert logic here to cause items to
' be selected from external modules

End Property
```

Notice that the Property Let has two arguments, the index and the new property value being passed in. For an indexed property, the index argument must always be declared before the value argument. In fact, the value argument for the Property Let must always be the *last* argument in the list. The methods needed by the form are:

Method	Arguments	Purpose
LoadList	None	After the database, recordset, and fields have been set, this method causes the list to be fetched from the database.
Clear	None	Clears out the selected items via an external call. Internal action is same as pressing the Clear button.

Here is the code for them:

```
Public Sub Clear()

cmdClear_Click

End Sub


Public Sub LoadList()

' Open database
Dim dbDatabase As Database
Set dbDatabase = OpenDatabase(msDatabaseName)

' open recordset
Dim rsRecordset As Recordset
Set rsRecordset = dbDatabase.OpenRecordset(msRecordSet)

lstSource.Clear

' Loop through the recordset, constructing
' items to add to list box
Dim sItem As String
Do Until rsRecordset.EOF

   ' always get the code field
   sItem = rsRecordset.Fields(msCodeField)
```

```
' only get description field if one is present
If msDescriptionField <> "" Then
  sItem = sItem & vbTab & _
          rsRecordset.Fields(msDescriptionField)
End If

' Add the item to the list box and get
' ready for the next one
lstSource.AddItem sItem
rsRecordset.MoveNext

Loop

' Note that the recordset and database objects are local.
' That means they will go away when the method is finished.
End Sub
```

Step 4 — Set Up the OK and Cancel Buttons

The OK and Cancel buttons are the last controls to be fixed up. They don't really need to do anything except set the user's action and hide the form:

```
Private Sub cmdOK_Click()

mnAction = actionOK

Me.Hide

End Sub


Private Sub cmdCancel_Click()

mnAction = actionCancel

Me.Hide

End Sub
```

WHY HIDE THE FORM INSTEAD OF UNLOADING IT?

Both the OK and Cancel buttons hide the form rather than unloading it. That's because this sequence of events has to occur:

1. The calling code loads and sets up the selection list form.
2. The calling code shows the selection list form (usually modally). That transfers execution to the form's code.

3. The selection list form allows the user to select items.

4. The user presses OK or Cancel. This hides the form and returns control to the calling code.

5. The calling code checks the Action property to see what the user did. If the user pressed OK, the calling code can get the selected items and process them.

If the form were unloaded at step 4 instead of hidden, then step 5 could not take place. The calling code would not be able to check the properties of the selection list form because it would be gone. (Actually, attempting to check the properties would cause a new version of the form to be loaded, but it would not have the information just entered by the user.)

Step 5 — Set up the Code to Load and Use the Form

The calling code which will load and use the form can be set up anywhere in a project, but for testing, we will put it in Sub Main.

First, insert a module into the project. It will be called Module1 by default, and that's fine. In that module, insert a single subroutine named Main. (Experienced Visual Basic developers should be familiar with this operation.)

For testing, we will use a table out of the Biblio.mdb sample database that comes with Visual Basic. Our Main subroutine should look something like this:

```
Public Sub Main()

Load frmSelectionList
With frmSelectionList
  .DatabaseName = "c:\progra~1\DevStudio\vb\biblio.mdb"
  .Recordset = "SELECT * FROM Titles"
  .CodeField = "ISBN"
  .DescriptionField = "Title"
  .Description = "Select books:"
  .LoadList
  .Show vbModal
End With

Dim nBookIndex As Integer

If frmSelectionList.Action = actionOK Then
  For nBookIndex = 1 To frmSelectionList.ItemCount
    Debug.Print frmSelectionList.Selection(nBookIndex)
```

```
      Next nBookIndex
   Else
      Debug.Print "User cancelled"
   End If

   End Sub
```

You should be familiar with the With statement in Visual Basic. If not, you should look over the Visual Basic help reference on the With statement.

You may need to change the line that sets the DatabaseName to point to an appropriate location for Biblio.mdb. If you don't have a handy copy of Biblio.mdb, you can get one from the /Examples directory of the enclosed CD.

Don't forget to change the project properties to make Sub Main the startup object for the property. Then run the project. It should load a list of titles into the selection list form and allow them to be selected. When OK is pressed, the selected titles will be printed to the Debug window. If the user cancels, that information will be printed to the Debug window.

Suggested Enhancements

This form could be enhanced with several features, including the ability to:

- Use drag-and-drop capabilities between the list boxes
- Set selected items from outside the form
- Display a progress bar while the list is loading
- Use grids instead of list boxes for the source and accumulator lists. This would allow as many fields as desired to be put in the list for display, with each field in a separate column. There could also be a property which specified which column contained the value to return in the Selection property
- Include a pair of option buttons at the top. One could say "All items" and the other could say "Select from the list below." This would allow the user to specify that all items are to be included without going through the entire list

These capabilities would all be straightforward to add. Except for using grids instead of list boxes, adding these capabilities would not require changes to code which was already using the selection list form.

Remember from the previous chapter that multiple instances of the selection list form could be created. This would allow several selection lists to exist simultaneously in the project with only one form to code. Here is the code which would load and configure two instances of frmSelectionList, one for Vendors and one for Parts:

```
Dim frmPartSelectionList As Form
Set frmPartSelectionList = New frmSelectionList

frmPartSelectionList.DatabaseName = "/data/inventry.mdb"
frmPartSelectionList.Table = "Parts"
frmPartSelectionList.CodeField = "PartNumber"
frmPartSelectionList.DescriptionField = "PartDescription"
frmPartSelectionList.ListDescription = _
        "Select the parts you need"

frmPartSelectionList.Show

Dim frmVendorSelectionList As Form
Set frmVendorSelectionList = New frmSelectionList

frmVendorSelectionList.DatabaseName = "/data/inventry.mdb"
frmVendorSelectionList.Table = "Vendors"
frmVendorSelectionList.CodeField = "VendorNumber"
frmVendorSelectionList.DescriptionField = "VendorDescription"
frmVendorSelectionList.ListDescription = _
        "Select the Vendors you need"

frmVendorSelectionList.Show
```

An Introduction to Class Modules

I'm assuming that at this point you have read Chapter 9, "Custom Properties and Methods for Forms." In it, we looked at forms as objects, and how we could do custom properties and methods for forms.

We saw many examples of how custom properties and methods can be useful, and how they allow encapsulation of logic into nice packages. In the chapter immediately before this one, we did a detailed example of constructing such a form.

The Valid Drives Example

Think back now to the last example in Chapter 9. It was a form that gave us a list of valid drives. That example is key to what we are going to do next.

Recall that our frmValidDrives form *never needed to be visible*. In other words, it was just a container for data and logic.

Suppose we had another way of getting a list of valid drives rather than a drive list box. (There are actually API functions to do that.) Then the last reason for using a form at all in the frmValidDrives example fades away. We just need a different container for the methods, properties, and logic of the object.

We have one available in Visual Basic. It is called a class module.

A class module is a template for a type of object. As with all objects, sometimes we only need one instance of a class; in others we may need many. Remember that the same possibilities were true for forms. We only needed one instance of the valid drives form (example 5), but possibly multiple instances of the selection list form (example 4 and the detailed exercise).

Creating a Class Module

You have known for a long time how to create a form in Visual Basic. And you now know how to create custom methods and properties for the form. That furnishes the basic skills you need to create class modules.

A new class module is added to your project on the same menu used to add a form or BAS module. It is the Project menu, and it contains an entry called "Add Class Module."

When you are adding a form, there are lots of template forms you can use as starting points. There are fewer choices for adding a new class module. Assuming you have the standard Visual Basic installation, the dialog you see after selecting "Add Class Module" should look something like Figure 11–1, depending on what version of VB you are using.

We will not discuss the class builder at this point. We will look at it later in the chapter. If you select the first option (the one just labeled "Class Module"), what you get is just an empty code window. At first glance, it looks just like a BAS module. But there are several important differences:

- In a BAS module, you can only insert functions and subroutines. In a class module, you can also insert property procedures
- Public subroutines become methods in a class module the same way they do for forms
- A class module automatically has some built-in events, like a form does. It can also have custom events defined

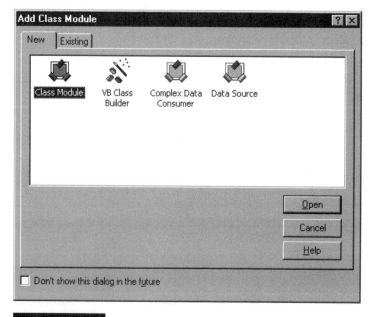

FIGURE 11-1   Add Class Module dialog box.

BUILT-IN EVENTS — INITIALIZE AND TERMINATE

We will discuss events for both forms and class modules in more detail later. For now it is enough to know that classes have two built-in events, Initialize and Terminate. These function very much like the Load and Unload events for forms. Anything you want to happen when an object is created from a class goes in the Initialize event and anything you want to happen when an object goes away goes in the Terminate event.

THE NAME OF A CLASS AND SOME NAMING CONVENTIONS

A class module has a name just as a form module does. When you create a class module, the first thing you should do is to put in an appropriate name, just as you would with a form. Classes are named in their property box, the same way forms are named.

It is conventional to use the prefix "c" or "cls" for a class module name. If we created a class module for valid drives to replace the form we looked at above, we might call it cValidDrives. An object created from such a class module might have a name like objValidDrives. We will use such conventions for all of our class module examples.

It is a good practice with classes to name their disk file with the same name as the class. Since such files use the extension ".cls," the classes above would typically be stored in files with the names cSettings.cls, cEmployee.cls, and cDiskFile.cls. VB will use such names by default.

▶ Why is it called a "class"?

All object-oriented systems refer to groups of related objects as "classes." This comes naturally from the "classification" that goes on in the real world. We understand intuitively that referring to the class of "houses" covers a lot of variation, but that there are certain things that the members of the class have in common.

A "class module" in Visual Basic defines a class of objects. The objects may vary in their properties, but they have some common underlying structure and capabilities.

If you recall the "cookie cutter" analogy in the previous chapter, the form module performed the role of the cookie cutter — it serves as a template to stamp out new "instances" of the form, which can then be customized. Class modules play the same role. They are the template to create new "instances" of the class, which are individual objects.

Using Classes in Code

Using classes in your code is much like using forms in your code. One big difference is that you can't just refer to a class module and start using it with a global reference (as you can with forms). To create (instantiate) an object based on a class, an object variable *must* be used.

There are two minor variations on the process:

VARIATION 1

```
Dim objMyClassObject as New cMyClass
.
.
.
objMyClassObject.Property1 = xxxx
Etc.
```

VARIATION 2

```
Dim objMyClassObject as cMyClass
.
.
.
Set objMyClassObject = new cMyClass
.
.
.
objMyClassObject.Property1 = xxxx
Etc.
```

What's the difference? Which one is preferable? The only significant difference is *when* the object is instantiated. In the first variation, the object is instantiated when the first property or method for the object is accessed (the Dim ... As New ... construct does not immediately instantiate an object). In the second variation, the instantiation happens when the Set statement executes.

Since any property or method can cause instantiation in the first variation, it may be hard to know exactly when an instantiation will occur. Therefore the second variation is usually preferred because the instantiation will always occur on the Set statement.

Building Classes with the Class Builder

With class modules, there is an option for creating methods and properties that is not available with forms — the class builder. This tool allows you to create a property for a class by specifying its name and data type. It allows you to create a method by specifying its name and arguments. When you have created all the properties and methods for a class, the class builder will then create "shell" code — code which contains all the declarations and member variables needed to implement simple properties and methods.

The class builder can certainly save you some significant time, but it has drawbacks, as we will discuss later. On balance, it is better than typing in all the code yourself, as long as you use it wisely.

Starting the Class Builder

Earlier in this chapter, we saw the screen (Figure 11–1) that appears when the "Add Class Module" option was selected. It has an icon to start up the class builder. If you select this icon, you'll get a screen which looks like Figure 11–2.

Note that the class builder shows you all the classes already in the project, if there are any. Despite the fact that you get to the class builder with "Add Class Module," you can also use it to change existing classes.

We will create a class named cSampleClass, and show the screens used to create properties and methods.

Adding a New Class to the Class Builder

To add our cSampleClass, select New on the File menu, then select Class. You'll get a screen which allows you to name a new class. After you fill in the name you want (in our case cSampleClass), the screen looks like Figure 11–3:

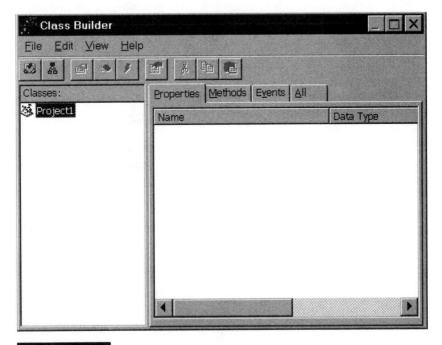

FIGURE 11-2   The initial class builder screen.

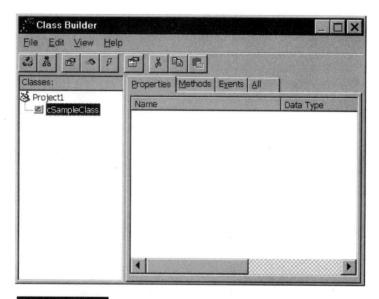

FIGURE 11–3   The class builder screen with a new class.

Adding New Properties and Methods to a Class

With cSampleClass highlighed, you can add a property to the class. On the File menu, select New, then select Property. The resulting dialog box requests property information. It looks like Figure 11–4:

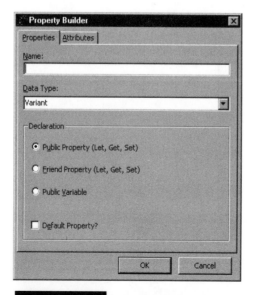

FIGURE 11–4   The dialog for a new property.

For a typical property, just fill in the name of the property and select the data type from the drop down list.

Similarly, if you open the file menu, select New, and then select Method, you will get a dialog to add a new method. It looks like Figure 11–5.

In this case, you need to supply the method's name, and its arguments, if any. To add an argument, press the plus button, and supply the argument type.

When you are finished adding classes, properties, and methods, select File, and then Exit. You will be asked if you want to update the project. If you select "Yes," the class builder will write shell code for the classes.

This quick introduction should get you started. As you learn more advanced techniques for methods and properties, you will use more of the options in the class builder.

Drawbacks to Using the Class Builder

While the class builder does save significant time in writing routine code for a class, it has some limitations. We'll be discussing these as they come up, but there is one you should know about right away — bad naming conventions.

The class builder prefixes all member variables with "mvar," regardless of data type. When I use the class builder to create a class, the first thing I do with the code is to fix all the variable names so that they have prefixes that correspond to their data type.

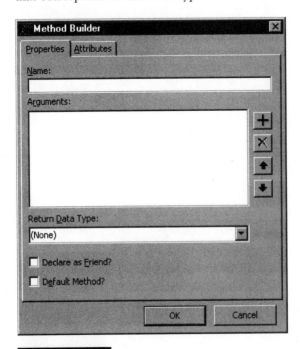

FIGURE 11–5 The dialog for a new method.

Chapter Summary

This chapter has introduced the concept of a class module in Visual Basic. At this point, you should have a basic understanding of a class module as container for logic and data, i.e., as an object. You also have been shown how to create and develop a class module, and how to use it to spawn objects of that that class in code.

The concepts involved are similar to the parallel concepts for forms. For your earliest understanding of class modules, it helps to think of them as forms with no visible manifestation. Later you will just think about them as templates for objects.

The next chapter will continue introducing VB syntax related to class modules, and we will look at a number of examples of useful class modules.

Examples of Objects and More Object Syntax

In the previous chapters, we looked at how objects are constructed in Visual Basic. We began with how we can modify built-in objects (forms) and built on that to see how to create brand-new, stand-alone objects (with class modules), and how to spawn instances of those objects with code.

In this chapter, we will start with some more examples of useful objects, and then we will look at the syntax used to do more manipulation of objects with Visual Basic code. In particular, we will look in more detail at the concept of an object variable.

Some More Examples of Objects

It is very important at this stage that you begin to understand why objects are a useful concept. Here are a few examples of situations in which an object approach yields obvious benefits over the typical structured programming approach.

A Settings Object

It is typical in VB programs to use several global variables to handle some critical pieces of information that are needed system-wide. The location of a database, for example, or settings of user preferences might be done this way. Often the information comes from a private INI file or from the system registry.

A better way of dealing with such information is to create a "settings" object. It can have properties for all of the information normally held in global variables. Only a single global reference would be needed, which is a global object variable pointing to the settings object.

There are many advantages to this approach. Let's examine some of them.

VERIFICATION OF SETTINGS

With a settings object, we can make the properties for the settings handle any necessary validation of the value of the setting. If a setting refers to a file name, for example, we could check to make sure that the file name is valid and that the file exists.

Any other routines dealing with settings could also be centralized in the settings object. If a property represents a social security number, for example, any formatting for the SSN could be placed in the code for the settings object.

MANAGEMENT OF SETTINGS

Management of the settings is also dramatically improved. We can do all of the initial loading of the property values in the Class Initialize event. Those values can come from INI files or the registry or anywhere else we like.

In some cases, we have properties that don't have a value in the INI file or registry. This might happen, for example, the first time a program is used. To deal with that, we set up any defaults we need. The Class Initialize code can check for properties which are not specified in the registry or INI file, and place appropriate values in them.

And we can arrange for current settings to be saved in the Class Terminate event. Then we no longer have to worry about making sure new settings are saved to disk when the program ends.

Here is the code for a simple settings object:

```
Option Explicit

'local variable(s) to hold property value(s)
Private msLastReportRun As String     'local copy
Private mnMaxPages As Long            'local copy

' needed to get and set Registry values
Dim msAppName As String
Dim msSection As String

Public Property Let MaxPages(ByVal nData As Long)
    mnMaxPages = nData
End Property
```

```
Public Property Get MaxPages() As Long
    MaxPages = mnMaxPages
End Property


Public Property Let LastReportRun(ByVal vData As String)
    msLastReportRun = vData
End Property


Public Property Get LastReportRun() As String
    LastReportRun = msLastReportRun
End Property


Private Sub Class_Initialize()

' Get current values from Registry

Dim sKey As String
Dim sValue As String

' First set our application name and section name
' for the registry. These are member variables because
' they are also used in Class Terminate
msAppName = "MyVBApp"
msSection = "MySection"

' get LastReportRun value - default is null string
sKey = "LastReportRun"
msLastReportRun = GetSetting(msAppName, msSection, _
                             sKey, vbNullString)

' get MaxPages value - default is 100
sKey = "MaxPages"
sValue = GetSetting(msAppName, msSection, sKey, "100")
mnMaxPages = Int(Val(sValue))

End Sub


Private Sub Class_Terminate()
' Place current values into Registry

Dim sKey As String
Dim sValue As String
```

```
' The application name and section name were set in
' Class Initialize event

' Save LastReportRun value
sKey = "LastReportRun"
SaveSetting msAppName, msSection, sKey, msLastReportRun

' Save MaxPages value
sKey = "MaxPages"
sValue = Str$(mnMaxPages)
SaveSetting msAppName, msSection, sKey, sValue

End Sub
```

You can test this settings object by doing the following:

1. Start a new VB project.
2. Create the class module in the project. Name it cSettings. Place the code listed just above in the class module.
3. On the default form created for the project, place two text boxes. Name one txtLastReportRun, and the other txtMaxPages. You may place labels on the form to identify these text boxes if you like.
4. In the Declarations section of the form code, place this line:

```
Private mobjSettings As cSettings
```

5. In the Form Load event, place this code:

```
Set mobjSettings = New cSettings

txtLastReportRun.Text = mobjSettings.LastReportRun
txtMaxPages.Text = mobjSettings.MaxPages
```

6. In the Form Unload event, place this code:

```
mobjSettings.LastReportRun = txtLastReportRun.Text
mobjSettings.MaxPages = Str$(txtMaxPages)
```

Now the form will load with the current values from the registry. Any values placed in the text boxes will be saved to the registry when the form is unloaded.

The settings object could have been made available throughout the project by changing the line in the Declarations section of the form from a Private declaration to a Public declaration.

The simple example above contains no validation of the registry values. However, it would be easy to add. For example, the Property Let for MaxPages could be changed to be:

```
Public Property Let MaxPages(ByVal nData As Long)

    ' We will only allow the maximum number of pages
    ' to be between 1 and 5000.
    If nData > 5000 Or nData <= 0 Then
        Err.Raise 380    ' invalid property value
    Else
        mnMaxPages = nData
    End If

End Property
```

Now the settings object "screens" the value of the MaxPages property to make sure it is more than zero and no more than 5000.

An expanded version of this example is included on the enclosed CD. I would encourage you to start using it right away. It contains instructions for modifying the information that is stored.

Encapsulating Records in Objects

Many books on objects refer to the fact that an object contains both data and the logic to operate on that data. The settings object above is an example. All the logic tied into settings data is placed in the object.

Objects can also encapsulate information from a database record, along with the information to operate upon that information. For example, we might construct an Employee object for a payroll application. This object could have properties representing the data fields in an employee record (EmployeeID, FirstName, LastName, etc.). It could also have properties that are not explicitly stored but are for tracking in the current program (a Dirty property, for example, which would say if there were any changes to the employee's data since the last time the record was stored, or an IsValid property to see if all of the current data in the record is valid.).

▶ Start using the settings object right away

Students in my class on objects often said that the Settings object was the first tangible object they used from the class. It is so easy to set up and offers so many benefits that it helps encourage constructive use of objects right away.

Think about your current project. If you do not already have some centralized way to deal with system settings, you should strongly consider creating a settings object. It will not take long, and you will save yourself lots of effort at other stages in your project.

To operate on the data, the Employee object could have various methods to change a status — firing the employee, for example. Or a method for calculation of pay could be available (probably called CalculatePay).

Such objects are often called "data objects." These types of objects are very common in some programming environments such as Powerbuilder™. They are less common in VB because they take more time to construct. But, depending on the situation, they can be very useful.

Another example of a data storage object is one for storing information about a disk file and taking actions on the file. A DiskFile object could have properties such as Size, Type, DateCreated, DataModified, PathName, etc. It could have methods such as Erase (or Delete), Clear, Move, etc.

A Database Sources Object

In a classic multi-tiered project, the location of the actual data is not coded into the client program (the program which runs on the user's machine). The location is routed at runtime by some intermediate component of the system.

Even in stand-alone situations, there are advantages to centralizing the "switching" of database locations. You can use a "DataSources" object for that. This object can contain all of the code that opens databases and recordsets. Each recordset is identified by an "alias." That is, you could have an alias of "Customers" that points to a local customer table, or a customer table somewhere on the network, or possibly even one of many customer tables on the system. Or, for a particular client, the definition of the recordset called "Customers" could include criteria to point only to customers in a particular region.

The "DataSources" object would read in the actual locations of all data sources from some configuration file. It would track what databases and recordsets are already open, and open unused ones as necessary.

Changing Object References

One of the more difficult challenges in adapting to objects is to gain a complete understanding of object variables. We have used them so far to instantiate objects. But they can be used for other kinds of manipulation.

Suppose our program uses a settings object, but it needs two very different settings objects because the program has to change on the fly from being used by an operator to being used by a supervisor. So we create two Settings objects, one called objOperatorSettings, and one called objManagerSettings. We do that with code very similar to the code we used before to create multiple instances of forms. It would look something like this:

```
Dim objOperatorSettings as cSettings
Set objOperatorSettings = new cSettings

Dim objManagerSettings as cSettings
Set objManagerSettings = new cSettings
```

Now at any particular time, one of these settings objects should be active and the other one should not be. (We might have a menu option to switch between them.) In old-style VB code, we might use a flag to indicate which one was active, and use the flag every time we need to access a setting. Such code might look like this:

```
' Don't use this code!!!
' Illustration of old-style way to decide which object
' to use.
If bOperator Then
   sFileName = objOperatorSettings.DataFileName
Else
   sFileName = objManagerSettings.DataFileName
End If
```

Fortunately, object variables make it much easier than that. An object variable can be created *which does not yet hold a reference to an object.* Then, instead of instantiating a new object, the object variable can simply be assigned to point to some object which already exists.

That means that we can declare another settings object variable and use it as our current settings object reference.

```
Dim objCurrentSettings as cSettings
   .

   .

   .
Set objCurrentSettings = objOperatorSettings
```

Take note! This does not create a new settings object! It just gives us a new reference to the Operator settings object. Let's look at some diagrams to reinforce that point.

When objOperatorSettings is first instantiated, we have the situation in Figure 12–1.

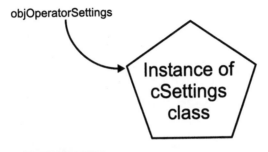

FIGURE 12-1   An object with a single reference.

That is, the object variable objOperatorSettings refers to a newly created object of the class cSettings.

Now suppose we carry out the code which declares and sets objCurrentSettings:

```
Dim objCurrentSettings as cSettings
.
.
.
Set objCurrentSettings = objOperatorSettings
```

Now our diagram looks like Figure 12–2.

We now have two object variables which both refer to the same object. There's only one object — it just has two ways that it can be referred to.

What does this do for us? We no longer need code with If statements to determine which object (objOperatorSettings or objManagerSettings) to refer to. We can set objCurrentSettings to whichever one is appropriate at a given time (with a menu option or other user interface element). That allows all of our code manipulating settings to look like this:

```
sFileName = objCurrentSettings.DataFileName
```

Compare that to the five lines of code above to accomplish the same thing. And note that we are no longer restricted to just settings for Operators and Managers. We could have an objAdministratorSettings added to the system with minimal intervention.

The capability for more than one object variable to refer to the same object is very useful, and it is important that you understand it before going much further with objects. An analogy with names and nicknames may help your understanding. I may call my spouse "Cindy," "Honey," or "Mom," depending on the circumstances, but it is still the same person. There's only one underlying "object" (though I hope she never finds out that I referred to her that way).

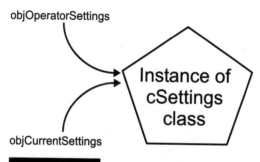

FIGURE 12–2   An object with a two references.

Similarly, I may have objCurrentSettings and objOperatorSettings referring to the same object. There is only one underlying object, but either reference can be used to get to it. Changing a property using one reference changes the value for the underlying object, and thus is reflected by both references.

For example, suppose both objCurrentSettings and objOperatorSettings are currently referring to the same object, and this line is executed:

```
objCurrentSettings.DataFileName = "c:\data\mainfile.mdb"
```

Then if this line is subsequently executed

```
Debug.Print objOperatorSettings.DataFileName
```

the debug window will print out "c:\data\mainfile.mdb."

This flexibility for object references is very important for manipulating collections, which we will take up later. For now, make sure you understand this key concept: object variables are merely pointers to the underlying objects, and you can have more than one pointer (reference) to a given object. Object variables do not "hold" the object the way data variables can be thought to "hold" a value.

Why is a Set Statement Necessary?

The syntax covered above leads to a common point of confusion. We have an object variable (objCurrentSettings) which is being assigned a reference to an existing object. The line to do that is:

```
Set objCurrentSettings = objOperatorSettings
```

Why can't we dispense with the "Set"? That is, why not just use this syntax:

```
objCurrentSettings = objOperatorSettings
' this won't work!!!
```

That would allow us to assign object references the same way we assign values. But the problem with that syntax is that it is ambiguous. Suppose we have a control on our form named txtAddress. Now suppose we write the following code:

```
Dim txtCurrentTextBox As TextBox
txtCurrentTextBox = txtAddress
```

This code is valid, but it does *not* assign an object reference. It actually assigns the Text property of txtAddress to the Text property of txtCurrent-TextBox. It does that because the Text property is the *default* property of the TextBox control.

Any kind of object can have a default property, including class modules you create. (We'll see how to assign a default property to a class in a later chapter.) That leads to the ambiguity. The following line:

```
objCurrentSettings = objOperatorSettings
' this won't work!!!
```

would assign the default property of objOperatorSettings to the default property of objCurrentSettings (if the cSettings class had a default property). This code cannot simultaneously be used to assign object references, because then the compiler would not know which of those two operations you really wanted when you wrote the code.

The Set keyword resolves all of this. The line

```
Set objCurrentSettings = objOperatorSettings
```

is unambiguous. It refers *only* to assigning object references.

Unfortunately, if you're like me, you will leave off the Set many times in your early work with objects. The error message you will typically get is "Object variable not set." You'll eventually get in the habit of using Set properly.

The Nothing Keyword

Sometimes it is desirable to have an object variable stop referring to a particular object. This is done with the Nothing keyword. The following line

```
Set objCurrentSettings = Nothing
```

terminates the connection between the object variable objCurrentSettings and the underlying object. This may or may not cause an object to go away. The discussion below on the life span of an object explains that in more detail.

You can also set an object variable to refer to a different object than the one it currently refers to. This was illustrated above in the example of operator settings and manager settings.

Object Variables with a Generic Type

Up to now, we have declared all our objects with a specific class name. That is, our declarations have looked like this:

```
Dim objCurrentSettings as cSettings
```

This syntax says that we know that the object variable objCurrentSettings will *always* refer to an object of type cSettings. It may refer to any cSettings object which has been instantiated, but it cannot refer to any other type of object. (We'll get a run-time error if we try.)

There are programming situations where we need an object reference that may need to refer to different object types at different times. For example, suppose we have a payroll application with a cEmployee class and a cSubcontractor type. These classes represent very different types of workers, and different information is needed about each one.

Now suppose we need an object variable named objCurrentWorker, which could be either an employee or a subcontractor. We can't declare objCurrentWorker with either of those types, because then it could not take on the other type.

Instead we declare it this way:

```
Dim objCurrentWorker as Object
```

Now objCurrentWorker can be assigned to reference any type of object. It could refer to an object of type cEmployee or one of type cSubcontractor, or to any other class name. It could even refer to a form or control.

This gives additional flexibility, but has some performance implications and some potential coding pitfalls. In general, you should only declare object variables this way in specific situations where the variable must refer to objects of different type.

Finding Out the Type of An Object

We've seen how an object variable can be declared with a generic type and then hold a reference to any type of object. Sometimes in code you need to find out the type of object currently being referred to by an object variable. We will see examples in the discussion of collections in the next chapter. For now, we'll just define two ways to do that.

The TypeName function returns a string expression that contains the object type. That is, if you had one of the Settings objects above named objCurrentSettings, then the statement

```
sObjectType = TypeName(objCurrentSettings)
```

would cause sObjectType to contain "cSettings."

If you are using an If statement, you can use the TypeOf keyword to look at the type of an object. Here is an example from the VB help files.

```
If TypeOf MyControl Is CommandButton Then
    Debug.Print "You passed in a " & TypeName(MyControl)
ElseIf TypeOf MyControl Is CheckBox Then
```

```
        Debug.Print "You passed in a " & TypeName(MyControl)
ElseIf TypeOf MyControl Is TextBox Then
        Debug.Print "You passed in a " & TypeName(MyControl)
End If
```

The Life Span of an Object

Every object goes through a life cycle, which has various stages. You need to understand what those stages are to control the objects you create. In particular, it is important to understand exactly when an object comes into being, and exactly when it goes away.

Here are the major events during the life span of an object:

1. An object variable is declared.
2. The object is instantiated.
3. The object is manipulated.
4. The object is terminated.

We'll look at each of these in turn.

Declaring the Object Variable

We already know that we declare an object variable the same way we declare any other variable, assigning an appropriate type to it. Our declaration might look like this:

```
Private mobjSettings As cSettings
```

This does not create the object. In fact, the object variable may later be assigned to point to an object that already exists and was created with some other object variable. But we must have the object variable before we can ever go on to creating the object.

The alternative way of declaring the object is:

```
Private mobjSettings As New cSettings
```

This does not create (instantiate) the object either, but it allows for the object to be automatically instantiated when any property or method of the object is referred to in succeeding code.

Object Instantiation

Depending on which form of object declaration was used, the object will be instantiated (created) by different actions. If the first declaration form above was used, then the object is created with this line:

```
Set mobjSettings = New cSettings
```

If the second form above was used, then the object will be created when it is referred to, such as in the following line:

```
mobjSettings.MaxPages = 200
```

In either case, instantiation causes the Class Initialize event in the class module to execute. That is the very first thing that happens when the object is instantiated.

Manipulation of the Object

The object may be manipulated in various ways. Properties may be set or fetched. Methods may be run.

Additional references to the object may be created, as we saw a few pages earlier. We may have mobjSettings and objCurrentSettings referring to the same object.

This leads to the idea of a "reference count." The reference count for an object is the number of active object variables that point to the object. Suppose we have the following code:

```
Dim mobjSettings As cSettings
Set mobjSettings = New cSettings
Dim objCurrentSettings as cSettings
Set objCurrentSettings = objOperatorSettings
```

When this code finishes, there is only one object, but the reference count for the object is 2.

The reference count for an object decreases whenever an object variable stops referring to the object. This could happen in three main ways:

1. An object variable falls out of scope.
2. An object variable is set to Nothing.
3. An object variable is set to refer to a different object.

The reference count for an object can rise and fall as many times as necessary. The reference count changes each time a new reference to the object is created, or an existing reference to the object goes away.

Termination of the Object

In normal program execution, there are two ways that an object can stop existing:

1. The reference count for the object goes to zero.
2. The program terminates normally.

When a program terminates normally, it basically sends all object variables out of scope, so all objects in the program are terminated.

The main thing that happens during object termination is that the Class Terminate event fires. That gives you a chance to take care of any clean-up work associated with the object. For example, our settings object used the Class Terminate event to write current values for the settings back to the registry.

Collections

The chapter provides an introduction to the concept of collections. A collection is a group of related objects. Just as variables are much more valuable because you can create arrays, objects become much more useful when grouped into collections.

A Collection — A Special Type of Object

A collection is an object in and of itself, but it has a limited number of properties and methods. It always has a Count property to indicate how many items are in the collection. It will typically have an Add method to place new items in the collection, and a Remove method to take items out. (We'll cover each of these in more detail below.)

Elements in the collection can be referred to by the syntax:

```
colMyCollection.Item(i)    '(or more commonly)
colMyCollection(i)
```

where "i" is the item number. For Each loops (discussed below) provide another way to access items in a collection. Later we will discuss indexed collections, which provide yet another way to refer to items.

> Notice that we use the prefix "col" for collection objects, rather than the generic "obj." This is consistent with the naming conventions used by most development shops, and will be used throughout the book.

The Forms collection and the Controls collection are examples of built-in collections in Visual Basic.

Forms Collection

Every VB project has a Forms collection. It is a collection whose elements represent each loaded form in an application.

This collection could be used, for example, to loop through all the forms and minimize or unload them all. Or it could be used to loop through the forms and see if a given form is loaded.

Controls Collection

Each form has a Controls collection. The items in this collection are all of the controls on the form.

You can use this collection to reposition all the controls on a form. That's not as simple as it sounds, however, since controls must be treated differently if they are contained in another control (such as a frame or tab control). Controls which are directly on the form have their positions respective to the form. Controls which have a container control have their positions respective to the container.

Syntax to Access Collections

One type of code used to access collections is similar to the code used to work with arrays. Here's a typical example:

```
For nItemIndex = 0 to colMyCollection.Count - 1
    colMyCollection(nItemIndex).Visible = false
Next nItemIndex
```

This syntax should look familiar to experienced Visual Basic developers. Collections which are part of the DAO (Data Access Objects) model, for example, are often accessed in this fashion. If you have ever used DAO for working with data, you have probably coded lines like these:

```
For nField = 0 to rsEmployees.Fields.Count - 1
    Debug.Print rsEmployees.Fields(nField).Name
    Debug.Print rsEmployees.Fields(nField).Value
Next nField
```

This code manipulates a collection. A recordset (rsEmployees in the example above) has a Fields collection. That collection has a Count property (rsEmployees.Fields.Count), and individual Field objects have properties like Name and Value.

This distinction between a collection and the objects in the collection is important. You should clearly understand that when you use "rsEmployees.Fields.Count," you are referring to the Count property of the Fields *collection*. But when you use the similar syntax "rsEmployees.Fields(nField).Name," you are using the Name property of an individual Field *object*, that is, a member of the Fields collection.

For Each Loops

There is another way to access collections which is better in many circumstances, and that's with For Each loops. Using this technique, the first example above would look like this:

```
For Each objItem in colMyCollection
    objItem.Visible = false
Next objItem
```

and the second example above would look like this:

```
For Each objField in rsEmployees.Fields
  Debug.Print objField.Name
  Debug.Print objField.Value
Next objField
```

These loops share many characteristics with regular For loops. Exit For is available to exit the loop, for example. And if there are no items in the collection, the loop does not execute.

If the loop does execute, then each time through the loop, the "index object" (objField in this case) takes on a reference to a different object in the collection. The first time through, objField will refer to the first object in the collection. The second time, objField will refer to the second object in the collection, and so on.

Just as For Next loops require their index to be properly declared, For Each loops need their "index object" to be declared. Before the code above could run, there would need to be a line somewhere which declared objField. It might look like this:

```
Dim objField As New Field
```

For Each loops work best when there is no need to know how many items there are to be processed, and when the order of the processing is not important. Most collections designed in true object-oriented fashion will typically meet these requirements.

Another advantage of For Each loops is that you don't have to worry about whether the collection numbering begins with 0 or 1. There are different conventions for different types of collections. The DAO collections begin with 0, for example, while other collections begin with 1. We'll discuss these inconsistencies in more detail later.

Here's another example using the Forms collection built into Visual Basic:

```
Dim frmCurrentForm as Form
For Each frmCurrentForm in Forms
    If Instr(frmCurrentForm.Caption, "Options") <> 0 Then
        frmCurrentForm.Hide
    End If
Next frmCurrentForm
```

This code would hide any active form which had the word "Options" in its caption (remember that the caption for a form shows up in the title bar of the form).

Create Your Own Collections

Any kind of object can be placed in a collection. The examples above use collections built into VB, but you can define your own collections and put any objects you like in them — either objects from your own class modules or objects built into VB. Following are some examples of hypothetical cases in which collections could be useful.

A Report Columns Collection

Suppose you want to define a report in terms of the columns that will appear in the report. The definition for each column could be placed in a column object.

Each column object would have typical properties such as "Heading," "Position," "DataSource," etc. There could be only one type of column (only one class module which is used to spawn all columns), or there could be multiple types. The collection could work in either event, since all the objects in a collection do not have to be of the same type.

In Chapter 15, "More About Objects," we will construct such a collection and see how code to generate the report is dramatically simplified by using the collection structure for the report.

A Collection of Projects

A project management system might internally represent projects as objects. Since a user may be working on more than one project at a time, the application would have a collection of projects. When a new project was opened, it would be added to the collection. This allows the application to have user interface elements that balance projects against one another.

An Employee Scheduling Example

If you are working on an employee scheduling system, you might have an employee object to represent individual employees, and then load the employees into an employee collection.

Alternatively, if employees need to be grouped by department, you could add a Department object, and a Departments collection. Each Department object could then hold a collection of Employee objects.

Exercise 13.1

Choose either the project management example or the employee scheduling example above. Make a list of typical properties and methods you would expect such objects to have. Which of these properties and methods might be accessed in a For Each loop for the whole collection?

Implementing Collections in Code

We have said that a collection is just a special type of object. That means a collection is created very much like any other object. This declaration line creates a new collection object named colMyCollection:

```
Dim colMyCollection as New Collection
```

The collection is immediately instantiated. Just as a newly created form has built-in properties and methods, a new collection automatically has the built-in properties and methods we discussed above:

Count property — the number of items in the collection

Item property — used to refer to objects that are placed in the collection

Add method — used to place objects in the collection

Remove method — used to remove objects from the collection

Let's take a look at how each of these works.

Add Method

When the collection is first created, it is empty. That is, it contains no objects. An object is added to a collection with code like this:

```
colMyCollection.Add objSomeObject
```

This presumes, of course, that objSomeObject has been defined, which is done as with any other object (creating a class module, instantiating it, etc.).

The Add method has several optional parameters, which we will discuss later.

▶ Collections and the object's reference count

Placing an object in a collection increases the object's reference count. We previously discussed in Chapter 12 ("Examples of Objects and More Object Syntax") how the life span of an object is determined by its reference count.

When a collection object is destroyed, the objects in the collection all have their reference counts decreased by one. If there are no current references to an object outside the collection, that would cause the object's reference count to go to zero, and the object will then terminate.

Count Property

When we create a collection, its Count property is zero. That is, this code

```
Dim colMyCollection as New Collection
Debug.Print colMyCollection.Count
```

would cause the number 0 to be printed in the debug window. But this code

```
Dim colMyCollection as New Collection
colMyCollection.Add objSomeObject
Debug.Print colMyCollection.Count
```

would cause the number 1 to be printed in the debug window. At any time, the Count property represents the number of objects in the collection, much as the ListCount property of a Listbox represents the number of items in the Listbox.

Item Property and the Index of an Item

If you use the Add method with no optional parameters, then the first item in the collection gets an index number of 1, the second gets an index number of 2, and so forth. These index numbers can be used to refer to the individual items with the Item property.

We saw previously how individual items in the collection can be referred to with the Item property of the collection. Here's that code again:

```
colMyCollection.Item(i)      '(or more commonly)
colMyCollection(i)
```

Or we could use specific numbers:

```
colMyCollection.Item(2)
```

Any number up to the Count property can be used. A number greater than the Count property (or less than one) will generate a runtime error.

Remove Method

Items can be removed with the Remove method, which requires the index number of the item to be removed. This line will remove item number 2:

```
colMyCollection.Remove 2
```

We will see an alternative way to use the Remove method in the section on indexed collections below.

Creating a Collection with a Class Module

Using collections as we discussed above has one big disadvantage. There is no restriction on what objects can be added to the collection. If some errant code tried to add a Form to your Employees collection, Visual Basic would think this was just fine.

In the real world, you typically want your collections to contain just one type of object. Such collections are called type-safe collections.

The only way to create such a collection is to write your own class module to "supervise" the collection. That is, your class module serves as a container or "wrapper" for the collection.

Your class module should have *the same properties and methods* as a normal collection. For example, the Count property of your class module actually refers to the Count property of the collection your class is containing. But you have the opportunity to add more logic to the properties and methods. Figure 13–1 illustrates how this works.

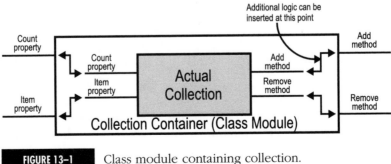

FIGURE 13–1   Class module containing collection.

Here's an example of the code for such a collection. This collection allows only employee objects to be added to it:

```
Private colEmployees as New Collection

' The Add method must be modified to verify the object type
' before adding an object to the collection
Sub Add(objEmployee as Object, Optional Key, _
        Optional Before, Optional After)
    ' If the object is an employee,
    ' add it to the collection
    If TypeName(objEmployee) = "cEmployee" Then
        colEmployees.Add objEmployee, Key, Before, After
    Else
        ' could raise an invalid object type error here
    End If
End Sub

Sub Remove(Index)
    colEmployees.Remove Index
End Sub

Function Item(Index) as Object
    ' Use the Set statement to return an object reference.
    Set Item = colEmployees.Item(Index)
End Function

Property Get Count() As Integer
    Count = colEmployees.Count
End Property
```

Such a programmer-defined class module is really a "wrapper" for a real collection. Notice how the properties and methods of the class module refer to the properties and methods of the "wrapped" internal collection.

Sometimes a collection object created in VB (and not wrapped up with your own class module) is called a *bare collection*. We will use that terminology for the rest of this book.

We will also use the generic term *collection* to include your own class modules which are specifically created to contain bare collections.

Adding Intelligence to Wrapped Collections

Besides controlling the type of objects allowed, another great reason to use wrapped collections is to add more intelligence to the collection. As mentioned above, collection classes need to have the basic collection properties and methods (Count, Item, Add, and Remove). But since we are constructing a Visual Basic class to hold the collection, we can add any additional properties and methods to it that we want.

For example, suppose we have a collection of employee objects. Each of these objects might have a Salary property. We could create a new property of the collection class called TotalSalary. It would loop through the collection, adding together the salaries from each individual object.

Such collection properties are usually read-only properties because they derive their values from the collection.

There can also be custom methods for the whole collection, but this is less common. Some situations call for a Clear method (as opposed to destroying the collection and re-creating it). And if all the objects in a collection have a particular method (say PrintCheck), then the collection can have a similar method which just fires the method for each member of the collection.

We will see a great example of adding intelligence to collections in the next chapter, which is an exercise using collections.

Naming Suggestions

We have already mentioned that class modules should have a "c" or a "cls" prefix. (This book uses "c.") However, classes being used to wrap collections can have a different prefix. Some developers use a prefix of "col" for this kind of class. However, that can be confusing if you also use "col" as the prefix of an instantiated collection object. It's not a good idea to use the same prefix for a class and instantiations of that class.

My solution is to use the prefix "ccl" for collection class modules, that is, class modules used to wrap collections. You may want to try that convention if your location does not already have standard naming schemes for class modules.

Inconsistent Numbering and Conventions

Microsoft is not consistent in numbering for collections. Most built-in collections (Forms, Controls, DAO collections) are zero-based. However, collections created with class modules are one-based.

While the Remove method is semi-standard for removing items from a collection, it is not universal. Some collections use a Delete method instead. And, of course, unloading a form removes it from the Form collection. In some other (more formal) object-oriented languages, unloading a form is actually done by using the Remove method on the Forms collection.

It's tough enough to keep this straight without making it worse. Try to be as consistent in your own code as possible. That normally means using one-based collections for the ones you create. And stick with the Remove method as a standard name.

Collections vs. Arrays

Collections are used in object-oriented design in many instances for purposes that would have required arrays in older design methods. The advantages of collections over arrays include:

- More dynamic allocation
- No empty slots when an item is removed
- Less concern about order

However, collections consume a lot more memory than arrays, so there are cases where it is definitely better to use arrays instead of collections.

Indexed Collections

We've already mentioned that the Add method has some optional arguments. These allow more flexibility in the ways we can refer to items in the collection. Here are the optional arguments for the Add method:

Key	a string expression that uniquely identifies this element in the collection
Before	a numeric index or a string index indicating the element this addition should be placed in front of
After	a numeric index or a string index indicating the element this addition should be placed in back of

The Key Argument for the Add Method

The optional Key argument, if used, must be a string. It is used to assign a unique key to an object in the collection.

Here's a simple example of using unique keys in a collection. Suppose we have a collection of book objects. Each book has a Title property, and we'll assume that book titles are unique. We will call the book collection colBooks and an individual book object objBook.

We could add books to the book collection with lines like this:

```
colBooks.Add objBook, "Moby Dick"
```

or

```
colBooks.Add objBook, objBook.Title
```

Now suppose we knew that "Moby Dick" was in the book collection, but we did not know which number it was. We would like to find out its author. We could do that with the line:

```
Debug.Print colBooks.Item("Moby Dick").Author
```

This should print out "Herman Melville" in the debug window. How does this work? The expression "colBooks.Item("Moby Dick")" gives us an object reference to the book object we want. Then the "Author" property on the end gets us the author.

The string used for the key must be a unique string for the collection. That is, two different objects in a collection cannot have the same key.

Before and After Arguments

As we have seen, collections are ordered. Normally, the order is determined by the order the objects were added to the collection.

The Before and After arguments are used to override this ordering. Only one of these can be used when adding an object.

The Before and After arguments are variants. They can hold either a string or an integer.

Using the Before argument indicates that you want the new object to be inserted *before* the object indicated by the Before parameter. For example, to insert "Moby Dick" into position number 5 of the books collection, we would use the line:

```
colBooks.Add objBook, "Moby Dick", 5
```

The new book object would take up position 5, and push whatever was there before into position 6, and so on down the line.

That's an example of using an integer argument for Before. We can also use a string:

```
colBooks.Add objBook, "Moby Dick", "Modern Times"
```

Now the object would be added to the position in front of the book identified as "Modern Times," no matter where that title occurred in the collection.

The After argument works the same way except that the new object takes up the position after the object specified by After.

Since you can't use Before and After at the same time, to use After, the syntax would look like this:

```
colBooks.Add objBook, "Moby Dick",,"Madame Bovary"
```

Notice the two consecutive commas. Similarly, the Key argument could be left out. A book could be added to position 4 (without a key identifier) with this line:

```
colBooks.Add objBook,,,3
```

In this case, we have skipped both the Key argument and the Before argument, and used 3 as the After argument.

In all cases, the index used for Before or After must correspond to an existing item in the collection, or an error occurs.

Some Terminology

All collections are indexed by the numeric position of the items. However, when we refer to "indexed collections," we typically mean collections that have string indexes established for each item in the collection.

For such items, they can be fetched from the collection using the syntax:

```
Set objThisItem = colMyCollection.Item("a string index")
```

or

```
Set objThisItem = colMyCollection("a string index")
```

The second syntax is more commonly used. In fact, Visual Basic developers often see such syntax with built-in objects based on DAO (Data Access Objects), RDO (Remote Data Objects), or ADO (ActiveX Data Objects). In DAO, for example, you might fetch a person's last name from a recordset of employees with the line:

```
Debug.Print rsEmployees.Fields("LastName")
```

▶ Using optional arguments to alphabetize a collection

Suppose you have a collection of book objects named colBooks. You have a new book object named objNewBook, which is in the class cBook. The cBook class allows a Title property, which is used to hold the title of the book. The Title property is used to index the colBooks collection.

You would like to insert objNewBook into the collection in its proper alphabetical order, by title. Write code which would accomplish that.

ANSWER

```
Dim objBook as new cBook

For Each objBook In colBooks
  If objNewBook.Title < objBook.Title Then
    colBooks.Add objNewBook, objNewBook.Title, objBook.Title
    Exit For
  End If
Next objBook
```

More On Collections

This section contains some additional information and useful techniques for creating collection classes.

Use Wrappers

As we saw, there are two ways of handling collections. "Bare" collections (those created with Dim … as New Collection) have predefined properties and methods. "Wrapped" collections are those that are created within a class module and only available through the methods and properties of the class.

In VB4, there were a couple of reasons to use bare collections. Only bare collections supported the Item method as the default (which made syntax using wrapped collections a bit more cumbersome), and only bare collections could be manipulated with For Each loops.

Both of these issues are addressed in later versions, so it is recommended that you wrap all but the simplest collections. The class builder does a good job of creating an initial wrapper very quickly, so there is very little additional work and a lot of available flexibility in working with wrapped collections. You can create type-safe collections and you have an obvious centralized point to add logic that works with the entire collection.

NewEnum Method

The NewEnum method is used to make wrapped collections compatible with For Each. You normally don't have to worry about NewEnum because it is taken care of automatically. However, if are working with older collection class modules developed under VB4, or collection class modules that were typed in from scratch, these classes will not have a NewEnum method in them. If you need to use these classes with For Each, you can retrofit the class modules. The NewEnum routine should look like this, assuming the name of the collection is mCol:

```
Public Property Get NewEnum() As IUnknown
    'this property allows you to enumerate
    'this collection with the For...Each syntax
    Set NewEnum = mCol.[_NewEnum]
End Property
```

The _NewEnum method is built into bare collections. The underscore indicates that it is a hidden method, that is, it does not show up in the object browser.

Once this method is created, it must have two procedure attributes set. Both are set in the Procedure Attributes dialog. To get to it, access the Tools menu. Select Procedure Attributes and press the Advanced button. The two attributes you need to set for NewEnum are Procedure ID and Hide this member. Procedure ID is a combo box, and you need to type −4 into it (don't ask why). Hide this member is a check box, and it should be checked. This obscure procedure should be enough to convince you that it's better to let the class builder take care of this if possible.

▶ The Add method as created by the class builder

If you use the class builder to create a collection class module, it will place an Add method in the code. But the code for the Add method may not work the way you want.

The Add method as created by the class builder requires an argument for *every property* of the class used for individual collection objects. It then creates the object, adds it to the collection, and returns a reference to the object to the calling code. Because it returns a reference, the Add method done by the class builder is a function, not a subroutine.

I do not care for this structure for most of my objects. Especially if there are several properties for the objects in the collection, this technique is clumsy. So I usually replace the Add method created by the class builder with one of my own. I usually make my Add method mimic the Add method of bare collections, the way we discussed earlier in this chapter.

Default Item Property

We've seen that we can access objects inside collections like this:

```
Set objStudent = colMyCollection("Billy")
```

instead of like this:

```
Set objStudent = colMyCollection.Item("Billy")
```

Why does this work? Because the Item property is usually the default property of a collection. You are probably familiar with default properties of controls. A text box, for example, has its Text property as the default property, so that this line:

```
Debug.Print txtName.Text
```

does exactly the same thing as this line:

```
Debug.Print txtName
```

Bare collections automatically have the Item property as the default. For your wrapped collections, the Item property will be set as the default property if you use the class builder to create your collection class. However, if you ever need to create a default property (of any class, not just collection classes), then go to the property procedure and access the Tools menu. Select Procedure Attributes and press the Advanced button. The Procedure ID drop-down will probably show {None}, and you should change it to {Default}.

Be careful about creating default properties. They can compromise readability of the code. But making the Item property the default for collections is an established convention, so it's OK. And if you are wrapping or imitating other system objects that have default properties, you may want your wrapper or imitation to have the same default property as the system object to which it corresponds.

Changing the Key for an Object in a Collection

If you using an indexed collection with unique string keys, remember that there is no connection between the object's properties and the object's index in the collection. That is, suppose you have a collection of students indexed by name. You have one object in the collection with the Name property "Sue Smith," and "Sue Smith" was used as the index when the collection was created. If you change the object's Name property to Sue Jones, that *does not* change the index to the collection automatically, and there's no way to change it manually. To change an item's index in a collection, you must remove the item and then re-insert it.

An Example

You may be familiar with the concept of database "bookmarks," which are pointers to particular records. Bookmarks are used to keep up with the location of records, so that a particular record can be recalled later.

Suppose I want to keep a set of bookmarks for a user doing data file maintenance. Users will be adding bookmarks and deleting bookmarks dynamically. This is an ideal situation for a collection.

Exercise 13.2..........

Design such a bookmark collection. Note that this requires designing two objects — the individual bookmark object and the collection object. For each of these, what should their properties and methods be?

The collection could be used to fill up a list box with bookmarks. This could be done in regular code, with a For Each loop. It could also be done by placing the For Each logic in a method of the collection and passing the list box reference to the collection. Which way would you prefer?

FOURTEEN

A Detailed
Objects
Example —
Selecting
Records

You've now covered the basic concepts of objects in Visual Basic. You've seen how to extend built-in objects such as forms with custom properties and methods, and how to create new objects via class modules. You understand the basics of properties and methods.

You've also looked at collections of objects. Now it's time to look at a detailed exercise that ties a lot of these concepts, particularly the ones concerning collections, all together.

To do that, we will work through a program which selects records out of a database. If you are experienced with using Visual Basic for data access, you have probably written programs to do something similar. Typically such programs contain a lot of code to construct SQL statements, and the SQL statements are used to fetch the data.

This example assumes you know the rudimentary syntax of SQL. It only uses SELECT and WHERE clauses, so you don't have to be a SQL guru to follow it.

The Problem Statement

We want to create a simple query screen for the Titles table of Biblio.mdb, which is a sample database included with Visual Basic. The Titles table contains information about books, including their title, the year published, the book's ISBN (standard identification number), and the subject of the book.

Figure 14-1 shows what we would like the form to look like.

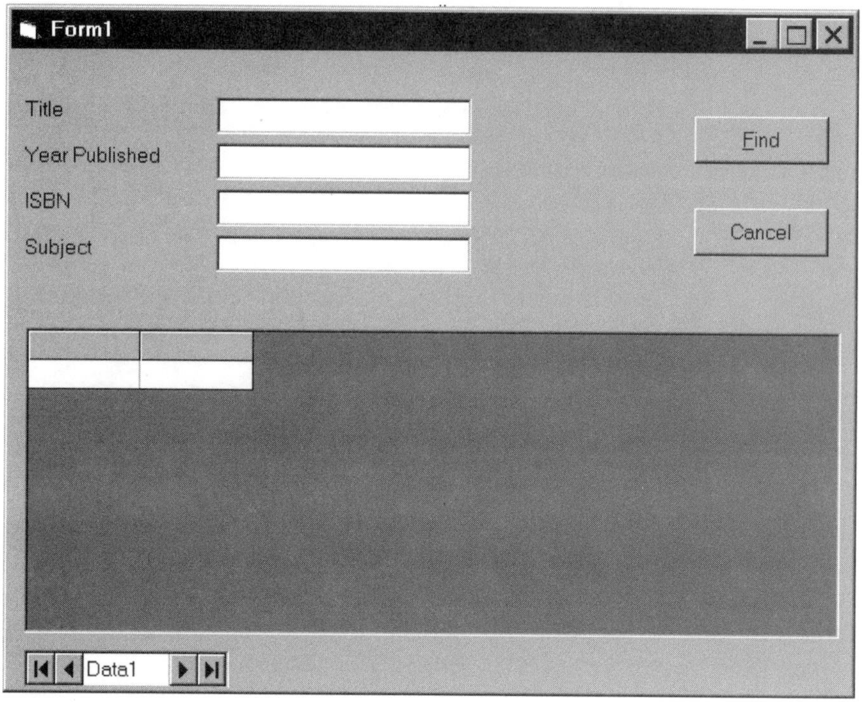

FIGURE 14-1 Query screen for the Titles table.

The user should be able to type in information to use for matching in any of the fields above. The information would then be used on a "partial match" basis. For example, if the user entered "CO" in the Title textbox, and "199" in the Year Published textbox, the program would find all the books with a title beginning with the letters "CO" and published in a year beginning with "199."

The user can use as many fields as needed.

For simplicity, a data bound grid is used to display the titles.

▶ Biblio.mdb for data access

All of the examples in this book that do data access use Biblio.mdb. It is typically installed by Visual Basic in one of the following locations:

```
c:/Program Files/DevStudio/VB (for VB5)
c:/Program Files/Microsoft Visual Studio/VB98 (for VB6)
```

The examples in the book use the first location above. If any of the examples fail on the line pointing to Biblio.mdb, then the location probably needs to be changed before the program will run.

If you need a fresh copy of Biblio.mdb, it is on the enclosed CD. Look in the /Examples directory.

Constructing the Program

We will go through the construction of this program step-by-step. First, we'll construct a form that just shows all the records in the Titles table. Then we will add enhancements for selection.

Note that this exercise, like all the ones in this book, is available on the enclosed CD. You can get the entire exercise off the CD, or just the starter form which is constructed in the next step. This exercise is in /Examples/VB5/TitleSearch and /Example/VB6/TitleSearch.

Creating the Form

You can skip this section by getting this form from the enclosed CD. Or you can create it yourself by following the steps below.

We'll avoid getting too detailed here, since this is standard VB stuff. Start a new project, and work with the default Form1 that it automatically creates. Construct the form with the following controls, with a layout like that shown above in Figure 14-1:

Control Type	Name	Special Properties
Textbox	txtTitle	
Textbox	txtYearPublished	
Textbox	txtISBN	
Textbox	txtSubject	
Label	lblTitle	Caption = "Title"
Label	lblYearPublished	Caption = "Year Published"
Label	lblISBN	Caption = "ISBN"
Label	lblSubject	Caption = "Subject"
Command Button	cmdFind	Caption = "Find"
Command Button	cmdCancel	Caption = "Cancel"
Data Control	datTitleTable	DatabaseName = "C:\Program Files\DevStudio\VB\Biblio.mdb" (or other location for Biblio.mdb)
MSFlexGrid	grdSelectedItems	DataSource = "datTitleTable"

In the Click event for cmdCancel, place the single statement "End". In the Click event for cmdFind, place the following code:

```
Dim sDataSource As String
sDataSource = "Select Title, [Year Published], ISBN, _
          Subject From Titles "
datTitleTable.RecordSource = sDataSource
datTitleTable.Refresh
grdSelectedItems.Refresh
```

The form will now work in a minimal fashion. If you start up the project and press the Find button, the grid will fill up with all the records in the Titles table. Try to make sure that there's nothing wrong up to this point.

The most likely thing to go wrong is that Biblio.mdb is not in the right place. If you have problems, check that first.

Create Objects to Handle Selection Criteria

If you were using a traditional approach, the next thing you would do is place some logic behind the Find button which would construct a SQL statement to get the appropriate records. You have probably written a lot of such code. It contains a lot of string manipulation to tie the parameters entered in the text boxes into the SQL statement. You probably write such code more or less from scratch every time you need to construct some SQL on the fly.

Such code is messy. It is easy for bugs to creep into it. It's tough to maintain. And it's not reusable for other projects.

We will handle the construction of the SQL statement with objects. This approach will yield code which is far clearer and more maintainable. It will also be reusable for other projects. This object approach will take a little longer to implement, but the benefits are well worth the small amount of extra time.

HOW THE OBJECT APPROACH WORKS

The foundation for our approach is to create a class of objects which can hold selection criteria. Each object in the class can hold the selection criteria from *one* text box.

Those individual objects are then placed in a collection. Each object in the collection will be able to generate a *piece* of a WHERE clause and make it available in a property.

The collection will have the capability to assemble the entire WHERE clause by getting the individual pieces from the objects in the collection, and putting them together in the right way.

For example, suppose the Title text box has "CO" entered in it, and the Year Published text box has "199" entered in it. The collection would hold two objects. The first object would generate a piece of the WHERE clause that said:

```
" Title LIKE 'CO*' "
```

and the second object would generate a piece of the WHERE clause that said:

```
" [Year Published] LIKE '199*' "
```

Then the collection would combine these pieces to get:

```
" WHERE Title LIKE 'CO*' AND [Year Published] LIKE '199*' "
```

This approach encapsulates and reuses the logic needed to create small pieces of WHERE clauses. It also distributes the intelligence needed to generate the entire WHERE clause. Both the individual objects and the collection object have clearly defined roles, and clearly defined logic to carry out those roles.

Here are the steps that will need to be done to construct these objects:

CREATING THE SELECTION CRITERIA OBJECT

This object will hold selection criteria from a single text box, and it will only be able to do partial matches. (We will discuss how to extend it for other cases at the end of the exercise .)

1. First create a blank class module named cSelectionCriteria. It should have three string properties:

    FieldName   The name of the field in the recordset which is used for selection.

    SearchString   The partial string to match against the field.

    WhereClause   A read-only property that generates the WHERE clause for this individual field.

    You can start from scratch and type in the code yourself, or use the class builder.

    The FieldName and SearchString properties should be simple store-and-retrieve properties. They look something like this:

```
Public Property Let SearchString(ByVal sData As String)
    msSearchString = sData
End Property


Public Property Get SearchString() As String
    SearchString = msSearchString
End Property


Public Property Let FieldName(ByVal sData As String)
    msFieldName = sData
End Property


Public Property Get FieldName() As String
    FieldName = msFieldName
End Property
```

    Don't forget to put the declarations for the member variables in the Declarations section of cSelectionCriteria. They look like this:

```
Private msFieldName As String 'local copy
Private msSearchString As String 'local copy
```

If you use the class builder, this code will be inserted for you, though the naming conventions will be different. (The class builder gives all member variables the prefix "mvar.")

2. Write a customized WhereClause property for the cSelectionCriteria class. It should construct a piece of a WHERE clause using the information from the FieldName and SearchString properties. Here's some typical code to accomplish this:

```
Public Property Get WhereClause() As String

  WhereClause = "[" & msFieldName & _
                "] LIKE '" & msSearchString & "*'"
End Property
```

We need the brackets around the field name because some field names have embedded spaces.

Notice that WhereClause is a read-only property. That is, it doesn't make sense for some external module to tell the object what its WHERE clause is. The object must construct the WHERE clause from information fed to it. You can either leave the Property Let off entirely, or place a single line in the Property Let which raises an error, like this:

```
Public Property Let WhereClause(ByVal sData As_
    String)
  Err.Raise 383          ' read-only property
End Property
```

If you are using the class builder, you will need to replace the code it places in the Where-Clause property with your own code.

And that's it for the first object. Now we'll create the collection.

CREATING THE COLLECTION OF SELECTION CRITERIA OBJECTS

Now we will create the collection class module to hold the cSelectionCriteria objects. This is to be a "wrapped" collection. In this case the "wrapping" gives us the ability to add intelligence to the collection.

The collection class should be named cclCriteria. It is suggested that you use the class builder to create it. If you do, the cclCriteria class should be defined as a collection of cSelectionCriteria objects. It will need the usual properties and methods for a collection (which will be created automatically for you), and will require an additional property besides the defaults. That's the WhereClause string property.

Unfortunately, the class builder uses a completely different approach for the Add method. Some developers prefer it, but I don't like it. As we discussed in the previous chapter, it both creates a new object and adds it to the class in one operation. But this is clumsy if the object has lots of properties, and it limits your flexibility in using optional arguments to index and order your class. I recommend against using the class builder technique except for collections of very simple objects.

So if you use the class builder, replace the Add method it generates with the Add method shown below.

1. Using the class builder, create a new collection. Name it cclCriteria. Make it a collection of cSelectionCriteria objects.

   Since the class builder will generate the usual collection properties and methods, you only need to add the additional string property WhereClause.(Don't be confused that both the collection object and the individual criteria objects have a WhereClause property. The properties serve different purposes. The individual objects create pieces of WHERE clauses with their WhereClause property. The collection object creates an entire WHERE clause with its WhereClause property. If you find this confusing, you can name the WhereClause property for the individual objects something like WhereClausePiece.)

2. Let the class builder generate the code for the collection class. In the resulting code, notice that the class builder names the internal (bare) collection mCol. This is a silly generic name, so let's change it to something more appropriate. Using Edit Replace, change the mCol to mcolCriteria throughout the module.

   Then replace the Add method with the code below:

```
Public Sub Add(objCriteria As Object, Optional Key, _
Optional Before, Optional After)

    ' If the object is of the right type,
    ' add it to the collection
    If TypeName(objCriteria) = "cSelectionCriteria" Then
      mcolCriteria.Add objCriteria, Key, Before, After
    Else
      Err.Raise 425 ' invalid object use
                    '(change this error # if desired)
    End If

End Sub
```

3. Replace the WhereClause property generated by the class builder with the code below:

```
Public Property Get WhereClause() As String

Dim objCriteria As cSelectionCriteria
Dim sTempWhereClause

sTempWhereClause = ""
```

```
For Each objCriteria In mcolCriteria

    ' If this is not the first piece, it needs
    ' an "AND" in front of it.
    If sTempWhereClause <> "" Then
        sTempWhereClause = sTempWhereClause & " AND "
    End If
    sTempWhereClause = sTempWhereClause & _
                        objCriteria.WhereClause

Next objCriteria

' If any selection criteria are present, put
' a "WHERE" in front of them.
If sTempWhereClause <> "" Then
  sTempWhereClause = " WHERE " & sTempWhereClause
end if

WhereClause = sTempWhereClause

End Property

Public Property Let WhereClause(ByVal vNewValue As
    String)

Err.Raise 383            ' read-only property

End Property
```

As before, if you prefer, you can leave out the Property Let procedure.

Notice what the code in the Property Get procedure does. We start with a temporary variable to hold the WHERE clause (sTempWhereClause). As we loop through the collection, we add pieces to this temporary version of the WHERE clause, inserting the "AND" operator before each piece except the first one.

For example, if we had two elements in the collection, and they generated individual WHERE clause pieces of:

```
" [Title] LIKE 'CO*' "
```

and

```
" [Year Published] LIKE '199*' "
```

Then at the end of the loop, sTempWhereClause would have the value

```
" [Title] LIKE 'CO*' AND [Year Published] LIKE '199*' "
```

Then all we need to do is put the WHERE keyword on the front. However, we do need to check and make sure that we have some pieces. If the collection is empty, at the end of the loop sTempWhereClause is empty, too. In that case, we don't want to pass back a WHERE clause that just says "WHERE," because the SQL interpreter will choke on that. So we only put a WHERE keyword on the front if we have a non-empty WHERE clause.

Then we send the value of the temporary variable sTempWhereClause back as the property value, and we're done.

Special notes if you are not using the class builder — The class builder automatically inserts all the plumbing needed to make the collection class work with For Each classes. It creates a NewEnum hidden property, and makes the Item property the default. If you choose to create the code for your collection class from scratch, you'll have to take care of these tasks manually. The preceding chapter has information on how you do that.

4. Now we are back to the inquiry form. We need to enhance the logic in the Find button. Click event to create the collection and extract the WHERE clause from it. Here is what that logic might look like:

```
Private Sub cmdFind_Click()

' Create selection criteria collection
Dim colSelectionCriteria As cclCriteria
Set colSelectionCriteria = New cclCriteria
Dim objCriteria As cSelectionCriteria


If txtTitle.Text <> "" Then
   Set objCriteria = New cSelectionCriteria
   With objCriteria
     .FieldName = "Title"
     .SearchString = txtTitle.Text
   End With
   colSelectionCriteria.Add objCriteria
End If

If txtYearPublished.Text <> "" Then
   Set objCriteria = New cSelectionCriteria
   With objCriteria
     .FieldName = "Year Published"
     .SearchString = txtYearPublished.Text
   End With
   colSelectionCriteria.Add objCriteria
End If

If txtISBN.Text <> "" Then
   Set objCriteria = New cSelectionCriteria
   With objCriteria
     .FieldName = "ISBN"
     .SearchString = txtISBN.Text
   End With
   colSelectionCriteria.Add objCriteria
End If


If txtSubject.Text <> "" Then
   Set objCriteria = New cSelectionCriteria
   With objCriteria
     .FieldName = "Subject"
```

```
                    .SearchString = txtSubject.Text
                End With
                colSelectionCriteria.Add objCriteria
            End If


            Dim sDataSource As String
            ' Here is the new line for DataSource
            sDataSource = "Select Title, [Year Published], " & _
                          "ISBN, Subject From Titles " & _
                          colSelectionCriteria.WhereClause

            datTitleTable.RecordSource = sDataSource
            datTitleTable.Refresh
            grdSelectedItems.Refresh

            End Sub
```

Finally, test the program, and debug as necessary. Check the copy on the CD if you have trouble making the example work — you may have made a minor error entering the code.

This is Just the Beginning

There are several obvious extensions to this project. You would ideally like your selection criteria to handle things like exact match, range of numbers, and other types of criteria.

The beauty of the object approach is that it's easy to add such capabilities to this foundation. Right now, we just have a single type of selection criteria class — cSelectionCriteria. But we could rename that to cPartialMatch, and then produce variations of it with names like cExactMatch, cSelectionRange, and so forth. The collection of criteria could have any combination of these. Each such class only needs to know how to produce its own little piece of a WHERE clause, and then it can be plugged into the overall scheme.

The cclCriteria class would only need to be changed to permit those types of classes to be added to the collection. And the logic behind the Find button would need to specify (for a given control or set of controls) which type of criteria object to create.

This example came from a real-world programming project. We eventually supported all the types of selection criteria I just named, plus several more. It made our selection screens much cleaner and more bug-free. And it actually took less time to write it this way than with the traditional "grind-it-out" types of SQL statement construction.

More About
Objects

In this chapter, we cover some more object concepts. We are finally going to get around to the terminology that most object books do in the first five pages. I have intentionally delayed talking about these matters until you have a more intuitive understanding of what an object is.

The Concepts of Inheritance and Polymorphism

Sometimes two different objects need to have similar but not identical structures. For example, suppose we are building a real estate application that uses a House object. We might also need a MobileHome object, which would have slightly different properties from a House. (Can you name some?) How can we set things up so that the characteristics that House and MobileHome have in common are only coded once?

In true object-oriented systems, this is done with the capability for inheritance. Typically, a "generic" class that has the stuff in common is created. For our example above, we might call this a "Dwelling" class. Then other classes (objects) are created which are based on Dwelling.

For these true object-oriented systems, all of the objects based on Dwelling have all of Dwelling's properties and methods, but they can add their own. Such an object is called a "subclass" of Dwelling. A House object and a MobileHome object could be subclasses of Dwelling. We say that the subclasses "inherit" the capabilities of the original object.

Unfortunately, Visual Basic does not have any direct capabilities for such inheritance. This is why many object developers dismiss VB as "not truly object-oriented."

They have a point, but you can still do very good object development in Visual Basic. You do have to deal with inheritance, because it's a common programming situation. We'll see how to do that below. First, though, we need to discuss multiple levels of inheritance.

Class Hierarchies

Our Dwelling class above might itself be a subclass of another class called Building. The Building class would hold the logic and data appropriate to all buildings, such as square footage and price.

If we combine this with our House and MobileHome subclasses, we see how the different classes are related in a tree structure, as shown in Figure 15–1.

This kind of a structure is called a "class hierarchy." A class that descends from another class, as we have seen, is called a sub-class. A class from which another class inherits properties and methods is called a "superclass."

In such a situation, the House class does not just inherit from the Dwelling class — it also inherits from the Building class by way of the Dwelling class. Changes to any of the classes in the class hierarchy which are superclasses of House may affect the House class.

As we move down the class hierarchy, classes can add properties and methods at each level. The Dwelling class may support some properties not needed by the Building class, and the House class may have properties that are not needed by the generic Dwelling class.

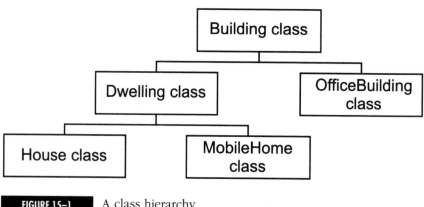

FIGURE 15–1   A class hierarchy.

Simulating Inheritance

There are several ways to simulate inheritance in Visual Basic. The brute-force approach is to create the generic object and then make copies of it to use for the subclasses. This, of course, means duplication of code, which is undesirable.

Here are two approaches that I recommend for inheritance situations.

USING A "TYPE" PROPERTY

You can create a generic object, and then give it a Type property which is used to set the subclass. That is, all the subclasses are actually coded in the same class module, with the Type property determining which subclass a particular instance is supposed to be.

For the code in common to all subclasses, nothing special has to be done. But there will be parts of the code that vary based on the subclass. For these situations, you can use If statements and Select Case blocks based on the Type property. That allows the code to execute appropriate logic for the subclass.

This approach causes a lot less code redundancy than using the brute-force "copying" approach. It works reasonably well if the differences between the subtypes are fairly minor. That means most of the code applies to all subclasses, and not much logic has to look at the Type property to determine what to do.

For example, a Person object could have Man and Woman subtypes. The Pregnant property could have logic like this:

```
Public Property Let Pregnant (bNewValue as Boolean)

If bNewValue = True Then
  If mnSubType = classtypeMale Then
    Err.raise 380      ' invalid property type
    Exit Property
  End if
End If


MbPregnant = bNewValue
```

or like this:

```
Public Property Let Pregnant (bNewValue as Boolean)

Select Case mnSubType

  Case classtypeMale
    If bNewValue = True Then
      If mnSubType = classtypeMale Then
```

```
        Err.raise 380        ' invalid property type
        Exit Property
    End if
        Else
          mbPregnant = false
    End If


    Case classtypeFemale
       MbPregnant = bNewValue

    End Select
```

WRAPPING THE BASE CLASS

The alternative approach involves a lot more work. It also incurs much more of a performance hit. But it gives maximum flexibility. This approach can actually be used to simulate just about any standard object configuration involving a class hierarchy.

This approach places code for the base class in its own separate class module. That is, in our example above with Dwelling and House, we would create a cDwelling class module with the properties and other attributes that were common to all dwellings.

A different class module is created for each subclass. Each subclass would then create an instance of the base class. Then the methods and properties that were in the base class would just be "passed along." That is, they would refer to the base class.

This approach effectively "wraps" the base class the same way we used a class module to wrap collection objects. You may recall how the "wrapper" passed the Count property directly to the wrapped collection. The collection wrapper class had no member variable or other location to store the Count property — it could only get the value of the Count property from the wrapped collection object.

Subclass wrappers work the same way. If the subclass has a property which is implemented just fine in the base class, then the property procedures in the subclass just use the same properties of the base class. Figure 15–2 diagrams the possibilities.

In Figure 15–2, the Depth property is passed straight to the base object. The Color property (which is not implemented in the base object) has its own property procedures in the subclass. And the Twist method has additional logic specific to the subclass, but is also passed to the base class at some point.

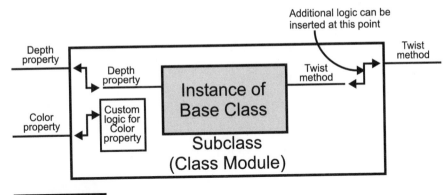

FIGURE 15–2   A subclass wrapper.

Here's an example of how the code would look. If the "wrapped" base object were named mobjBase, and it contained a Depth property, then the subclasses would have routines like this:

```
Public Property Get Depth () As Double
Depth = mobjBase.Depth
End Property

Public Property Let Depth (dblNewValue as Double)
mobjBase.Depth = dblNewValue
End Property
```

Similarly, if a method inside the subclass needed to refer to the Depth property, it would refer to mobjBase.Depth rather than, say, mdblDepth.

Notice that the wrapped base class could itself be the wrapper of another class further up the class hierarchy. So we can implement most any object design, even those that depend heavily on inheritance, with this approach.

The downside is that the more object calls we make, the bigger performance hit we take. If a simple Property Get has objects calling objects calling other objects, then the operation is slow. If such operations are inside a loop, the impact on response times can be serious.

But if there is a lot of variation in the subclasses, this method is preferred.

Notice that this technique allows "overriding" of methods and properties in the subtypes. That is, if the House object needs to handle the Price property differently from the Dwelling object, then the House class can have its own code for the Price property instead of just linking directly to the wrapped Dwelling object.

If you find all of this confusing, a detailed example may help. The next chapter (Chapter 16, "The Prisoner's Dilemma — An Exercise in Inheritance") contains such an example.

Polymorphism

Polymorphism is a related concept. Whenever two different objects display a common interface element (a property or a method), they are implementing polymorphism. If both House and MobileHome objects have a MarkSold method, that's an example of polymorphism.

The difference between polymorphism and inheritance is that polymorphic interfaces don't have to have any underlying logic in common at all. If I have a Contractor class and an Employee class, they both need a CalculatePay method. But the methods can implement wildly different logic.

What polymorphism does for you is to allow you to access objects without knowing their exact type. A given action can be taken for a collection of objects that may have considerable differences from one another, but have an interface element in common. An object may have a "Save" method, which may save to a text file, a relational database, a binary proprietary format, or an indexed flat file. A collection of these objects can be saved in a loop without the loop being concerned about how each object saves itself.

If you recall the Selection Criteria object (Chapter 14, "A Detailed Objects Example — Selecting Records"), one of the suggested enhancements was to create many selection criteria objects for different types of matching. The properties for these objects could vary, but all such objects would need a WhereClause property. That allows all of them to be accessed in the collection to assemble a complete WHERE clause. This is another example of polymorphism.

How Objects Fit into Programs

Most of the objects we have discussed so far could be called in-project objects. They are modules in the project. The code for them is compiled as part of the program's executable.

However, there are other alternatives for producing objects that your program can access. The three main possibilities are ActiveX components, in-process servers, and ActiveX controls.

We will not look at the exact processes needed to create such objects or components, but we will quickly go over why you might want to use them. There are many good books already available which discuss the nuances of creating these object types. (I don't recommend that you consult the Visual Basic documentation on creating these types of objects. The third-party books are quite superior.) Some of these books are mentioned in the Suggested Reading section at the end of this chapter.

If you feel you have gained a good basic understanding of objects up to this point, then you are ready to construct such objects when you need them. But an understanding of class modules, properties, methods, events, and instantiation are essential to moving on to these advanced topics.

Let's discuss what each type is good for.

ActiveX Components

Suppose you have a system which may have several programs loaded at once. You need to do activity logging on all of them, and the logging info needs to go in the same file.

You can do this by having logic compiled into each program to access the log (either function/subroutine or object style). But each program must open the log on each attempt, and close it as soon as logging is finished to release the log for other programs. And sometimes two programs will hit at the same time, so the logging routines have to handle that.

A better structure is to have a logging server. It sits around in memory and takes requests to put things in the log. It is the only application that has the log open, and it can keep it open all the time. Other programs communicate with it to get information in and out through OLE calls to its methods and properties.

Any time many programs need functionality which should only be resident in memory once and shared among several programs, an ActiveX component is the answer.

Note that such components are accessed exactly the same way Excel is accessed as an object. Excel can also be an ActiveX component.

Such components are sometimes referred to as out-of-process servers because their execution is not within the process of the calling program(s). They have their own thread of execution. While they will be instantiated if they are not available when called, they don't disappear when the calling process is through with them. They have to explicitly shut themselves down, typically in response to an external request to do so.

These components are compiled as EXE files. One such EXE could have several objects (representing several different classes) with exposed interfaces. ActiveX components may or may not have a visual interface.

This type of component has become much more popular with the advent of Active Server Pages as a tool for Internet development. Since ASP is limited to scripting rather than true software development, complex logic is often placed in an ActiveX component which runs on the same NT server that is handling the website. Then the Active Server Pages use the object as an out-of-process server. The ActiveX component is faster (because the code is compiled) and easier to manage (because it is created with a real, industrial-strength development tool).

ActiveX components are often called COM components because they are constructed using Microsoft's Component Object Model (COM) standard. We'll talk a bit more about COM in Chapter 23, "Additional Design Topics."

In-Process Servers

Some objects need to be available in a repository accessible by several programs. Just as a DLL provides functions that several programs can call, an in-process server provides objects that several programs can use (and in fact they are compiled as DLLs).

The main difference between this case and the standard ActiveX component discussed above is that in-process servers run their logic inside the calling process, which results in much better performance.

How do you decide which is better? Besides performance considerations, if several programs need access to the same instance of an object (as in the logging example), then an ActiveX component is required. But if each program will be creating its own instance of an object, it should typically be in an in-process server.

ActiveX Controls

One of the most eagerly anticipated capabilities of Visual Basic 5 was the creation of custom controls inside VB. You can package VB's built-in controls with your own logic and then embed the result just as if it were a standard control from a third party. Such an object is compiled as an OCX.

Consider our generic selection list form. Another approach to packaging that functionality would be to make that form into an ActiveX control, which would then be embedded into other forms. All the logic for transferring objects between the list boxes would be wrapped up in the control.

The difficulty in this case would be handling resizing. All the VB controls in the ActiveX control would have to dynamically size themselves, based on the overall size of the control at that time.

Object Tags

If you have a collection of objects and something is going wrong with one of them, VB will of course show the code where the problem is coming up. But VB doesn't tell you which instance of a class is being accessed by the code.

There's a reason for that. Regardless of how many instances of a class module are created, the code for the class module is only in memory once. Thus that code is referenced for any instance of the class.

Sometimes, there's an obvious property which can tell you which particular instance is active. In a House class, for example, the Address property would presumably be unique (and necessarily unique if it was used as the index to a Houses collection). But in some cases, there is no such obvious property.

In those cases, classes should have a Tag or Name property implemented. This property is not necessarily ever accessed outside the object (except to set it). It's just to enable the programmer to find out quickly what object is currently active.

Enumerated Constants

Sometimes properties have only certain values that are valid. In our example on the selection list form, for example, the Action property can only have two values — 1, which means that the selection was completed, or 2, which means the user cancelled.

You may have noticed that we did not use named constants for these values. Instead we used what are called enumerated constants. The declaration for these constants was done with this code:

```
Public Enum enuAction
  actionOK = 1
  actionCancel = 2
End Enum
```

The Action property was then declared to be of type "enuAction." So was the member variable (mnAction) used to hold the property value.

When an enumerated type is defined, a variable declared to be of that type can only take on values listed in the definition. That is, since mnAction is defined as type enuAction in its declaration,

```
Public mnAction As enuAction
```

means that mnAction can only hold the values 1 or 2. Attempting to assign any other value to mnAction will result in a runtime error.

This is a major advantage. There is no need to code a lot of logic to screen the values that can get into mnAction — only 1 or 2 will ever get in there.

Another advantage is that the individual enumerated constants are self-documenting. A line which says:

```
mnAction = actionCancel
```

has a self evident purpose, whereas this line would not:

```
mnAction = 2
```

This line is syntactically valid, but is still poor programming practice. (In fact, using any hard-coded numbers like "2," "37," or "3.14159" in the main body of a program is poor practice. These are sometimes called "magic numbers" and they result in problems with code readability and maintainability. Any such numbers should be assigned to named constants or enumerated constants.)

One final advantage of enumerated constants is that they work transparently with Intellisense™ in Visual Basic. If you are typing a line to assign a value to mnAction, after you type the equal sign, you'll get a window with the possible enumerated values. The screen would look something like the one shown in Figure 15–3.

The list of enumerated constants for a given enumerated type can be as long as you like. The values assigned to the constants can be any long integer value, positive or negative. You can even leave the values off of all the constants, and the values will then be assigned sequentially.

Note that the value of the enumerated constants above *cannot* be changed at runtime. They are assigned at compile time. That is, this line would generate an error:

```
actionCancel = 7
```

Enumerated constants in classes or forms are often declared "Public" to make them globally available. That makes it easy to put constants that are needed with a class in the declarations section of the class, but have them available throughout any project that contains the class.

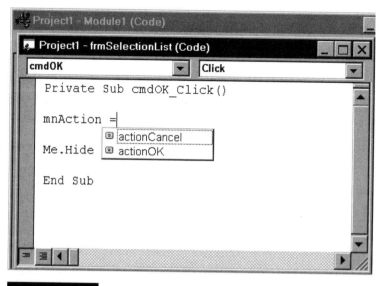

FIGURE 15–3 Intellisense™ with enumerated constants.

The Property Set Routine

Most properties contain values. Just about all of the ones we have looked at so far fit this description. We have integer properties, string properties, boolean properties, and so forth, but they all fundamentally return a *value* of some kind.

But there is a need in some circumstances for a property that returns an *object reference* rather than a value. For example, suppose an object which processes data needs to expose its underlying recordset. That's an object reference — a recordset is an object, not a value.

Such a property, which contains a reference to another object instead of a value, is implemented with a Property Set routine is instead of a Property Let. They are quite similar in other respects.

A property which is of type Variant may require both a Property Let and a Property Set. If you create Variant properties with the class builder, it will insert both property procedures into your shell code.

Public Functions as Methods

All of the example methods up to this point have been public subroutines in a class module or form. But public functions can also be used to construct methods. Such methods return a value which corresponds to the value of the function.

The syntax of such a method actually looks like a property is being used. For example, suppose we have an object which represents the dashboard of a car. We have other objects which represent things which can go on a dashboard (speedometer, tachometer, fuel gauge, and so forth). We want to assign dashboard objects to dashboard slots.

Our dashboard object might have a method to remove the least important item from the dashboard arrangement to make room for another object. We could call the method ForceSlot. In this case, we might want ForceSlot to tell us which slot it opened up. The syntax would look like this:

```
nDashboardPosition = objDashboard.ForceSlot
```

ForceSlot is a public function in the dashboard class module. It returns the value which will be placed in nDashboardPosition.

Such a method strongly resembles a Property Get in construction. The differences are that (1) there is no corresponding Property Let, and (2) the method not only fetches a value, but it also performs some kind of action.

Programming Events

Objects can have properties and methods, and can generate events. Up to now we have concentrated on properties and methods, but there are programming situations where events are very useful.

You are already familiar with the concept of an event. Forms and controls have many built-in events. You would not be able to get very far in Visual Basic without understanding the nature of a Click event. Here is a sequence of steps which you have done many times to work with an event:

1. Place a control on the form.
2. In the editor window, the control shows up in the left hand drop-down box (the one with "(General)" at the top). Figure 15–4 shows a typical screen.

   Click on the control (cmdSave, for example) in this list.
3. The right-hand dropdown in the editor now contains the events that are available for the control. Figure 15–5 shows a typical screen.

   Select one of these.
4. The editor creates shell code for the event, and places the cursor in the event procedure for further editing.

That event procedure is then executed when the event is "fired," which is typically in response to some system event such as a mouse click or keypress.

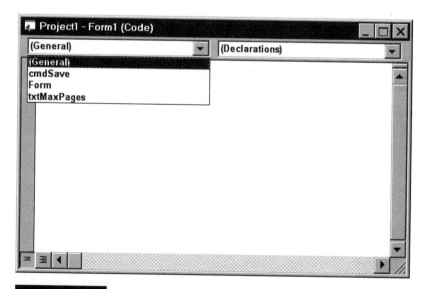

FIGURE 15–4 Editor screen for selecting a control.

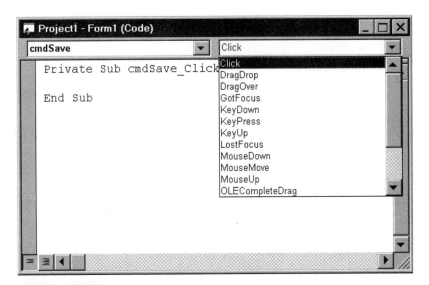

FIGURE 15-5   Available events for a control.

Event procedures may have arguments that are passed in when the event is fired. For example, the KeyPress event passes in an argument to indicate the key that was pressed.

Custom events (which you define in your class modules) are used much the same way. But first those events must be defined.

Setting Up a Class to Fire its Own Events

To make a class fire an event, first the event must be declared. For example, suppose our cSettings class needed to fire an event when the MaxPages setting was changed. We might want to do this because we have an options form which might need to update its user interface with the new value.

To *declare* the event in the cSettings class, we insert this line in the Declarations section of the class module:

```
Public Event MaxPagesChanged()
```

Now we can *raise* the event anywhere in the class module. Of course, the most likely place to do that would be the Property Let procedure for MaxPages. You may recall that this procedure looked like this:

```
Public Property Let MaxPages(ByVal nData As Long)

    ' We will only allow the maximum number of pages
    ' to be between 1 and 5000.
```

```
        If nData > 5000 Or nData <= 0 Then
            Err.Raise 380    ' invalid property value
        Else
            mnMaxPages = nData
        End If

    End Property
```

To raise an event, we use a command called simply "RaiseEvent." To make the procedure above raise an event when the MaxPages values was changed, we could change it to look like this:

```
Public Property Let MaxPages(ByVal nData As Long)

    ' We will only allow the maximum number of pages
    ' to be between 1 and 5000.
    If nData > 5000 Or nData <= 0 Then
        Err.Raise 380    ' invalid property value
    Else
        ' see if the value is really changing - otherwise
        ' don't raise the event
        If mnMaxPages <> nData Then
            mnMaxPages = nData
            RaiseEvent MaxPagesChanged
        End If
    End If

End Property
```

The MaxPagesChanged event will now be fired whenever the Max-Pages property is changed.

Forms and other classes which declare a cSettings object can now be set up to process this event. For example, suppose we have an options form called frmOptions. It declares a public cSettings object, which it calls gobjSettings. To have frmOptions process events for the object, we change the way the object is declared. As we have seen, the object would normally be declared like this:

```
Public gobjSettings As cSettings
```

▶ Watch your code sequence!

Be careful with this type of coding. Usually, you will want to make sure that raising the event is the *last* thing you do in the Property Let.

Why? The event will be processed in another module. That module might ask for the value of the MaxPages property while processing the event! So it's important that the property value be set before raising the event.

To cause events to be processed, instead we declare it like this:

```
Public WithEvents gobjSettings As cSettings
```

If you declare an object this way, it will actually appear in the same drop-down list in the editor that controls appear. The list might then look something like the one shown in Figure 15–6.

And if the object is selected in that drop-down list, the other drop-down list will contain the events for the class. The screen would look like the one shown in Figure 15–7.

Now the options form has a procedure to process the event, and you can place any code there which should be executed when the event fires. The screen above assumes that the text box holding the maximum number of pages needs to be updated with the current value, so it executes a single line, doing just that.

Who Receives an Event?

When an object fires an event, such as the MaxPagesChanged event above, all forms and classes that have included WithEvents in their declaration for the object will have the event fired. A single RaiseEvent may cause events to fire in many forms and classes which refer to the object firing the event.

When a RaiseEvent is executed, all the forms and classes which receive the event must process it before execution can continue after the RaiseEvent statement.

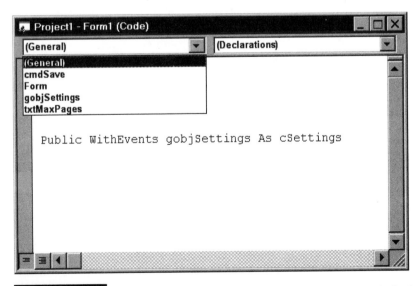

| FIGURE 15–6 | Editor screen containing an object (gobjSettings) declared with events. |

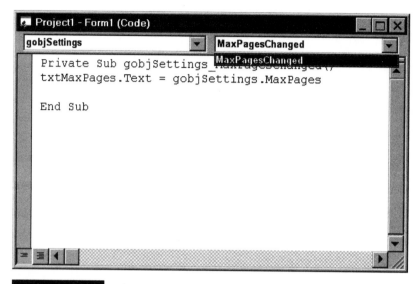

MaxPagesChanged

FIGURE 15-7 Displaying the events for a class.

Events with Arguments

The simple event we defined above had no arguments. But events can be defined with arguments, just as built-in events (such as KeyPress) have arguments.

To define an event with arguments, just place the arguments in the event declaration. If we wanted the MaxPagesChanged event to include the new number of maximum pages as an argument, we could change the event declaration to look like this:

```
Public Event MaxPagesChanged(nMaxPages as Long)
```

We could then change the Property Let procedure to look like this:

```
Public Property Let MaxPages(ByVal nData As Long)

    ' We will only allow the maximum number of pages
    ' to be between 1 and 5000.
    If nData > 5000 Or nData <= 0 Then
        Err.Raise 380    ' invalid property value
    Else
        ' see if the value is really changing - otherwise
        ' don't raise the event
        If mnMaxPages <> nData Then
            mnMaxPages = nData
            RaiseEvent MaxPagesChanged(mnMaxPages)
```

```
        End If
    End If

End Property
```

Now the event procedure in the options form would look like this:

```
Private Sub gobjSettings_MaxPagesChanged(nMaxPages As
Long)

txtMaxPages.Text = nMaxPages

End Sub
```

When to Use Events

If you find that you are writing a lot of code in your class modules and forms to track when changes are made and when various logic needs to be run, then an event-driven design may help simplify your code. For example, in our options form above, we have now centralized all the logic needed when the MaxPages property of the settings object changes — no matter how the changes were made.

Alternate Interfaces

We have previously discussed different classes which share methods or properties in common. Such classes might be needed because we are simulating inheritance, or just because we need polymorphism.

If we know that a set of classes will have a lot of interface elements (properties and methods) in common, then Visual Basic provides a way to *declare* such an interface. Such an interface is sometimes called an alternate interface.

An alternate interface is often used to declare the properties and methods which are in a superclass. Our House and MobileHome classes above might need to share all the properties and methods in a Dwelling class, for example.

In this case, the House class might have a boolean property named Basement which did not appear in the Dwelling class. Our MobileHome class doesn't need the property, so there's no reason to make the property common to all dwellings. Similarly, the MobileHome class might have a Manufacturer property that does not appear in the Dwelling class.

The subclasses (House and MobileHome) thus have two types of properties — those descended from the Dwelling class, and those specific to the subclass. The ones specific to the subclass must be created in the standard way that we have been using (inserting property procedures). But the properties descended from the Dwelling class can be handled differently, with an alternate interface.

Here's how to create an alternate interface for the House class:

1. Create the Dwelling class (give it the class name cDwelling).

2. Insert into cDwelling all the properties and methods that are needed by both House and MobileHome. That would include properties such as Address, Price, and NumberOfBedrooms. If we do that with the class builder, that would give a class with the following code:

```
Option Explicit

'local variable(s) to hold property value(s)
Private mvarAddress As String 'local copy
Private mvarPrice As Currency 'local copy
Private mvarNumberOfBedrooms As Integer 'local copy

Public Property Let NumberOfBedrooms(ByVal vData _
                                    As Integer)
   mvarNumberOfBedrooms = vData
End Property

Public Property Get NumberOfBedrooms() As Integer
   NumberOfBedrooms = mvarNumberOfBedrooms
End Property

Public Property Let Price(ByVal vData As Currency)
   mvarPrice = vData
End Property

Public Property Get Price() As Currency
   Price = mvarPrice
End Property

Public Property Let Address(ByVal vData As String)
   mvarAddress = vData
End Property

Public Property Get Address() As String
   Address = mvarAddress
End Property
```

3. Create the House class (we'll use the class name cHouse). Insert any properties (such as Basement) needed just for cHouse.

4. In the cHouse class, place this line in the Declarations section of the code:

```
Implements cDwelling
```

This line declares that House needs to have all of the properties and methods present in cDwelling. *However, those properties and methods only inherit an interface from cDwelling — they do not inherit any of the code present in cDwelling.*

5. Now code the cDwelling properties in the cHouse class. To get to those properties, use the left hand dropdown in the editor window for cHouse. Your screen will look something like the one shown in Figure 15–8.

If you select cDwelling in the drop-down list and then access the right-hand dropdown, the screen will look like the one in Figure 15–9.

Even though we are in the cHouse code module, we see the properties that were originally included in the cDwelling module. The single line "Implements cDwelling" is all that is needed to see these property procedures.

But note once again that all the property procedures are empty. Only the property types were "inherited" from cDwelling. No actual code from cDwelling can be seen in cHouse.

Only the interface (property names, types, and arguments) was included from cDwelling. But this at least ensures that all the property declarations are consistent for each class that implements the cDwelling interface. Use of such alternate interfaces allows you to:

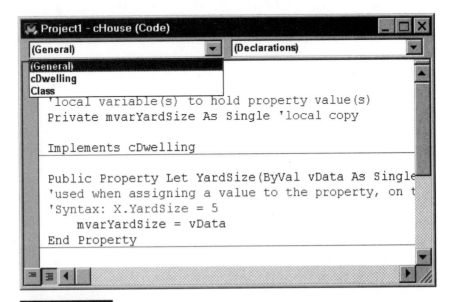

FIGURE 15–8   Editor screen in a class module — compare to Figure 15-4.

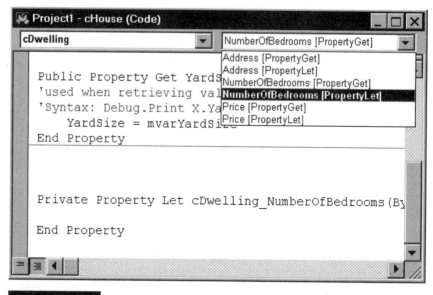

FIGURE 15-9 Editor screen for alternate interface — compare to Figure 15-5.

- Organize and simplify interfaces
- Ensure interface commonality among several classes
- Add new functionality without redefining existing interfaces
- Define an interface for a COM implementation

The Available Interface Depends on the Declaration

One of the limitations of alternate interfaces is that the properties and methods you can access for an object depend on how the object variable is declared. For example, if we create an instance of a cHouse object this way:

```
Dim objHouse As cDwelling
Set objHouse = New cHouse
```

then *the only properties and methods we can get to are those implemented using the cDwelling interface.* If we try to set "objHouse.Address," we'll be fine. But if we try to set "objHouse.YardSize," we will get a "Method or Data Member not found" error. Even though the cHouse class supports the Yard-Size property, an object variable declared as cDwelling can't get to it.

Similarly, if we do our declaration this way:

```
Dim objHouse As cHouse
Set objHouse = New cHouse
```

we can only access properties or methods that are part of the cHouse interface, not those that are implemented through the cDwelling interface.

This limitation is not well documented. It definitely limits flexibility when using alternate interfaces. But you can usually structure your code to use object variables of the "generic" type, especially when looping through collections. That allows access to the properties the objects have in common.

This limitation explains in some sense why they are called "alternate interfaces." The object can only show one interface at a time. The objHouse object can show its own special interface (if the object variable objHouse was declared as type cHouse), or it can show an *alternate* interface derived from the dwelling class if objHouse was declared as type cDwelling.

You Must Code All Elements of the Interface

If you implement an alternate interface, all the properties and methods in the interface must have corresponding routines in the class module which implements the interface. The procedures for these properties and methods can be empty of logic, but the procedures must be at least declared.

We'll see an example of this in the advanced exercise on inheritance in the next chapter.

An Advanced Exercise

Chapter 16, "The Prisoner's Dilemma — An Exercise in Inheritance," contains a detailed exercise which uses alternate interfaces in the context of simulating inheritance in Visual Basic. Going through this exercise will give you a hands-on understanding of interfaces and the Implements keyword.

The Object Browser and Documentation of Objects

If you go to the property window for a VB object, you will see descriptions of the properties when you click on one. A more organized way to see the properties and methods of the entire project is to use the object browser. The object browser is accessible from a button on the standard Visual Basic toolbar.

The object browser lists all the classes and object types your project can access. When a new class module is created or imported into your project, it shows up in the object browser.

When a particular class is highlighted, another window shows all the properties and methods for that class. This is useful in and of itself. However, even more detail is available when a method or property is highlighted. A description of it appears in a description window below the list, and an option is available to edit the description.

It is very good programming practice to add such comments to all the methods and properties for classes you create. It is much easier to locate the appropriate method or property in the object browser than by looking in the code window. These comments can be added in the object browser, or in the class builder.

Some Final Object Examples

A Reporting Example

The next example is simplified from a real project in which we needed to produce a lot of straightforward reports, but we did not want to include the Crystal Report report engine, nor did we want to use Microsoft Access reports. So we wrote our own report writer.

Here's the general structure of such a program. The report is an object, and it includes a collection of column objects. A typical set of methods and properties for the report and column objects might look like this:

THE REPORT OBJECT — CLASS CCLREPORT

Property	Type	Purpose
Count	Integer	Collection count.
Item	Object	Give reference to items in collection.
DataSource	String	The database name for reporting.
RecordSource	String	The SQL string to get a recordset for reporting.
DefaultFont	String	The default font to use on the report.
OutputObject	Object	The object (printer or screen element) to which the report will be output.
ReportTitle	String	The title to appear at the top of the report.

Method	Purpose
Add	Add column to report collection.
Remove	Remove column from report collection.
ReportPrint	Begin output of report.

THE COLUMN OBJECT — CLASS CREPORTCOLUMN

Property	Type	Purpose
Alignment	Enumerated type	Left, Right, Center, Decimal alignment.
CurrentTotal	Double	The object keeps up with its own total. This read-only property exposes that total.
DataField	String	The data field to use for the value.
FontBold	Boolean	If true, print the data in bold.
FontName	String	The font to use for this particular column (if empty, use report's default font).
Heading	String	The title to put in the heading line of the report columns for this column.
Offset	Long	A read-only property calculated from the Alignment and Print Value properties. Offset tells how far from the beginning of the physical column to start printing the value (to ensure proper alignment).
OutputObject	Object	The object (printer or screen element) to which the report will be output. The column needs to know this to be able to calculate the Offset property.
PrintValue	String	The value to print on the report.
Totalled	Boolean	Is this column totalled?
Width	Long	Width of the column, expressed in twips.

Method	Purpose
Total	Add current value of PrintValue to the member variable exposed by CurrentTotal

PROCESSING LOGIC FOR THE REPORT WRITER

Now let's suppose we want to write the processing logic for the application. We first set up the report object and the columns collection by instantiating objects and filling in appropriate properties. Then we get ready to print.

Once the rest of the methods and properties for both objects are set up, here is the code that prints the entire report, which is in the PrintReport method of the report object:

```
Public Sub ReportPrint()
  ' We'll need to know the height of a line.
  Dim nLineHeight As Long
  nLineHeight = mobjOutputObject.TextHeight("A")

  ' We'll need to hang on to the beginning column position
  Dim nColPosition As Long

  ' First open the data source and recordset.
  ' We'll leave off error checking, etc. for simplicity
  Dim dbReportDatabase As Database
  Set dbReportDatabase = OpenDatabase(msDataSource)
  Set mrsReportRecordset = _
      dbReportDatabase.OpenRecordset(msRecordSource)

  ' Print the report title
  mobjOutputObject.CurrentX = 0
  mobjOutputObject.CurrentY = 0
  mobjOutputObject.Print msReportTitle;

  mobjOutputObject.CurrentX = 0
  mobjOutputObject.CurrentY = mobjOutputObject.CurrentY + _
                             nLineHeight

  ' Now print the column headings
  Dim objColumn As cReportColumn
  mobjOutputObject.CurrentX = 0
  If Me.DefaultFont <> "" Then
    mobjOutputObject.FontName = Me.DefaultFont
  End If
  For Each objColumn In mcolReportColumns
    nColPosition = mobjOutputObject.CurrentX
    objColumn.PrintValue = objColumn.Heading
    mobjOutputObject.CurrentX = _
                              mobjOutputObject.CurrentX + _
                              objColumn.Offset
    mobjOutputObject.Print objColumn.Heading;
    mobjOutputObject.CurrentX = nColPosition + _
                              objColumn.Width
  Next objColumn
```

```
' Now print the data
Do Until mrsReportRecordset.EOF
  mobjOutputObject.CurrentX = 0
  mobjOutputObject.CurrentY = _
                    mobjOutputObject.CurrentY + _
                    nLineHeight

    ' could put logic here to change font for each field
    If Me.DefaultFont <> "" Then
      mobjOutputObject.FontName = Me.DefaultFont
    End If
    For Each objColumn In mcolReportColumns
      nColPosition = mobjOutputObject.CurrentX
      ' could put additional logic here
      ' for formatting values
      If IsNull _
      (mrsReportRecordset.Fields(objColumn.DataField)) Then
        objColumn.PrintValue = ""
      Else
        objColumn.PrintValue = _
            mrsReportRecordset.Fields(objColumn.DataField)
      End If
      mobjOutputObject.CurrentX = _
                            mobjOutputObject.CurrentX + _
                            objColumn.Offset
      mobjOutputObject.Print objColumn.PrintValue;
      mobjOutputObject.CurrentX = _
                            nColPosition + _
                            objColumn.Width
      ' Tell the column object to total itself
      objColumn.Total
    Next objColumn
  mrsReportRecordset.MoveNext

Loop

' Show Totals
mobjOutputObject.CurrentX = 0
mobjOutputObject.CurrentY = _
                    mobjOutputObject.CurrentY + _
                    nLineHeight
mobjOutputObject.Print "Totals............";
mobjOutputObject.CurrentX = 0
mobjOutputObject.CurrentY = _
                    mobjOutputObject.CurrentY + _
                    nLineHeight

If Me.DefaultFont <> "" Then
  mobjOutputObject.FontName = Me.DefaultFont
```

```
End If
For Each objColumn In mcolReportColumns
  nColPosition = mobjOutputObject.CurrentX
  objColumn.PrintValue = objColumn.CurrentTotal
  mobjOutputObject.CurrentX = _
                      mobjOutputObject.CurrentX + _
                      objColumn.Offset
  If objColumn.Totalled Then
    mobjOutputObject.Print objColumn.PrintValue;
  End If
  mobjOutputObject.CurrentX = nColPosition + _
                      objColumn.Width
Next objColumn

End Sub
```

This is not much logic for a complete generic report writer, even if it does handle only simple reports. Notice that the For Each loops (which loop through the report columns) all look very similar, and none are very long.

A working example of this program is on the enclosed CD. It would be worth some time for you to examine the logic above, and add enhancements. The working model does not change fonts for individual columns, for example. It's a good exercise for you to add that capability.

Many other enhancements were in our production version, including columns with values derived from other columns, and subtotals. All of them were easy to add to the object design above.

A Layered Data Maintenance Example

The classic multitier architecture for client-server projects is best implemented with objects. Typically, the three layers look like those shown in Figure 15-10.

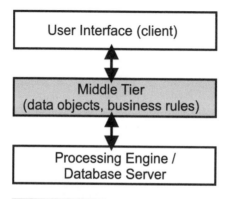

FIGURE 15–10   Client-server multitier architecture.

In some cases, more layers may be added.

The best form of communication between layers is to implement an object interface with properties and methods. It is also advisable to insulate layers, that is, to only allow interaction with adjacent layers.

This technique is a standard method of providing encapsulation of logic not germane to other layers. The user interface, for example, can be written in total ignorance of where the data is residing. There could even be multiple user interfaces, with one being complex and one simple, or one written in Visual Basic and another based on a browser. The data can even be moved without the top layers needing to know. (Some of the middle layers would provide the reconfiguration.)

The prevalence of this architecture is enough in and of itself to make it desirable to be proficient with objects. Within the Microsoft operating environment, such a layered architecture requires a component-based approach.

Testing Objects

Objects are not typically tested the same way as functions and subroutines. Structured routines are often written as they are needed, and are tested against the code that will actually call them. That means there is typically no special effort in creating a "testbed" for these routines.

With objects, it is common to create such a testbed. This can be a minimal user interface which is specifically created to manipulate the properties and methods of the object, and to display the results.

Why do you need such a testbed? Often, objects are written completely independently of the calling code. The calling code may be the responsibility of another team member. You can't afford to wait until the actual production calling code is finished to test the object.

The testbed can be very rudimentary. Here is where the ease of creating user interfaces in Visual Basic really pays off. Just crank up a form, throw some controls on it, and start feeding information to object properties and methods. Remember to try lots of potential combinations of manipulations. Don't forget to test invalid property values and operations to see if the object raises errors correctly.The end result of such testing is typically a much more robust piece of code.

Going to the Next Stage

No short presentation on objects can truly communicate how to use objects effectively when doing software development. The best you can hope for is to gain enough exposure to start doing it on your own and gradually acquire the expertise you need.

Your early attempts will often not be any better than traditional approaches (and occasionally will be worse). But experimentation and experience will eventually yield situations where you effectively use objects.

Eventually, you will reach a point where you see something you need to do which will be easy to do in objects and hard to do any other way. That will be the turning point. From then on, you will always consider object approaches when designing software.

Note that you don't have to be a slave to objects. Using object techniques does not mean that you never write another function or BAS module. But, especially early in your object-based work, you should stop every time you do that and ask yourself if there is an object-based technique which would work as well or better.

Recommendations to Go from Here

SUGGESTED READING

There are many books on programming objects, but most are for C++, Java, Smalltalk, and other pure object languages. *Doing Objects in VB5* (Deborah Kurata) is the best of the books aimed at Visual Basic developers.

To understand the object philosophy, you should take a look at *The Tao of Objects* by Gary Entsminger; it is helpful for getting you to think of software design in terms of objects. You may have trouble finding it since it is out of print.

GETTING HELP

To accelerate your own efforts, submit your early object attempts to an experienced object developer for critique. Also look at projects which were developed with object techniques to get ideas on doing your own.

Also remember that objects don't relieve you of traditional tasks which often aren't done well in software development — design, documentation, testing, etc. While objects will typically produce more robust, bug-resistant software, and more reusable software, they need documentation in their code just like functions and subroutines. And they need to be effectively designed before they are written.

The most important point I would recommend is not to give up if your early efforts do not seem to be giving you a payoff. The eventual result will be worth the extra effort during your early object work.

TWO IN-DEPTH EXERCISES

The two chapters which follow this one present two in-depth exercises on objects. These will help you gain a better hands-on understanding.

However, they take time. Don't expect to just read them and have it all sink in. You need to work through the code for these exercises in detail.

The first exercise demonstrates the "wrapper" approach to simulating inheritance. It does this in the context of a simulation game. The exercise spells out what you need to do in some detail. This exercise is in Chapter 16, "The Prisoner's Dilemma — An Exercise in Inheritance."

The second exercise is different. You are not told exactly what to do — that's what you have to figure out. The exercise presents you with an object design and a set of steps to accomplish, but detailed code is not included. However, if you get stuck, there is an appendix which contains the detailed code that completes the exercise. This exercise is in Chapter 17, "Object Workshop — Programming the Data Maintenance Object."

The Prisoner's Dilemma — An Exercise in Inheritance

We discussed in the previous chapter that Visual Basic does not support true inheritance. We also covered two ways to simulate inheritance in VB.

This chapter is a detailed exercise in simulating inheritance by "wrapping" a generic class in class modules representing the subclass. Our exercise is a simulation game which has a variety of players and strategies. We create a generic player class, and it then becomes the basis for creating individual player subclasses, each with its own playing strategy. Then we allow the strategies to play against one another, allowing us to see how they fare.

The game is called the Prisoner's Dilemma. It is interesting in and of itself, so we will spend some time understanding the game before proceeding with the exercise of writing the game simulation. For those of you who hated math, you may be tempted to skip all this. I actually have to show you a couple of small matrices. Stick with it. I promise to keep the theoretical material to a minimum, and understanding the Prisoner's Dilemma game itself is very enlightening.

Game Theory — A Branch of Mathematics

One of the new types of mathematics created in the twentieth century was game theory. Don't let the name fool you — mathematicians consider war just another game. Game theory has found broad applications in the real world.

Game theory is concerned with mathematical analysis of strategies. Much of game theory works with two-player games.

In game theory, every game is considered to have "moves." Players each select their move for a given turn of the game, and then the results are calculated according to a "payoff matrix."

Here's a simple example. Suppose you and I are playing the old game of "odds and evens," except that instead of flipping coins, we get to choose heads or tails on each turn. You have odds and I have evens. That means if we choose the same thing on a turn, I win. If we choose different things, you win.

Let's assume the loser pays the winner two dollars for each turn. In game theory, the payoff matrix for this game would look like the table below. Each combination of moves has a pair of numbers representing the amount of gain or loss for each player.

		You	
		Tails	Heads
Me	Tails	You get two dollars I lose two dollars	You lose two dollars I get two dollars
	Heads	You lose two dollars I get two dollars	You get two dollars I lose two dollars

What is a good strategy for this particular game? It depends. If your opponent is predictable, it is better to base your move on what you think he will do. But if your opponent is smart and unpredictable, then you should be unpredictable too. That usually means choosing your move on a particular turn at random.

So a "strategy" for the above game might be to select Tails 50% of the time and Heads 50% of the time, using some random means to select Heads or Tails on each turn.

Of course, there are other strategies. I could just select Heads all the time. But this strategy allows the other player (once he figures me out) to win a lot of money.

Often, one of the key questions about a game is "what is the best strategy?" That is, what strategy will yield the largest number of points (the highest payoff)?

The Prisoner's Dilemma Story

Game theoreticians have a number of theories that help them decide, based on a given payoff matrix, what the best strategy is (assuming the other player also chooses his or her best strategy). However, one game had a payoff matrix that seemed to yield strange results.

The payoff matrix comes from a story about two prisoners who have been caught by the police. They have been charged with possession of stolen goods. The police suspect that the prisoners committed burglary to get the goods, but they have no proof of that. So they make this offer to each of the prisoners:

"Look, we've got you cold on the stolen goods charge, so you're going to jail for that. We think you did the burglary too, but we have no proof. You have two choices. You can keep quiet, or you can squeal on your partner.

"If you both stay quiet, you'll probably both get a year in jail. If you squeal and your partner stays quiet, well, we'll let you out on probation, and he'll get five years. If you both squeal, you'll probably both do three years because we'll have you both dead to rights on the burglary.

"Both of you must decide what to do without talking to the other one, and without knowing what the other one had done. So what do you want to do? Squeal on him, or stay quiet?"

If a prisoner squeals, we'll call that "defecting" against his partner. If a prisoner stays quiet, we'll call that "cooperating" with his partner. Let's look at the payoff matrix for this situation. (Negative numbers are used for payoffs, because presumably the prisoners consider more time in jail to be bad.)

		Player 1's move	
		C (cooperate)	D (defect)
Player 2's move	C (cooperate)	Player 1 gets –1 points	Player 1 gets 0 points
		Player 2 gets –1 points	Player 2 gets –5 points
	D (defect)	Player 1 gets –5 points	Player 2 gets 0 points
		Player 1 gets –3 points	Player 1 gets –3 points

What's the best strategy for each player? A typical game theoretical analysis would go like this. Suppose your opponent cooperates. Then if you cooperate too, you get –1 (1 year in jail). If you defect, you get 0 (no jail time). 0 beats –1 so the logical choice is to defect if your opponent cooperates.

On the other hand, suppose your opponent defects. Now your possibilities are to cooperate and get –5 (five years in jail), or to defect also and get –3 (three years in jail). –3 beats –5, so the logical choice is to defect if your opponent defects.

In both cases, defecting is your best strategy. That is, no matter what your opponent does, your logical choice is to defect.

So with two completely logical players, both would choose to defect, and end up with three years in jail. It's rather amusing, then, that if the players were "irrational" and both chose to cooperate, both would only get one year in jail!

That's the paradox of the Prisoner's Dilemma. What appears to be the logical strategy actually yields undesirable results. So it looks like cooperating is a better strategy. But only if both players do it!

This game has become a metaphor for many real-life situations where what seems the correct choice for an individual is not the correct choice when the group is considered as a whole. For example, if I like wildflowers, I get the most benefit personally if I pick them and take them to my house. But if everyone does that, the wildflowers are quickly destroyed, so the group as a whole suffers.

The Iterated Prisoner's Dilemma

This game gets even more interesting if you assume that the two players interact (we don't use the word compete for reasons which will become obvious) over many turns. We take away the jail scenario, and just use a similar payoff matrix to define the game.

We can consider this game with just two players who interact with each other for a certain number of rounds. But things get really fun if we have a bunch of players, all of whom are playing with every other player on each turn.

The objective for each player is to amass the highest number of points for themselves. Note that they should not care how many points other players get — they just want to maximize their own points.

For each round, each pair of players takes a turn with one another. Each player can elect to Cooperate with the other player, or Defect. (These are typically referred to as C and D moves.)

The number of points each player receives is determined by a payoff matrix which is revised to make most of the payoff values positive:

		Player 1's move	
		C (cooperate)	D (defect)
Player 2's move	C (cooperate)	Player 1 gets 3 points Player 2 gets 3 points	Player 1 gets 5 points Player 2 gets –1 points
	D (defect)	Player 1 gets –1 point Player 2 gets 5 points	Player 2 gets 0 points Player 1 gets 0 points

There are many strategies for playing this game, and we can give appropriate names to each strategy. Here are some of the possible strategies:

Name of strategy	How strategy works
Ruthless (also known as All D)	Always defect no matter what the other player does
Sucker (also known as All C)	Always cooperate no matter what the other player does
Bully	Defect until the other player defects on you, then always cooperate after that
Random	Choose defect or cooperate at random (each 50% of the time)
Tit for tat	Start by cooperating on the first turn. On each succeeding turn, do to the other player whatever he did to you last time. That is, cooperate with him as long as he cooperates. Once he defects, you defect on the next turn. If he goes back to cooperating, then you return to cooperating also.
Tit for two tats	Like tit for tat, except that the opponent has to defect on you twice in a row before you will defect on the next turn.

It turns out in computer simulations with a wide variety of players (these strategies and many others) that tit for tat performs well in most scenarios. Tit for Tat usually wins or comes in close to the top of the list.

The results of this game are not just for entertainment value. As we mentioned earlier, there are many real-world situations that resemble the Prisoner's Dilemma, especially the iterated (multiple round) version. For example, suppose you are a building contractor who specializes in doing kitchens. You can do bathrooms too, but you are the best in town at doing kitchens. You know another contractor who is the best in town at bathrooms, but is capable of doing kitchens.

In such a situation, you may make the most money by doing the kitchens and subcontracting the bathrooms to the other contractor. He may reciprocate and subcontract his kitchens to you. Both you and he come out ahead.

Now for each contract you get with both a kitchen and a bathroom, you have to make a choice. Do you subcontract (cooperate) and both do what you are best at? Or do you do it all (defect) and make a little extra money on this job, but possibly lose future jobs from the other contractor?

Computer simulations suggest that your best strategy (long-term) is to cooperate until the other guy defects against you. Then you should retaliate to let him know that you won't be taken advantage of. If, however, he then goes back to cooperating, then you should forgive him and return to cooperation yourself. Of course, the real world is always more complicated, but the Prisoner's Dilemma simulation can help us understand why some approaches usually work better than others.

The First Computer Simulations of the Prisoner's Dilemma

The original computer tournaments for the Prisoner's Dilemma were done by Robert Axelrod, and he has written them all up in his book, *The Evolution of Cooperation*. He uses that title because the iterated Prisoner's Dilemma suggests that it is possible for cooperation to arise spontaneously in situations (like the contracting example above) which start out with pure competition.

(I have dramatically simplified the whole story in this chapter, as you might expect. If this piques your interest, I strongly suggest you get Axelrod's book or other books on the Prisoner's Dilemma to learn more.)

In the early 1980s, Professor Axelrod asked many game theoreticians to submit strategies, and he played them all against one another. He would manually run the programs (many of which were in different languages), and manually tally the results. As we mentioned earlier, Tit for Tat did well in his original simulations.

Writing Your Own Computer Simulation

It took Robert Axelrod a long time to carry out his "tournament" which compared competing strategies for the Prisoner's Dilemma. The time frame was the early eighties. Most of the "players" were coded in traditional FORTRAN or BASIC. Fortunately, you have much better tools at your disposal. And the game is a natural fit for an object-based design.

If you want to do a computer simulation of this game in VB, the best way to do it is to construct player objects which implement the various strategies. Player objects need methods to generate moves and update scores, and properties to tell the player object who the current other player is and what the other player does on a turn.

Once several players are constructed (each with its own strategy), a collection of players can be created. It can contain multiple copies of some strategies if desired. You could have a collection with four Tit for Tat players, three Ruthless players, a Bully, and a Sucker, for example.

To play the game do a For Next loop for the desired number of rounds, and inside of it, use loops to make every player in the collection play against every other player for a round. Then display the results. We will go through an exercise which carries out all these steps.

▶ A preliminary exercise

Before getting into the object-based design for this game, you might spend a few minutes thinking about how you would design it using traditional structured design (functions and subroutines). You would probably have a lot of arrays. The playing engine would need to have some large Select Case structures to handle the different players. And setting up for different player configurations would probably involve some coding.

Our design will be much cleaner, and will allow you to define the mix of players without additional coding, assuming that all the different player class modules have been created.

Traditional ways of programming this game make playing rounds or changing players cumbersome. With this structure, it's very easy. You can investigate various mixtures of players quickly and easily.

The Prisoner's Dilemma — An Exercise in Object Design and Programming

Let's develop a system to simulate playing the Prisoner's Dilemma. Our design will include the following elements:

A user interface to run the game and display results

A generic player object which encapsulates functionality needed by every player

Specific player objects for four strategies:

- Ruthless (all D — always defects)
- Sucker (all C — always cooperates)
- Bully (starts by defecting, then switches to total cooperation when the opponent defects for the first time)
- Tit for Tat (cooperates on first move, thereafter does whatever opponent did last time)

Our development process is to first develop the generic player object. During the real project, I worked with a temporary user interface to test its properties and methods, and you may wish to do the same.

Then we develop one or two specific player objects. Again, testing is easiest with a temporary interface.

Then we create an interface to allow us to create a collection of players, allow them to play against each other, and display the results.

Finally, we develop the remaining player objects, and integrate them into the system. This stage can be extended with the development of other player objects, including Random and Tit for Two Tats, and other variations.

Since the individual player classes resemble one another a lot, we will use a simulated form of inheritance. The method we will use for simulating inheritance is discussed in Chapter 15, "More About Objects," and is the second inheritance method discussed in that chapter — the one which "wraps" a base class.

Developing the Generic Player Object

We will call the generic player class module cPlayer.cls. It will serve two purposes: (1) as the interface definition for all classes, and (2) as a "base class" which will be wrapped by the specific player classes.

There are lots of ways we could define the interface for the generic player object. I have designed an interface for the generic player class which consists of the following properties and methods:

Property	Type	Purpose
Description	String	A descriptive field used to identify the type of player in human-readable lists.
Opponent	Integer	The index of the next opponent in the game.
CurrentMove	Enumerated type — enu-Move, which is 1 for Cooperate and 2 for defect	The selected move against the current opponent for the current round.
OpponentPrevious-Move(nIndex)	Enumerated type — enuMove	The move made by an opponent against this player for some turn in the past — the turn is identified by nIndex. This is needed because strategies for players may depend on any or all previous moves. The generic player object will keep a record of all previous moves for all opponents in an array.
TurnsWithOpponent	Integer	The number of turns played against the current opponent so far — this helps in indexing the previous property. A specific player strategy could examine all the turns from 1 to TurnsWith-Opponent, which gives the most recent turn number.
TotalScore	Long	Keeps the running score for a specific player. We assume that computerized players don't cheat and keep their own score honestly.

To reiterate — the generic player class cPlayer defines these properties and methods both to encapsulate functionality needed by all players and to define the interface for all players.

Method	Arguments	Purpose
GenerateMove	None	Determines the next move against the current opponent. In the generic player object, all this does is update the index for the latest round against the current player. In the individual player strategies, this method is where the logic implementing the strategy goes.
UpdateScore	nOpponentsMove (enuMove)	Tells the player object what the opponent did, and requests a calculation of the points for the current round and accumulation of those points for the total score.

There are several arrays which are needed to keep up with the history of moves against each opponent. To simplify the code, these arrays have set sizes. This is not recommended coding practice, but is just done to keep the code in the example as simple as possible.

Here is the code for the generic player class module cPlayer:

```
' This class module holds the generic player object. It
' has all the logic needed to keep up with the player's
' score and the move history of opponents. It is also used
' as a template (via the Implements keyword)
' for the interface
' of all other player objects.

' The individual player objects descended from this class
' differ mainly in the GenerateMove method. This
' method for the generic class is empty, and should never
' be accessed.

Private mnTotalScore As Long        'local copy
Private mnOpponent As Integer       'local copy
Private mnDescription As String     'local copy

Public Enum enuMove
  moveCooperate = 1
  moveDefect = 2
End Enum
```

```
Private mnCurrentMove As enuMove

' This array holds all the previous moves. This is a
' brute force approach to simplify the rest of the code.
' We will support up to 200 players and up to 200 moves.
' Change these limits if you like.
Private mnMoveHistory(200, 200) As enuMove

' This array holds the move # for each opponent (how many
' turns have been played with this opponent).
' It is limited to 200 opponents.
Private mnMoveIndex(200) As Integer



Public Sub UpdateScore(nOpponentsMove As enuMove)

' This routine in the generic player encapsulates the
' payoff matrix for the game.

Select Case nOpponentsMove
  Case moveCooperate
    Select Case mnCurrentMove
      Case moveCooperate
        ' reward - mutual cooperation
        mnTotalScore = mnTotalScore + 3
      Case moveDefect
        ' temptation to defect
        mnTotalScore = mnTotalScore + 5
    End Select
  Case moveDefect
    Select Case mnCurrentMove
      Case moveCooperate
        ' sucker's payoff
        mnTotalScore = mnTotalScore + 0
      Case moveDefect
        ' punishment - mutual defection
        mnTotalScore = mnTotalScore + 1
    End Select
End Select

' record the opponents move in the history array
mnMoveHistory(mnOpponent, mnMoveIndex(mnOpponent)) = _
            nOpponentsMove

End Sub

Public Property Let Description(ByVal vData As String)
    mnDescription = vData
End Property
```

```
Public Property Get Description() As String
    Description = mnDescription
End Property


Public Property Let CurrentMove(ByVal nData As enuMove)
    mnCurrentMove = nData
End Property


Public Property Get CurrentMove() As enuMove
    CurrentMove = mnCurrentMove
End Property



Public Property Let Opponent(ByVal nData As Integer)
    mnOpponent = nData
End Property


Public Property Get Opponent() As Integer
    Opponent = mnOpponent
End Property


Public Property Let TotalScore(ByVal nData As Long)
    mnTotalScore = nData
End Property


Public Property Get TotalScore() As Long
    TotalScore = mnTotalScore
End Property


Public Sub GenerateMove()
mnMoveIndex(mnOpponent) = mnMoveIndex(mnOpponent) + 1
End Sub


Public Property Get _
        OpponentPreviousMove(nIndex As Integer)  As enuMove

OpponentPreviousMove = mnMoveHistory(mnOpponent, nIndex)
End Property


    Public Property Let _
```

```
      OpponentPreviousMove(nIndex As Integer, _
                       ByVal nNewValue As enuMove)

   Err.Raise 383      ' read only property
   End Property


   Public Property Get TurnsWithOpponent() As Integer
   TurnsWithOpponent = mnMoveIndex(mnOpponent)
   End Property


   Public Property Let _
            TurnsWithOpponent(ByVal nNewValue As Integer)

   Err.Raise 383      ' read-only property
   End Property
```

Developing a Specific Player Object — Tit for Tat

The individual player classes get their interface from the cPlayer class. They also "wrap" an instantiation of the cPlayer class. This allows them to pass along the generic work done by all players into a single class module.

The first player we will develop is to implement the Tit-for-Tat strategy. We will call the class cTitForTat.cls.

Since individual player classes use the same interface as cPlayer.cls, we don't have to define it again. Instead, the declarations section of each player subclass contains this line:

```
Implements cPlayer
```

That gives each player the correct interface, but each player class needs to have *all* the necessary properties and methods coded. Remember, Implements does not cause any code to be inherited by the subclass — only the interface is inherited.

Most of the properties and methods of the individual player classes merely wrap the base object. The base object is instantiated as mobjPlayer.

The one place where the different player classes vary is in the GenerateMove method. This routine contains the "strategy" for the class.

Here is the code for the properties and methods in cTitForTat.cls:

```
Implements cPlayer

' private copy of generic player (for pseudo-inheritance)
```

```
Private mobjPlayer As cPlayer

Private Sub Class_Initialize()

Set mobjPlayer = New cPlayer

End Sub

Private Property Let cPlayer_CurrentMove(ByVal nMove _
                                        As enuMove)

mobjPlayer.CurrentMove = nMove

End Property

Private Property Get cPlayer_CurrentMove() As enuMove

cPlayer_CurrentMove = mobjPlayer.CurrentMove

End Property

Private Property Let cPlayer_Opponent(ByVal nOpponent _
                                      As Integer)

mobjPlayer.Opponent = nOpponent

End Property

Private Property Get cPlayer_Opponent() As Integer

cPlayer_Opponent = mobjPlayer.Opponent

End Property

Private Property Let cPlayer_Description(ByVal _
                        sDescription As String)

mobjPlayer.Description = sDescription

End Property

Private Property Get cPlayer_Description() As String

cPlayer_Description = mobjPlayer.Description

End Property

Private Sub cPlayer_GenerateMove()
' This method should be called when the current opponent
```

```
' has been set and it is time to play a round

With mobjPlayer
' First, increment the opponent's move index
' (current turn #)
  .GenerateMove

  '******** This begins the section that will be
  '******** different for each player type.

  ' See if we are on the first turn - if so, cooperate
  If .TurnsWithOpponent = 1 Then
    .CurrentMove = moveCooperate
    Exit Sub
  End If

' Otherwise see what this opponent did last time
' and do it to him this time.
  .CurrentMove = .OpponentPreviousMove(.TurnsWithOpponent _
                                        - 1)
  End With
End Sub


Private Property Let cPlayer_OpponentPreviousMove(nIndex _
                As Integer, ByVal RHS As enuMove)

End Property


Private Property Get cPlayer_OpponentPreviousMove(nIndex _
                As Integer) As enuMove

End Property


Private Property Let cPlayer_TotalScore(ByVal RHS As
Long)

Err.Raise 383      ' read-only property

End Property


Private Property Get cPlayer_TotalScore() As Long

cPlayer_TotalScore = mobjPlayer.TotalScore

End Property


Private Property Let cPlayer_TurnsWithOpponent(ByVal _
                RHS As Integer)
```

```
End Property

Private Property Get cPlayer_TurnsWithOpponent() As Integer

End Property

Private Sub cPlayer_UpdateScore(nOpponentsMove As enuMove)

mobjPlayer.UpdateScore nOpponentsMove

End Sub
```

Notice how simple most of this code is. The Class Initialize event creates an instance of the cPlayer class to "wrap." Then most of the remaining properties and methods just pass their information on to that wrapped instance of cPlayer.

But take a close look at cPlayer_GenerateMove. It calls on the base class, too, but remember that all the base class does in GenerateMove is increment the round number for an opponent. The method in the individual classes has the responsibility of deciding what the actual move should be and then telling the generic player what it has decided.

Note that cPlayer_TurnsWithOpponent has no code in it. Only the base class (cPlayer) needs this property. However, since the base class has it, the subclasses have to have it too — Visual Basic requires that. But the property doesn't have to have any code in it and should never be used. In fact, you can place code in the property procedures for cPlayer_TurnsWithOpponent to raise an error if you like to ensure that this property will never be accessed in the subclasses.

For the strategy in this case, there are two possibilities — the first round and all succeeding rounds. On the first round, the Tit-for-Tat strategy says the move should be to cooperate. On all succeeding rounds, the code looks to see what the opponent did last time, and that becomes the current move for Tit For Tat.

It is of paramount importance that you understand the relationship between the generic class cPlayer.cls and the specific strategy class cTitFor-Tat.cls. If you do, you have gained a real understanding both of what inheritance is supposed to do and how to implement it in Visual Basic.

Developing the Other Player Strategy Classes

Now that cTitForTat.cls is created, the other player classes are easy. They are all exactly the same as cTitForTat.cls except in the cPlayer_GenerateMove method. All you need to do is make a copy of cTitForTat.cls, change the class name, and replace the cPlayer_GenerateMove method code.

Here is the cPlayer_GenerateMove method for Ruthless:

```
Private Sub cPlayer_GenerateMove()
' This method should be called when the current opponent
' has been set and it is time to play a round

With mobjPlayer
' First, increment the opponent's move index
' (current turn #)
  .GenerateMove

  '********* This begins the section that will be ********
  '********* different for each player type.   ********


  ' We're mean, so we always defect
  .CurrentMove = moveDefect

End With
End Sub
```

And here's the one for Sucker:

```
Private Sub cPlayer_GenerateMove()
' This method should be called when the current opponent
' has been set and it is time to play a round

With mobjPlayer
' First, increment the opponent's move index
' (current turn #)
  .GenerateMove

  '********* This begins the section that will be ********
  '********* different for each player type.   ********


  ' We're nice, so we always cooperate
  .CurrentMove = moveCooperate

End With
End Sub
```

This is for Bully:

```
Private Sub cPlayer_GenerateMove()
' This method should be called when the current opponent
' has been set and it is time to play a round

With mobjPlayer
```

```
' First, increment the opponent's move index
' (current turn #)
 .GenerateMove

'********* This begins the section that will be ********
'********* different for each player type.    ********

' Bully checks to see if the opponent has ever
' defected. If it has, Bully plays cooperate.
' Otherwise, Bully defects.
Dim nMoveIndex As Integer
Dim nTempMove As enuMove

' set default of defect
nTempMove = moveDefect
For nMoveIndex = 1 To .TurnsWithOpponent
  If .OpponentPreviousMove(nMoveIndex) = _
                          moveDefect Then
    ' We found a previous defection, so cooperate
    nTempMove = moveCooperate
    Exit For
  End If
Next nMoveIndex

 .CurrentMove = nTempMove

End With
End Sub
```

Notice that Bully is the only one so far that uses the whole history of the opponent to determine the current move.

Developing an Interface to Run the Game

To run the game, we need to implement two capabilities:

- Select the players for the current simulation.
- Play the rounds and display the scores.

We could do this on the same form, but instead we use a variation of our selection list form which we developed in a previous chapter for the selection function. Then we develop a form from scratch to run the game and display the results.

I'll leave the details of modifying the selection list form to you. There's a completed version on the enclosed CD in the PrisonersDilemma directory of \examples\VB5\ or \examples\VB6. The changes from the earlier selection list include:

- Hard-coding the list elements (player strategies) instead of getting them from a database.
- Allowing each player strategy to be selected more than once.

The form which will run the game looks like the one in Figure 16–1. Here are the controls to construct this form:

Control Type	Name	Special Properties
Label	lblScores	Caption = "Scores for this session"
Label	lblRounds	Caption = "Number of rounds"
Textbox	txtRounds	Text = "100" (default number of rounds)
MS Flex Grid	grdPlayerScores	Rows = 2
		Columns = 2
		FixedCols = 0
		(other grid properties fixed at run time)
Command Button	cmdSelectPlayers	Caption = "Select Players"
Command Button	cmdStart	Caption = "Start Simulation"
Command Button	cmdCancel	Caption = "Cancel", Cancel = True

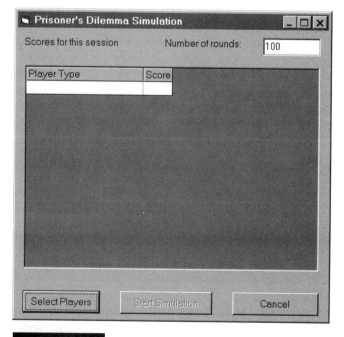

FIGURE 16–1 Form for running Prisoner's Dilemma

And here is the code needed behind these controls:

```
' put constants for the player types here

Private Const gsTIT_FOR_TAT = "Tit for tat"
Private Const gsTIT_FOR_2_TATS = "Tit for two tats"
Private Const gsRANDOM = "Random"
Private Const gsBULLY = "Bully"
Private Const gsRUTHLESS = "All D (Ruthless)"
Private Const gsSUCKER = "All C (Sucker)"
' may need to add to this list

Private Sub cmdCancel_Click()
End
End Sub

Private Sub cmdSelectPlayers_Click()

frmSelectionList.Show vbModal
If frmSelectionList.Action = actionOK Then
  cmdStart.Enabled = True
Else
  cmdStart.Enabled = False
End If

End Sub

Private Sub cmdStart_Click()

Dim colPlayers As New Collection
Dim objPlayer As cPlayer
Dim nPlayerIndex As Integer

For nPlayerIndex = 1 To frmSelectionList.ItemCount

  ' for each selected player, instantiate a player object
  ' and add to players collection
  Select Case frmSelectionList.Selection(nPlayerIndex)
    Case gsTIT_FOR_TAT
      Set objPlayer = New cTitForTat
    Case gsBULLY
      Set objPlayer = New cBully
    Case gsRUTHLESS
      Set objPlayer = New cRuthless
    Case gsSUCKER
      Set objPlayer = New cSucker
  End Select
  objPlayer.Description = _
          frmSelectionList.Selection(nPlayerIndex)
```

```
        colPlayers.Add objPlayer

Next nPlayerIndex

' Now we have a collection of players.
' Let's play them against one another.
' We'll have to use the collection index
' to make this work.

Dim nRoundNumber As Integer
Dim nFirstPlayerIndex As Integer
Dim nSecondPlayerIndex As Integer
Dim objFirstPlayer As cPlayer
Dim objSecondPlayer As cPlayer

For nFirstPlayerIndex = 1 To colPlayers.Count
  Set objFirstPlayer = colPlayers(nFirstPlayerIndex)
  For nSecondPlayerIndex = nFirstPlayerIndex + 1 _
                      To colPlayers.Count
    Set objSecondPlayer = colPlayers(nSecondPlayerIndex)
    objFirstPlayer.Opponent = nSecondPlayerIndex
    objSecondPlayer.Opponent = nFirstPlayerIndex

    For nRoundNumber = 1 To txtRounds.Text
     objFirstPlayer.GenerateMove
     objSecondPlayer.GenerateMove
     objFirstPlayer.UpdateScore objSecondPlayer.CurrentMove
     objSecondPlayer.UpdateScore objFirstPlayer.CurrentMove
    Next nRoundNumber
  Next nSecondPlayerIndex
Next nFirstPlayerIndex

' Now we are finished playing.
' Place the results in the flex grid.

' First clear the grid and erase the rows
grdPlayerScores.Clear
Dim nRow As Integer
For nRow = grdPlayerScores.Rows - 1 To 2 Step -1
  grdPlayerScores.RemoveItem nRow
Next nRow

' Now fill in the headers and player scores
grdPlayerScores.TextMatrix(0, 0) = "Player Type"
grdPlayerScores.TextMatrix(0, 1) = "Score"

For Each objPlayer In colPlayers
  grdPlayerScores.AddItem objPlayer.Description & vbTab _
                    & objPlayer.TotalScore
```

```
Next objPlayer

End Sub

Private Sub Form_Load()
Load frmSelectionList
With frmSelectionList
  .Description = "Select players:"
  .AddItem gsTIT_FOR_TAT
  .AddItem gsRUTHLESS
  .AddItem gsSUCKER
  .AddItem gsBULLY
End With

cmdStart.Enabled = False
grdPlayerScores.ColWidth(0) = 2000
grdPlayerScores.ColWidth(1) = 500
grdPlayerScores.TextMatrix(0, 0) = "Player Type"
grdPlayerScores.TextMatrix(0, 1) = "Score"


End Sub
```

All of this logic is routine Visual Basic except for the cmdStart click event. Let's look at this routine in detail. It starts with these declarations:

```
Dim colPlayers As New Collection
Dim objPlayer As cPlayer
Dim nPlayerIndex As Integer
```

We will be creating a collection of players, so we declare it as a collection. It's a pretty simple collection, so we don't take the trouble to wrap it.

We also need a player object. It is declared of the type cPlayer. This is important. Since objPlayer is declared as type cPlayer, it can be set to instantiate or reference any class which implements the cPlayer interface. All of our individual strategy classes do that.

And then we need an index for the loop of selected players. Now we are ready for the fun part — building the collection. Here's the code for that:

```
For nPlayerIndex = 1 To frmSelectionList.ItemCount

  ' for each selected player, instantiate a player object
  ' and add to players collection
  Select Case frmSelectionList.Selection(nPlayerIndex)
    Case gsTIT_FOR_TAT
      Set objPlayer = New cTitForTat
    Case gsBULLY
      Set objPlayer = New cBully
```

```
      Case gsRUTHLESS
        Set objPlayer = New cRuthless
      Case gsSUCKER
        Set objPlayer = New cSucker
   End Select
   objPlayer.Description = _
            frmSelectionList.Selection(nPlayerIndex)
   colPlayers.Add objPlayer

Next nPlayerIndex
```

We loop through all the selected items in the selection list form. For each one, we check to see what player type it is. We instantiate a player of that type, set its description (which we will need for later display), and add the player to the players collection.

We are now ready for the players to play against one another. First we need some declarations:

```
Dim nRoundNumber As Integer
Dim nFirstPlayerIndex As Integer
Dim nSecondPlayerIndex As Integer
Dim objFirstPlayer As cPlayer
Dim objSecondPlayer As cPlayer
```

The next part is a bit tricky. We need to go through the players collection, having the players play against one another. But we can't just crank up a For Each loop because that would have players playing against themselves, and some other problems. Instead we need to construct a loop that matches up each pair of players once and only once. Here's the logic which does that:

```
For nFirstPlayerIndex = 1 To colPlayers.Count
   Set objFirstPlayer = colPlayers(nFirstPlayerIndex)
   For nSecondPlayerIndex = nFirstPlayerIndex + 1 _
                         To colPlayers.Count
      Set objSecondPlayer = colPlayers(nSecondPlayerIndex)
      objFirstPlayer.Opponent = nSecondPlayerIndex
      objSecondPlayer.Opponent = nFirstPlayerIndex

      For nRoundNumber = 1 To txtRounds.Text
         objFirstPlayer.GenerateMove
         objSecondPlayer.GenerateMove
         objFirstPlayer.UpdateScore objSecondPlayer.CurrentMove
         objSecondPlayer.UpdateScore objFirstPlayer.CurrentMove
      Next nRoundNumber
   Next nSecondPlayerIndex
Next nFirstPlayerIndex
```

The first loop goes through the entire collection. But for each trip through the first loop, the second loop only gets players with a higher numeric index. A little thought (and maybe a few hand-compiled runs through the loops) should convince you that this will get each pair of players once and only once.

When we have a pair of players, we tell each player who the opponent is. Then we loop for the number of rounds. On each round, we have the players generate moves, and update their scores for that round.

The remaining logic is routine Visual Basic code to display the results in the grid. We have to delete rows in the grid for each time the game is run — otherwise rows will just be added at the bottom.

Once all these elements are in place, you can run the program and select a mix of players. Then run the simulation and see how the various strategies fare. With lots of ruthless players and suckers, Tit for Tat does not do well. But as the mix of players increases, Tit for Tat does better and better.

If you want to implement other strategies, by all means do so. You may want to try your hand at improving on Tit for Tat. Here's a hint — if you put logic in Tit for Tat to detect when the opponent is random, or is not responsive to an offer of cooperation (such as Ruthless) and then have Tit for Tat switch to an all defection strategy *just for that opponent*, then Tit for Tat will just about beat all comers. This reflects the fact that, in the real world, we stop trying to please someone whose opinion we cannot affect.

Moving Beyond Tit for Tat — Fuzzy Communications

The original computer tournaments for the Prisoner's Dilemma assumed clear communication among players. That is, if a player cooperated with another player, both players clearly recognized this. But in the real world, sometimes communication is not so clean. I became interested in the possibility of fuzzy communications. That is, I wondered what would happen if there was a small random chance that a move would be miscommunicated. In this case, Player A might choose cooperation, but his opponent player B might be told that Player A had defected instead. This was touched on in Robert Axelrod's book, but was not explored in detail — probably because simulations were so hard to run in his environment.

The above simulation is very easy to modify to deal with such fuzzy communications. Here's all you have to do:

1. Put another text box on the game form to get the amount of "fuzziness," that is, the percentage of times opponents moves will be misreported. ".05" is a good default value to place in the text box. Notice that a fuzz factor of zero equates to the original game above.

2. In the code for running the game above, replace this section:

```
objFirstPlayer.GenerateMove
objSecondPlayer.GenerateMove
objFirstPlayer.UpdateScore objSecondPlayer.CurrentMove
objSecondPlayer.UpdateScore objFirstPlayer.CurrentMove
```

with this code:

```
objFirstPlayer.GenerateMove
objSecondPlayer.GenerateMove
nFirstPlayerMove = _
            Fuzz(objFirstPlayer.CurrentMove, _
                sngFuzzFactor)
nSecondPlayerMove = _
            Fuzz(objSecondPlayer.CurrentMove, _
                sngFuzzFactor)
objFirstPlayer.UpdateScore nSecondPlayerMove
objSecondPlayer.UpdateScore nFirstPlayerMove
```

You'll need to declare the variables nFirstPlayerMove and nSecondPlayerMove as type enuMove. The sngFuzzFactor comes from the text box which holds the amount of fuzziness.

1. Add this function to the form:

```
Public Function Fuzz(nMove As enuMove, sngFuzzFactor As
  Single)

If Rnd < sngFuzzFactor Then
  If nMove = moveCooperate Then
    Fuzz = moveDefect
  Else
    Fuzz = moveCooperate
  End If
Else
  Fuzz = nMove
End If

End Function
```

It's interesting to play around with different communications fuzz factors and see how that affects the viability of strategies. With moderate fuzz factors (around 10%), Tit for Two Tats does very well because it doesn't start retaliating so fast. Of course, when the fuzz factor is above 50%, all strategies essentially behave like a random strategy.

Some Final Comments on the Prisoner's Dilemma

This exercise is a great one to study inheritance in Visual Basic. It uses the base class both to encapsulate functionality and to enforce a common interface.

The completed version of the Prisoner's Dilemma simulation on the enclosed CD implements several additional strategies and fuzzy communications.

I hope that the subject matter is interesting enough for you to want to play around with the simulation. This will help give you a solid hands-on understanding of alternate interfaces and inheritance in Visual Basic.

Object Workshop — Programming the Data Maintenance Object

Developing objects is like any other skill. You can't learn to hit a baseball by reading about hitting technique, or how to ride a bicycle without getting on one and pedaling. And you can't really learn how to write objects without writing them.

But you can do your first attempt with "training wheels," and that's what this exercise is designed to do. It was created for my object class to give them hands-on experience with a fairly complicated object structure.

This exercise is not like previous object exercises in this book. All the ones up to this point have told you exactly what to do at each step, showing all code needed. In this exercise, you are presented with a brief specification, and an outline of the steps needed to write the objects to fulfill the specification. The steps do not tell you exactly what code to write — they just tell you what you need to accomplish at each step.

The good news is that there is a backup strategy if and when you get stuck on a particular step. Appendix A of the book has code samples which will accomplish the various steps in the exercise. Many steps will refer to these "code references." You only have to refer to them if you need them.

This is a long exercise. I allotted four hours for my class to do it, and most of them took about that much time. But many students commented that it was time well spent because it involved real development work on a complex, real-world object.

The Scenario

I once had to do a project which involved many data maintenance screens which resembled one another overall, but had differing details. All the screens were supposed to have the same general layout, with the same buttons for typical database operations. Figure 17–1 is a simple example of such a form.

The project would need over a dozen such forms which only differed in the database fields to be managed. The options typically considered for a VB project with such a challenge would be:

1. Write one of the forms completely. Copy it for each additional form needed. This results in duplicate code in each form for the standard database operations. If a problem is found, it has to be corrected in all forms that descended from the original.

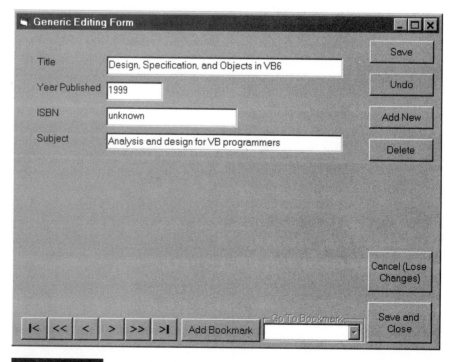

FIGURE 17–1   Example of a data maintenance screen.

2. Use data binding to minimize the logic needed for database operations. (Experienced Visual Basic developers are familiar with the limitations of data binding, so I won't go into them here.)

Neither option was satisfactory, so the development team found a third alternative. We wrote objects which wrapped up the database manipulation logic, and attached an instantiation of the objects to each form.

The resulting forms were very much like one another. They had different controls for their different fields, of course, but all of the logic behind the buttons was *exactly the same* for each form. And there was not that much logic behind the buttons. The buttons mostly called methods in the attached objects.

You may be wondering how this could possibly work. How can a generic object handle recordsets that have differing database fields in them?

The key is that the main database maintenance object contained a Fields collection. The collection contained all the information about the database fields that the database maintenance object needed to carry out its tasks. In particular, the Fields collection contained a reference to the actual control on the form in which the field was displayed and edited.

Figure 17–2 is a diagram showing the relationships of the forms and the objects graphically.

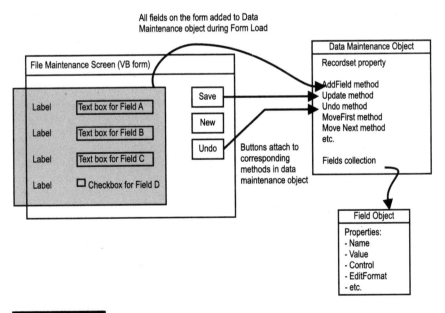

FIGURE 17–2 Relationships of the forms and objects for data maintenance.

The data maintenance object is a key component in a generalized data file maintenance architecture. It allows individual editing forms to be simple in construction because they contain no significant data manipulation code. Such code is centralized in the data maintenance object.

The concept behind the data maintenance object is very similar to that of using a data control in VB and then "binding" controls to data fields. However, building the data maintenance object allows the use of unbound controls and provides precise control over the logic used in manipulating fields and records.

When an editing form is loaded, it must create its own instance of a data maintenance object, and set up the object. In particular, the form must tell the object what data fields the form contains, which control holds each field, and other field-related information. The data maintenance object must also know what recordset the edit form is using. (This is basically the same information that would be used to bind a data control and editing controls to a recordset.)

Once the data maintenance object contains this information, it is capable of handling record navigation, record saving, default editing of fields, clearing and reloading of fields on the edit form, and many other actions. The form does not need logic for these actions, which makes coding an edit form much simpler. In fact, a generic template form will be created to hold the logic needed by any edit form, so edit forms created from that template will only need positioning and registration (binding) of fields to be ready to work. In our exercise, we will place this form in the proper directory to be used as a VB form template.

It is important to understand the data flow of this architecture. Information from the user is placed in the controls on the form. That information is transferred to the Fields collection (each Field object has a Value property to hold the field's current data value) as necessary by the data maintenance object. Then the data maintenance object transfers the information to the actual database record and does an update on the recordset as shown in Figure 17–3.

The information flows the other way when the record is read and displayed for editing. The data starts in the database record, and is first transferred to the Fields collection. Then the data is transferred to the appropriate controls on the form. That's just the reverse of the diagram in Figure 17–3, and is shown in Figure 17–4.

All these operations are carried out in the data maintenance object.

Data Maintenance Object — Properties and Methods

This section looks like an extract from a real technical specification document, and was in fact inspired by a real project. The specifications have been simplified and abbreviated to save time in the exercise. In particular, the only type of control that is to be considered valid for a field is a text box, whereas in the actual project several types of controls were supported (check boxes, list boxes, and labels for read-only fields, to name a few).

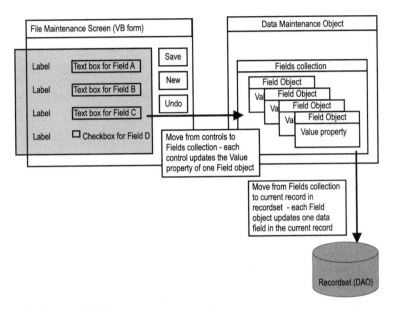

FIGURE 17–3   Data flow for entering or changing data.

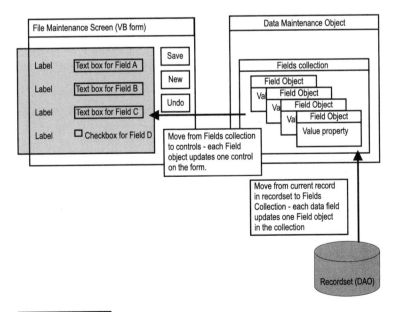

FIGURE 17–4   Data flow for display of data.

As we have discussed, the information about the fields on the form is contained in a Fields collection. This collection resides *inside* the data maintenance object. It is made of Field objects which are described after the explanation of the data maintenance object.

Now let's look at the properties and methods needed by the data maintenance object:

Property / method/ collection	How used
Recordset property	Contains object reference to the recordset being manipulated by the associated edit form.
Fields collection	Contains all information about the fields in the edit form. See details on the Fields collection below.
AddField method	Adds a new field to the fields collection. The name of the field is a required argument. This must be the actual name of a field in the current recordset. This method must create a new field object and return the object reference to the new object so that the Field object's properties and methods can be manipulated. (This method does not take a Field object reference as an argument. You should not create a Field object outside the Data Maintenance object and then try to add it to the Fields collection. Field objects should only be created by the AddField method. This technique is different from the way other example collections have worked.)
NewRecord method	Clears all fields and sets for a new record to be added to the recordset. Checks first to see if data will be lost in the current edit fields.
MoveNext method	Just like the recordset MoveNext method, except that it automatically updates the Fields collection on the form.
MovePrevious method	Just like the recordset MovePrev method, except that it automatically updates the Fields collection on the form.
MoveFirst method	Just like the recordset MoveFirst method, except that it automatically updates the Fields collection on the form.
MoveLast method	Just like the recordset MoveLast method, except that it automatically updates the Fields collection on the form.
LoadFieldValues method	Places the values from the current record in the recordset into the Fields collection.
UpdateRecord method	Performs the actual update to the recordset. Similar to the Update method of a Recordset object.
ClearForm method	Clears out the form for a new record. This method is called by the NewRecord method above. Note that controls on the editing form will either be empty or contain default values when this method is finished.
Undo method	Puts the current record back to its database values, throwing away any changes in editing controls which have been entered by the user.
RefreshForm method	Places values of fields for the current record in the editing controls. Called by several of the methods above (all the Movexxxx methods for example), and may also be called externally. May be used to initialize the controls when the editing form is first loaded.

Fields Collection and the Field Object — Properties and Methods

The field object (for insertion into the Fields collection) has the following properties and methods:

Property / method	How used
Name property	String property which contains the name of the field as specified in the database. This is also the index key to the collection.
Control property	Object reference property which specifies the edit control that the field is being editing in on the edit form. This could be a text box, combo box, list box, check box, or label. In this exercise, only text boxes will be supported.
Value property	Contains the current value of the field for insertion into the database. This must be a Variant property because it must hold many types of data. The database maintenance screen never has a reason to work with this property — it is only used by the data maintenance object.
Default property	The default value of the field for a new or cleared record. This value will be inserted into the associated control when the ClearForm method of the data maintenance object is invoked.
UseLastValue property	Boolean property which is optional and defaults to false. If set to true, then when a new record is begun, the value of the field in the last record accessed should be used for the new record.
Clear method	Reset the Value property to the default value for the field.

How Forms Use the Data Maintenance Object

Forms which use the data maintenance object can have code modules which are very similar. The form's visual layout may vary, of course, depending on the fields needed for editing. Simple editing forms might just present all the fields, and complex forms could used a tabbed interface.

The code modules differ only in the Form Load event. This is where the data maintenance object is instantiated and the Fields collection is defined.

Edit forms for a single project probably should be similar visually (though the data maintenance object doesn't really care). These forms will usually have the same buttons for record navigation and database operations, and these buttons will access methods in the associated data maintenance object.

The data maintenance object variable is declared at the form level. The suggested name for it is mobjDataMaintenance, and to keep all the code modules alike, this name should be used in every form using the data maintenance object.

The logic in the Form Load event for an edit form should look similar to this (we will look at such code in detail later in the exercise):

```
Dim mobjDataMaintenance as cDataMaintenance
Set mobjDataMaintenance = New cDataMaintenance
Set mobjDataMaintenance.Recordset = dbMyDatabase.
   OpenRecordset(sSQLStatement)

Dim objCurrentField as cField
Set objCurrentField = mobjDataMaintenance.AddField
With objCurrentField
    .Name = "FieldName"
     Set .Control = txtFieldControl
    .EditType = edittypeEnumeratedEditType
    .Default = "Some default value"
End With
' … repeat this for each control on the form
```

This code shows the necessary steps to set up the data maintenance object for use. First, it needs to be instantiated. Then, it should have its Recordset property set. Finally, the Fields collection should be built, one field object at a time, with each tied to a control on the form. Other properties of each field can be set as necessary.

Start of Exercise

In this exercise, you will program a complete initial version of the data maintenance object. It will support all the functionality described above, although it will be simpler than the one we actually developed for our real-world project.

Step 1

The first step in the exercise is to get the "shell" data entry form which will be used to create new data maintenance screens. It has all the buttons needed, but no controls for editing data (see Figure 17–5).

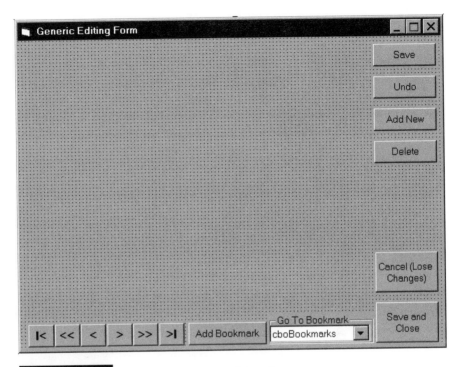

FIGURE 17–5 An empty generic editing form.

Notice that the form has controls for dealing with bookmarks. These controls are inactive at this point. There is an advanced portion of the exercise which explains how to make the editing forms work with bookmarks.

The only thing the shell data entry form needs is to be populated with fields, and to have these fields set up in the data maintenance object.

You can create this form, but it's easier to get it from the enclosed CD. It is in the Examples\VB6\DMObject\ directory, and is named EditForm.frm, and the shell project that goes with it is named dmobject.vbp.

If the CD is missing, or you just like to go through every step in the process, then you can create the form with the steps below. If you are going to use the form from the CD (which is recommended), then you can skip to the heading "Putting the generic form in the templates directory" below.

Creating the Generic Form

Open a new Visual Basic project and change the name of Form1 to frmEdit-Form. Then place the following controls on the form, with a layout like that shown above in the screen shot above:

Control Type	Name	Special Properties
Command Button	cmdSave	Caption = "Save"
Command Button	cmdUndo	Caption = "Undo"
Command Button	cmdAddNew	Caption = "Add New"
Command Button	cmdDelete	Caption = "Delete"
Command Button	cmdCancel	Caption = "Cancel (Lost Changes)"
Command Button	cmdSaveAndClose	Caption = "Save and Close"
Command Button	cmdFirstRecord	Caption = " |<", font size 10 point bold
Command Button	cmdFastRewind	Caption = "<<", font size 10 point bold
Command Button	cmdBack	Caption = "<", font size 10 point bold
Command Button	cmdForward	Caption = ">", font size 10 point bold
Command Button	cmdFastForward	Caption = ">>", font size 10 point bold
Command Button	cmdLastRecord	Caption = ">|", font size 10 point bold
Command Button	cmdAddBookmark	Caption = "Add Bookmark"
Frame	fmeGoToBookmark	Caption = "Go to bookmark"
Combo Box	cboBookmarks	Style = "2 - Dropdown List" Should be inserted into fmeGoToBookmark, not directly on the form.

Insert the following code for the respective click events:

```
Private Sub cmdSave_Click()

mobjDataMaintenance.UpdateRecord
mobjDataMaintenance.LoadFieldValues
mobjDataMaintenance.RefreshForm

End Sub


Private Sub cmdAddNew_Click()
mobjDataMaintenance.NewRecord
End Sub


Private Sub cmdBack_Click()
mobjDataMaintenance.MovePrevious
End Sub


Private Sub cmdCancel_Click()
Unload Me
End Sub
```

```
Private Sub cmdFastForward_Click()
mobjDataMaintenance.MoveFastForward
End Sub


Private Sub cmdFastRewind_Click()
mobjDataMaintenance.MoveFastRewind
End Sub


Private Sub cmdFirstRecord_Click()
mobjDataMaintenance.MoveFirst
End Sub


Private Sub cmdForward_Click()
mobjDataMaintenance.MoveNext
End Sub


Private Sub cmdLastRecord_Click()
mobjDataMaintenance.MoveLast
End Sub


Private Sub cmdSaveAndClose_Click()

mobjDataMaintenance.UpdateRecord
Unload Me

End Sub


Private Sub cmdUndo_Click()
mobjDataMaintenance.Undo
End Sub
```

Insert the following "generic" sample code in the Form Load event:

```
Private Sub Form_Load()

Dim rsMyRecordset As Recordset
Dim wsMyWorkspace As Workspace
Dim dbMyDatabase As Database
Dim sDatabaseName As String
```

```
Set wsMyWorkspace = DBEngine.Workspaces(0)
sDatabaseName = "insert your database name here"
Set dbMyDatabase = _
            wsMyWorkspace.OpenDatabase(sDatabaseName)
Set rsMyRecordset = _
            dbMyDatabase.OpenRecordset("Your table here")

Set mobjDataMaintenance = New cDataMaintenance
Set mobjDataMaintenance.Recordset = rsMyRecordset

mobjDataMaintenance.BookmarkField = _
                        "insert a field name here"

' Here's generic logic for adding a field to the
' collection.
Dim objField As cField

Set objField = _
    mobjDataMaintenance.AddField("a field in your database")
With objField
    Set .Control = txtYourControlName
    ' set other properties of objField if necessary
End With

' repeat with all your editing controls....


mobjDataMaintenance.LoadFieldValues
mobjDataMaintenance.RefreshForm

End Sub
```

And that's it. The generic form is now ready to use. We just need to put it in the templates directory.

Putting the Generic Form in the Templates Directory

Whether you got the form from the CD, or created it yourself, it needs to be inserted into the VB form templates directory. A typical path for this directory in VB5 is "c:\Program Files\DevStudio\VB\Template\Forms." For VB6, the path would typically be "c:\Program Files\Microsoft Visual Studio\VB98\ Template\Forms."

Once the form is in that directory, you can use the Add Form command on the Project menu to add a new copy of it to your project. That command gives you a window showing all the available templates, and the generic editing form will show up with "EditForm" as its name (underneath it).

Getting a Project to Work In

1. Start Visual Basic, and select a new project (Standard EXE).
2. On the resulting project, select Project — Add Form, and add a generic editing form to your project.
3. Rename the form to frmEditTitles.
4. On the Project Properties dialog, make the start-up object for the project frmEditTitles. If you wish, you can delete Form1 from the project at this point, since it is not needed.

Creating the Field Object

Up to this point, the exercise has been standard VB, and the steps have been clearly specified. Now the exercise presents you with more generic steps to accomplish, and you have to figure out how to write the code and what other operations you need to do to complete the step.

Remember, if you get stuck, you can look at the sample code references in Appendix A. There are references throughout the steps below to various code references.

STEP 1

Use the *class builder* to construct a Field class with the properties and methods shown in the design document above. Take care to get the property data types correct.

Use cField for the name of the class.

Have the class builder update the project, which creates the class.

STEP 2

Change the names of the member variables created by the class wizard to reflect their types. They all start with "mvar." This should be changed to "mn" or "ms" or whatever is needed for a particular type. The sample code references use correct prefixes, so changing them now will make using the sample code references much easier. These changes will need to be made throughout the class module.

STEP 3

The cField object will need to set some default property values in its Class Initialize event. The UseLastValue property should default to false, and the Default property should default to a null string.

Create the Data Maintenance Object

STEP 1

Use the ***class builder*** to construct a data maintenance class with the properties and methods shown in the design document above.

The Data Maintenance object can be considered as a collection of field objects, but you will find it easier to program if you do ***not*** have the class builder insert the Fields collection into the Data Maintenance object automatically because you would end up with some superfluous methods and properties. We will put those collections in the data maintenance object manually in the next step.

Take care to get the property data types correct, and to insert the proper argument for AddField. Also, set AddField as a method which returns a value.

Use cDataMaintenance for the name of the class.

Note that the class builder only knows one object type, namely "Object." Any properties which are object references will have to have their types changed later, after the class builder has generated the code. (There are steps for that below.)

Have the class builder update the project, which creates the class.

STEP 2

As with the Field object, change all the "mvar" prefixes created by the class builder to appropriate prefixes. Also, the member variable that holds Recordset (for cDataMaintenance) should have its type changed from Object to Recordset.

After these changes, the declaration for the member variable holding the Recordset property should look like this:

```
Private mrsRecordSet As Recordset      'local copy
```

STEP 3

Add the Fields collection to the data maintenance object. To do this, declare a private collection variable as a member variable for the data maintenance object. Name it mcolFields. The line should look like sample code reference #1.

The collection object should be instantiated in the Class Initialize event for the data maintenance object. The code for that is sample code reference #14.

Then implement the AddField method. This method builds the Fields collection. Note that this method is the only way items can be added to this collection.

AddField should look something like sample code reference #2. Note that AddField returns a reference to the created field, so it is a function and not a subroutine.

STEP 4

Add appropriate code for the following properties and methods:

ClearForm — This method needs to loop through the Fields collection, and place the default value of the field in the control. See sample code reference #5.

RefreshForm — This method needs to loop through the Fields collection, and place the current value of each field in the associated control. Be careful, because if a field has a null value (because of a null in the database), then it must be dealt with specifically by placing a null string in the control. (You can't place a null in a text box's Text property.) See sample code reference #6.

NewRecord — This method should do the following things: (1) Clear the form (ClearForm), (2) Set up the recordset for a new record with the AddNew method, (3) clear out the values of Fields collection (unless the UseLastValue property is true for a field), and (4) Refresh the form controls (RefreshForm). (Why refresh the form? Because the UseLastValue property may cause placement of values in some controls, and these values then need to be placed on the form.) See sample code reference #4 for an example.

Create the public LoadFieldValues method. It gets information from the record buffer into the fields collection. It should loop through the fields collection and find the associated field in the recordset for each one, and get the value of that field in the recordset. When all values are loaded out of the record buffer, an Edit method should be executed against the recordset to prepare for editing. Sample code reference #8 has an example routine.

MoveNext, MovePrev, MoveFirst, MoveLast — These all look a lot alike. They just implement the corresponding method on the recordset. Don't forget to check for BOF or EOF as appropriate, and to make sure you always have a current record. The code for MoveNext is in sample code reference #7.

UndoChanges — In our simplified version, all this needs to do is refresh the form with the current field values (which wipes out any changes the user has made). So just call the RefreshForm method.

Implement a *private* method called MoveControlValuesToFields. It should just loop through the fields collection, placing the value for the corresponding control in the field value. See sample code reference #10.

Implement a *private* method called MoveFieldValuesToRecordBuffer. This is the inverse of the LoadFieldValues method we did previously. Loop through the collection of fields, placing the field value in the corresponding recordset field. See sample code reference #11.

UpdateRecord — This is easy since the private methods above are done. It just needs to call MoveControlValuesToFields, and then MoveFieldValuesToRecordBuffer. Then do an Update method on the recordset. (There is one minor consideration caused by an oddity in the Microsoft Access Jet engine. If the record being updated is an added record, it will not be current, even after being added. So we need to make it the current record in the recordset. The sample code has a line to do that using the LastModified property of the recordset.) See sample code reference #9.

STEP 5

Now set up the form (frmEditTitles) to use the object.

All the coding you need to do is in Form Load. We will be using the Titles table of bibio.mdb again. You'll need to open the Biblio.mdb database (wherever it is on your system) and set the recordset as the Titles table. If you don't have a copy of Biblio.mdb, you can get one off the enclosed CD in the directory \Examples.

Draw labels and text boxes on the form for the following fields in the Titles table:

- Title
- Year Published
- ISBN
- Subject

Then set up each field with its associated text box in the data maintenance object's Fields collection. A generic example already present in Form Load will show you what to do.

STEP 6

You are ready to roll. Test and tweak the program. If you have problems making it work, check out the sample code references to see if your code looks similar. You can also see the completed project in action on the enclosed CD in Exercises\DMObject\CompletedProject.

If you want more experience, you may wish to do various enhancements: Here are some possible additions to try:

- Fast forward and rewind functions
- Implementing additional control types — check boxes, labels for read-only controls, combo boxes, etc.
- Implementing edit formatting for the Field object. This would require a property to specify the edit format and code to verify that the current value was of the correct type and/or formatted properly. For example,

the project above does not test the year to make sure it is numeric before placing it in the database. The edit formatting feature could check that before attempting to write the record.

There's also nothing to keep you from adding edit capabilities to the form directly. That is, the form you have created above, which uses the data maintenance object for much of its operation, can still have standard VB logic of its own. For example, you could place on-the-fly editing into control's click events. Or you could have your own verification routine that got called in the cmdSave click event before the calls to the data maintenance object.

There's another advanced feature that we discuss in detail below because it allows us to add another object to the project.

Advanced Feature — The Bookmark Object and the Bookmarks Collection

Many database systems allow the user to "bookmark" a record. That allows the user to return to that record after looking at some other records.

The Microsoft Access Jet database engine supports a Bookmark property for recordsets. It allows the saving of record references and using the reference to return to previous records. If you are not familiar with the Bookmark property, check it out in the help for Data Access Objects (DAO).

Using this bookmark property, we can add capability to our project above to support bookmarks for all of our forms. This will require us to add some logic to the generic form, since some buttons were intentionally left inactive to simplify the exercise to this point. We will also create a bookmark object, and add a bookmark collection to the data maintenance object.

Enhancing the Generic Form

To make the generic form work with bookmarks, open the form, and add the following logic to these two click events:

```
Private Sub cboBookmarks_Click()

If cboBookmarks.ListIndex >= 0 Then
   mobjDataMaintenance.GoToBookmark cboBookmarks.ListIndex
End If

End Sub


Private Sub cmdAddBookmark_Click()
```

```
mobjDataMaintenance.AddBookmark
mobjDataMaintenance.ListBookmarks cboBookmarks
If cboBookmarks.ListCount > 0 Then
   fmeGoToBookmark.Enabled = True
   cboBookmarks.Enabled = True
Else
   fmeGoToBookmark.Enabled = False
   cboBookmarks.Enabled = False
End If

End Sub
```

Creating the Bookmark Object

The bookmark object holds a pointer to a particular record, and also includes information needed to display and manage bookmarks. The bookmark object (for insertion into the Bookmarks collection) has the following properties and methods:

Property / method	How used
Name property	String property which contains the name of the bookmark. The name is constructed using the field in the BookmarkFields property. This is also the index key to the collection.
BookmarkValue property	This is a string property that holds the bookmark value returned by the recordset Bookmark property for the record. The property is used to set the current record on a GoToBookmark method in the DataMaintenance object.

Use the class builder or a blank class module to create the cBookmark class with the properties above.

Enhancing the Data Maintenance Object

The data maintenance object will need the following properties and methods to support bookmarks:

Property / method	How used
Bookmarks collection	A collection of bookmark objects (see above for a specification of a bookmark object).
BookmarkField property	This property tells which field should be used to construct the bookmark name for display in the combo box. It should typically be specified in the Form Load event of the editing form. (Note that this field should have unique values in the recordset. In our production system, we constructed the bookmark from the primary key plus the field specified in the BookmarkFields property.)
AddBookmark method	Adds a record pointer to the bookmark collection. The user can later select the option to go to a particular bookmark to return to any record in the bookmark collection. This method requires no argument — the current record is assumed.
ListBookmarks method	Requires a list box or combo box as an argument. This method fills the list box or combo box with the currently available bookmarks. The list is constructed using the field specified in the BookmarkFields property.
GoToBookmark method	Repositions a recordset to a bookmark. The bookmark number must be included as an argument, and is the position in the list box or combo box at which the bookmark appears.

To add these enhancements, carry out the following:

Add the Bookmarks collection. To do this, declare a private collection variable as a member variable of the data maintenance object, just like you did with the Fields collection. Name it mcolBookmarks.

The collection object should be instantiated in the Class Initialize event for the data maintenance object, just as the Fields collection was.

Then implement the AddBookmark method. It creates the bookmark, using the current record in the recordset. It is simpler than AddField. You can see it in sample code reference #3.

Then implement these methods:

ListBookmarks — This method places the current bookmarks in a drop-down combo box. See sample code reference #12.

GoToBookmark — This method repositions the recordset at a selected bookmark. The bookmark number from the combo box has to be passed in as an argument. See sample code reference #13.

Now set up your specific editing form for bookmarks. To do that, you just add a line to the Form Load event to set the BookmarkField property of the data maintenance object. If you are working with the same editing screen for the Titles table, I suggest you use the Title field.

And you're done. Test the new bookmarking capabilities.

Summary

This exercise has dramatically shown how objects can encapsulate logic. Rather than repeating the same logic over and over on similar forms, it can be combined into an object. Then each form can get its own instantiation of the object.

The key to the success of this approach is that an object doesn't just package logic — it also packages data. Each instance of an object can have its own data. In this case, each instance of the data maintenance object has its own Fields collection and Recordset property to tell it what data to operate on.

You might want to spend some time thinking about how you would duplicate the capabilities of the data maintenance object with just functions and subroutines. I think you'll agree after considering it for a while that it would be very difficult and probably not practical. Understanding the problems inherent in a traditional structured design will help you to appreciate the strong points of an object-based design.

Wrap-up on Objects

The journey to understanding objects is not easy. As we mentioned before, it is the classic example of a paradigm shift, and requires a complete readjustment of the way you think about creating software. It affects everything from the way you gather requirements to the way you roll out the system and document it

Is it worth it? Definitely. Let's revisit the reasons an object approach to software development is the obvious choice for Windows development projects.

You Don't Have a Choice

Today's multitier Windows development projects are all component-based. Unless you are going to be restricted to just producing user interfaces, you *must* know how to construct components, which is just another name for objects and groups of objects.

And the user interface portion is getting thinner. Where traditional client/server projects often had fat Visual Basic programs just for the client side, today's browser-based systems have very thin clients. The advantages for thinner clients are compelling — easier distribution, transparent maintenance, standardized interfaces, and complete geographic coverage, for starters. So sticking to just the user interface piece can be very career-limiting.

Let's pick one example. With the release of Visual Basic 6, the capability for webclasses was added. What are webclasses? They are simply a type of class module specially constructed to run on an Internet server and to output HTML. While constructing server components was less than straightforward with Visual Basic 5, now even comparatively inexperienced VB developers can create software to run on a server. But you can only journey into web-classes if you already know the fundamentals of class modules and objects.

I believe that learning the fundamentals is best done in a standard Visual Basic environment because that limits the number of new concepts to be absorbed at the same time. This book has been structured with that approach. But as soon as you do understand those fundamentals, you are ready to branch out to a wider application of them by creating ActiveX components, ActiveX controls, webclasses, and other advanced object forms.

Faster Development

The earliest textbooks on object-oriented methods estimated that an object approach consumed around twenty percent more time than traditional approaches. The justification for objects was supposed to be in the reusability and robustness of the software.

That does not match my experience. I believe an object approach speeds software development. In one real-world situation involving many of the same developers, a project in Visual Basic 3 (without objects) took over forty person-months. The next project was conceptually similar, but somewhat more complex. It was sufficiently different that virtually no code was used from the first project — everything was done from scratch. Using Visual Basic 4 (and an object approach), the second project took only *eighteen* person-months.

You may not get an improvement of that magnitude, but there are a lot of reasons that an object approach speeds development. Here are a few of them:

- Objects force better definition before coding.

- The encapsulation of functionality in objects allows clearer focus on each object. While a particular object is being written, the developer can dismiss most of what is going on elsewhere in the system.

- It's easier to test objects. They provide a package which accomplishes certain specific functions. If each of these functions is thoroughly verified, then the object should work just about anywhere it is plugged in.

- Dividing the work among team members is dramatically improved. Each team member has responsibility for clearly defined areas of functionality, and the interface to the functionality being developed by other team members is clear.

It is possible that in a very small project, an object approach will take slightly longer. I still believe the other advantages of objects would indicate that an object design is preferable almost all the time.

Dramatically Lower Bug Count

In the project mentioned above, as the project drew to a close, the bug count was far lower than comparable projects being done with traditional techniques at the same time. Towards the end of the development cycle, the object-oriented project was generating about one-tenth the number of bug reports as other projects offering simpler functionality. And the bugs tended to be simpler to find and easier to fix.

This factor alone would be enough in my opinion to demand an object approach. A persistent problem in our industry is unstable software. Building more robust software should be a priority for all developers.

Reusability

This one is typically first on the list in the object textbooks. It is important, but I have intentionally put it later in the list because I think the other factors are even more important.

It is true that well-designed objects tend to find uses outside their original purpose in life. Thinking about functionality in object terms forces you to abstract out the most important capabilities. The better abstraction makes objects more widely applicable than typical structured routines.

The quest for reusability can lead you astray, however. Some object textbooks recommend designing an exhaustive "object framework" before beginning serious development on a system. Placing reusability first on the list of reasons to do objects inspires this. Such efforts fail as often as they succeed, and it's easy to see why. Until you are solving real problems, it's hard to know exactly what functionality you'll need.

It is useful to think about base objects which are going to be widely applicable, especially if you are doing a series of related development projects. Just don't get carried away with that to the exclusion of developing the actual systems needed.

During and after a development project, you will spot objects that have potential capability for reuse. It's a good idea at the end of a project to look over the objects that were created for the project and pick out those that look to have wider applicability. Then document what these objects can do, and inform anyone who might be able to make use of them.

Less Expensive Maintenance

The encapsulation of logic by objects reduces the number of places that need to be touched for a typical change to a system. And the clear purpose of most objects makes it easier to find the places that need to be touched. Testing of the changes is also easier.

All these factors help reduce the expense of maintenance. Since more money is spent on maintenance for a typical system than was spent on the original development, the savings can be impressive.

Objects in Internet Development

Many Visual Basic developers are forced into learning more about objects when they get involved in Internet-related projects. The server-based architecture required for interactive websites dictates extensive use of objects.

Most Internet projects done with Microsoft technologies use Active Server Pages to generate the interactive web pages required. But Active Server Pages are only interpreted script. They cannot take the place of structured, compiled programs.

But Active Server Pages can instantiate and access objects. It is common to create such objects any time an Active Server Page needs to access significant functionality.

As a Visual Basic developer, don't be reluctant to get involved with Internet projects which use Active Server Pages. You are already well positioned to do that. A Visual Basic developer making the move to Active Server Pages basically needs to understand:

- Objects
- How web browsers work
- The basics of Hypertext Markup Language (HTML)

Webclasses

We previously discussed webclasses, which are basically compiled Active Server Pages. They are available with Visual Basic 6 and are an option to Active Server Pages for web development.

And, of course, you need to understand objects before you can use webclasses. However, if you have a good object understanding, the wizards and examples that come with Visual Basic 6 can get you started with webclasses.

Designing Objects

Knowing how to code objects is just one part of being an object developer. You also must be able to design objects. That topic is covered in detail in the third part of the book, which is on the general topic of design.

This section on how objects work in Visual Basic is a necessary prerequisite for discussing object design. That's why it's in the middle of the book. Once you have gained that basic understanding of objects in Visual Basic, you are ready to return to the main theme of the book — analysis and design.

Questions You Should Ask Yourself

Here are some questions you might ask yourself to decide what areas you need to look at next:

Do I have current projects where I could use form properties and methods to simplify program structure during routine maintenance?

Where could I make obvious use of a class module in my next project?

Do I understand how to code an object when I have a design?

How do I test objects when they are developed?

Suggestions for Further Reading

Perhaps the most exhaustive book on objects in Visual Basic is *Doing Objects in Visual Basic 5* by Deborah Kurata. It has been mentioned several times in this book. It will take some time to read through it, but if you are still hazy on some of the concepts, it can help. There should be a version for Visual Basic 6 by the time you read this.

Another good book on objects in VB is *Visual Basic 6 Object-Oriented Programming* by Gene Swartzfager, Ramesh Chandak, Purshottam Chandak, and Steve Alvarez. While using the traditional academic approach to objects, it will present additional examples which you may find enlightening. And it contains a good section on object design.

If you are just getting into Internet development, a good introduction is in *Active Server Pages Unleashed* by Steve Walther. It contains a basic introduction to HTML as well as the Microsoft technologies related to Active Server Pages.

The Design Phase

The Design Phase — Introduction

This part of the book covers the design phase of software development. As with the analysis phase, the emphasis is on concrete suggestions and ideas for Visual Basic developers to use in their projects.

Remember that we are following the 80/20 rule in this book. This presentation of ideas for design is definitely not intended to be exhaustive. The goal is to give you a good understanding of fundamentals, and to communicate some of the most valuable techniques.

It is also important once again to understand that not all suggestions are appropriate for all situations. The design phase offers a multitude of possible approaches for each subphase. Your circumstances will determine which techniques work best for you.

What vs. How — The Difference Between Analysis and Design

Recall that the central idea of the analysis phase was to discover *what* the software system is supposed to do. Now come the design and development phases. These phases are concerned with *how* the software will accomplish its tasks.

Once you have an excellent feeling for the "what," you are ready to determine the "how."

The Subphases of Design

Most design phases have several subphases, including:

- Database design
- User interface design
- Design of the objects which will make up the system

We will look at each of these phases in detail. We will also cover tools used for some design phases. Tools tend to be more important to the design phase than the analysis phase. Whereas most analysis doesn't need anything more complex than a word processor, design can benefit greatly from the appropriate tools.

At several points, the phases will discuss the Visio Enterprise™ tool for design tasks. A trial version of that system is on the enclosed CD. Visio™ is by no means the only design tools which can be used. Other design tools for various design-related tasks include Rational Rose™ from Rational Software, HOW™ from Riverton Software, Erwin™ from Logic Works, and Power-Designer™ from Powersoft.

What Documents are Produced During Design?

Many of the documents produced during the design phase are called "technical specifications." These documents consist of the description of the system to be produced from a technical point of view. Technical specification documents may include such elements as:

- Overall system architecture
- Detailed database layouts
- Object designs and interfaces
- Pseudocode for major processes in the system
- User interface screen designs

There is a lot of variation in the structure and content of design phase documents. In some cases, a single technical specification combines almost all of the documentation for the design phase. In other cases, the development team prefers to produce several documents concentrating on specific areas of design.

Because of this variation, this section does not give detailed suggestions for constructing the documents like those in the section for the analysis phase. There are some general suggestions, but I'm leaving the detailed organization up to you.

Who Does the Design Documents?

There is not usually much competition for those wanting to do technical design of software projects. Except for user interface design, users want no part of it. And many programmers don't like to do it either.

But the best case is for the design phase to be a team-based effort. Initial design can be done with the entire team, with individual team members then filling in detail on subsections of the design. That means the writing of the technical specification is typically shared among several members of the development team.

This discussion of design sometimes assumes that a multiperson team is involved, although most of the concepts are equally important if you are working alone.

Designing a System Architecture

One of the results of a design phase is a design of the overall architecture of the system to be developed. In-depth system architecture is beyond the scope of this book. But you should be aware that, on large projects, system architecture is a significant challenge.

Typical Visual Basic projects have a somewhat simpler system architecture. For these types of projects, here are some guidelines to follow:

Use Multitiered Architecture —
Even on a Single Platform

One of the advantages of object-based design is that even a stand-alone program which is self-contained on a single computer can still be implemented with a multitier design. The classic "three-tier design" should be used for all but the simplest systems.

This allows better object design for the initial development effort, and, as a bonus, makes it far easier to "break apart" the system into multiple physical tiers later, if it should be desirable to do so.

Keep the Client Thin

Visual Basic has produced some of fattest clients around for distributed database projects. There was an excuse for this in earlier days, but there is no longer an excuse. Try to keep the client layer of your design down to just user interface management. Push everything else into middle layers of objects, or into the database itself.

This is easier to do with modern, browser-based interfaces. These interfaces are so much easier to install and support that many development teams choose them over a classic Visual Basic interface; even an interface based on VB forms is far more flexible.

Don't be Afraid of COM

Modern distributed designs in the Microsoft universe depend on COM. If you are not proficient with COM, and you need to work in a distributed environment, you should make familiarization with COM a high priority.

There is a brief overview of COM in Chapter 23, "Additional Design Topics."

What are the Other Products of the Design Phase?

The design phase typically produces some prototypes and "proof-of-concept" programs. Prototypes are typically done for user interface designs. Proof-of-concept programs are another type of prototype. They may be for any element of the system, and consist of just enough development to show that a given design or technology will work for the intended purpose.

Methodologies and Best Practices

Chapter 24, "Methodologies and Best Practices," covers some overall good practices for the entire design and development process and some methodologies which assist in application of these practices. I believe that chapter contains some of the most important concepts in the book, and I would urge you not to leave it out of your reading.

Thinking Outside the Box

Chapter 25, "Thinking Outside the Box," deals with the subject of creativity, and how to stimulate it. The analysis phase doesn't require a lot of creativity. It is mostly descriptive. But the design phase definitely has a creative element. Using your creativity to maximum effect will definitely make you a better designer.

Data Design

Visual Basic was around for a couple of years before it started to be used in serious development efforts. It is easy to pinpoint the reason that Visual Basic started being successful. Version 3.0 added the built-in capability to get to relational databases.

The vast majority of Visual Basic projects manipulate some kind of data. Sometimes the data is already defined, and may exist on a system which is not even Windows-based (a mainframe or Unix system, for example). But many Visual Basic projects require the design of a database structure to hold the information to be manipulated by the system.

Data design should one of the earliest tasks in the design phase. Some high-level data design may even be done during functional specification.

Some object methodologies recommend designing the objects for the system before designing the database. There are projects where this will work better. But I find that typical data-intensive Visual Basic applications are better done by getting a handle on the database structures first. You may want to try both approaches and see what works best for you.

Persistent Information

With an object approach, the difference between data which is permanent and temporary becomes clearer. Information about object states (object properties and internal values) is used only during execution of the program. Permanent or persistent information is that information which must be held between executions of the program.

Sometimes it is necessary to store object states. This is one of the primary purposes of so-called object databases. But we will not go into that aspect of object development. When we talk about persistent information in this chapter, we are referring to information traditionally stored in databases.

Tools for Designing Databases

For simple systems, paper and pencil are quite sufficient for most of the definition steps below. Most modern relational databases also have an interface for designing database structures. Microsoft Access and SQL Server 7.0 both have adequate tools, for example. (SQL Server 6.5 has very limited tools for this purpose.) And Visual Studio 6 includes a database design feature that can access most ODBC-compliant databases.

For very complex database systems, there are data modeling tools which work better. Visio Enterprise™ and Visio Professional™ both include data design tools. (Trial copies of both are included on the enclosed CD.) Erwin™ (from Logic Works) and PowerDesigner™ (from Powersoft, a division of Sybase) are other available tools. These advanced tools have more flexibility for assistance during design, and also can take a graphical design and translate it into actual database structures in a variety of database formats.

Steps in the Process

The major steps in the process of defining database structures for your projects include:

- Definition of the system
- Analyzing the system for necessary data elements
- Organizing data elements into tables
- Determining relationships among tables
- Setting table indexes
- Normalizing the data
- Determining validation requirements for data fields
- Building queries or stored procedures

The first part in this book was about definition of the system, so we will presume that this step is done. Let's look at the other steps in some detail.

There are some similarities in the way you extract database definitions from a definition and the way you extract object definitions. You will see more about this commonality after reading the Chapter 22, "Designing Objects."

Analyzing the System
for Necessary Data Elements

To start this process, examine the system definition document (usually the functional specification), and look for the nouns used. You'll typically see terms like:

- customer
- incident
- order
- patient
- transaction
- employee
- facility

All of these are candidates for tables in your data definition. Such items are often referred to as "entities."

Also look for nouns which express attributes or pieces of information that the system needs to work with. These include words like:

- count
- date
- name
- address
- amount
- quantity
- color

These are candidates for data fields.

Organizing the Data Elements
into Tables

For each entity discovered in the previous step, decide if there is a need for persistent information about the entity. For example, you are just about sure to need permanently stored information on employees. But with transactions, you might or might not, depending on the nature of the application.

Then, for each entity which needs persistent information, start listing all the attributes or characteristics of the entity referred to anywhere in the definition. For an employee, this might consist of things like:

- first name
- last name
- address
- city
- state
- zip
- social security number
- date hired
- salary
- etc.

By the way, a great source of ideas on fields for typical entities is the table-building wizard in Microsoft Access. Even if you are using SQL Server or some other industrial-strength database instead of Access, taking a look at the wizard may cause you to develop a better list of fields.

Determining Relationships among Tables

The entities that give rise to tables usually have relationships defined by the requirements. Each order, for example, is for one and only one customer. A customer may have no orders on record, or may have one or many.

To document these relationships, I recommend "drawing" (on paper or on screen) a diagram of the entities and their relationships. The database design tools (discussed previously) are all good for this kind of operation.

At this point, it's only necessary to determine that the tables (entities) have relationships. We'll pin down exactly what fields are used to implement the relationship later.

TYPES OF RELATIONSHIPS

There are several types of relationships that entities can have. The most common ones are one-to-many and many-to-many.

ONE-TO-MANY RELATIONSHIPS

The customer-order relationship above is a good example of a one-to-many relationship. An order can only be related to one customer. A customer can be related to many orders.

MANY-TO-MANY RELATIONSHIPS

Many-to-many relationships are very common in modern systems. Here's an example from a university class registration system. There are two main entities in this system: students and classes. (We're talking about college classes here now. Put the object meaning of "classes" out of your mind for the moment.) Students can take many classes. An individual class can have many students in it. This is a classic example of a many-to-many relationship.

Relational databases do not support direct many-to-many relationships. An intermediate table is required to hold the individually related pairs. We will explore the student-class relationship as part of our detailed example at the end of this chapter.

ONE-TO-ONE RELATIONSHIPS

One-to-one relationships are less common, but are helpful in some circumstances. One-to-one relationships do not often arise from requirements. Often they arise a bit later in the process to get an effective and efficient database design.

Here's an example. Suppose our database needs to contain pictures of employees for our website. We know that we only have pictures for some employees, and we don't want to clutter up routine payroll processing by getting pictures involved. So we might implement an Employees table and an EmployeePictures table.

These tables would have a one-to-one relationship. Each Employee can have one and only one picture (though some employees might have no picture). If you need pictures in your recordset of employees, then the SQL to get those pictures would have a left join between the Employees and EmployeePictures table. This would get all of the employees, and would get pictures for any employees who had them. (If you are unfamiliar with SQL, you should become familiar with the basics before even attempting to design a relational database.)

Setting Table Indexes

After tables are defined from entities, and relationships are defined, it's time to set the indexes (or indices, if you like your Latin pure).

An index or key is a way to provide the right kind of access to the table. The physical order of the table is typically determined by the order the rows were placed in the table. An index allows a "logical" version of the table with the rows ordered by some field or combination of fields.

These logical tables provide surprisingly fast access to the data for processing. Accordingly, indexes are typically determined by the fields which are used for accessing the data (for looking up particular records). Names, phone numbers, and zip codes would be examples of such fields. Other fields, such as occupation, would not typically need to be used for indexing the data (unless the application did a lot of access of people with particular occupations).

PRIMARY KEY

Most tables need a primary key. You should be familiar with the concept that the primary key is a unique identifier of a record in a table. But it's a good idea to go a step further than that. I recommend that the primary key be, in a certain sense, meaningless.

Let me explain what that means. I've seen member management systems (for churches and the like) use the last name, with some arbitrary digits to enforce uniqueness, as the primary key. This had the advantage of being able to narrow down the members just by looking at the key.

But in modern relational systems, users don't need to look at the primary key. Your system should be able to fetch (using SQL) any data needed at various stages, with data elements and their relationships already resolved, and with only the data needed by the user displayed.

The problem with the example above is that last names can change (from marriage, divorce, and so forth). Changing the primary key in a relational system is difficult. In many of them, you can't change it directly — you can only delete the record and add it back with a new key. This requires lots of additional logic.

Better to make the primary key a meaningless number. Counter fields (in Access) and identity fields (in SQL Server) are available for this precise purpose. If the primary key contains no concrete, meaningful information about the actual entity, it will never need to be changed.

Even in tables where there is a potentially unique primary key, it is usually better to use made-up keys instead.

▶ Globally unique IDs

A globally unique ID, usually abbreviated GUID, is a 128-byte field which can be generated for you by the Windows operating system. It is, for all practical purposes, unique (hence the name). You have seen GUIDs used to register objects, because every component in Windows has a GUID to distinguish it from other components. Those long hexadecimal strings in the Windows Registry are often GUIDs.

GUIDs can also be good primary keys. Sometimes counter or identity fields cannot be used because records are being added in such a way that it is impossible to track a sequential key. For example, several remote laptops might need to add records to a table while being disconnected from the network.

SQL Server 7.0 offers a GUID field which is very useful for primary keys. It will automatically fetch the GUID and insert it into a new record.

OTHER INDEXES

Besides serving as the primary key, indexes are used in addition for two main purposes:

1. Indexing a foreign key to enforce a relationship
2. Indexing a field commonly used for sorting or access (to speed performance)

A foreign key is the field that points to a primary key in a related table. In our customer-order relationship, the order table would need a foreign key which was a customer number. That foreign key should be indexed. In a one-to-many relationship, the entity on the "many" side needs the foreign key and the entity on the "one" side needs the primary key.

Foreign keys are determined from the design work on relationships done in the previous step. Additional indexes are typically determined by looking at user interface lookup needs, and by looking at reporting requirements. If the users need to look up a record with a certain field, that field probably needs to be indexed. Similarly, if reports need to be ordered by a certain field, the field should be indexed unless the report is small and run very infrequently.

Normalizing the Data

Relational databases work best when they are organized properly, both from a performance point-of-view, and for ease of use within the programming environment.

The main principles of normalization are:

- No repeating information
- All data in a table should be related to the unique entity in a particular record
- No derived or dependent data in a table

NO REPEATING INFORMATION

Suppose our employees have up to three emergency numbers. You might be tempted to make a repeating field for those numbers. That is, you could construct EmergencyNumber1, EmergencyNumber2, and EmergencyNumber3.

I made this mistake several times early in my work with relational databases. I discovered that it presents several problems. The obvious one is that the requirements may change to support more emergency numbers. But less obvious is the impact on the code that accesses the data. My reports, for example, needed all kinds of custom logic to handle situations where EmergencyNumber1 was blank, but EmergencyNumber2 was filled in. And adding any new emergency number fields required changing not just the database, but also the code accessing it.

Instead, implement an EmergencyNumber table, and give it a many-to-one relationship with Employees. Then you can support an arbitrary number of emergency phone numbers, and the code will not need to change.

(Proper support of such relationships has other implications. You should make your interface support an arbitrary number of emergency numbers also, if at all possible. Otherwise, when the number of supported numbers changes, you still have to modify the program just to fix the interface.)

A variation on this mistake is to put several items of data in one field. I've seen designs where three or more phone numbers were stored in one field, with delimiters used to separate them. This has many of the same disadvantages for retrieving the data, and adds a new complexity. The code for breaking out the individual items has to be placed in every program that accesses the data.

The solution is the same as the one above — a separate table which can hold an arbitrary number of items.

ALL DATA IN A TABLE SHOULD BE RELATED TO THE UNIQUE ENTITY IN A PARTICULAR RECORD

Older database designs sometimes used various kludges to improve performance. A common one was to place records in a single table (actually, a single file in hierarchical systems) that were related to different entities.

For example, a record might represent a contractor or an employee, with some flag field indicating which one this particular record contained. The meaning of various fields might change, depending on whether a particular record was for a contractor or employee.

This is very poor design in a relational system. A table should represent a unique entity, and all the data fields in the table should relate directly to that entity.

NO DERIVED OR DEPENDENT DATA IN A TABLE

Suppose we often needed to know the total of all orders for a particular customer, or the date of the last order. We could keep fields in the customer table called "TotalOrders" and "LastOrderDate" and update them as necessary. Then a query against the customer table would contain this information.

In older systems, this was sometimes done for performance reasons, and in very isolated instances it might be used even today. But such design is contrary to good relational principles. Better to derive the value for the orders total when it is needed. Today's relational database engines can handles such tasks surprisingly quickly.

Also avoid dependent data. For example, our orders table could contain both the customer number and the customer name, which would simplify lookup. But the customer name is dependent on the customer number, and can be found if the number is known. So the customer name has no place in the orders table in a good relational design.

Another reason to leave off dependent data is because it minimizes the impact of changes to the data. The customer might change their company name, for example. If the customer name is in each order record, it has to be changed in all of them. If the customer name is only in the master customer record, it only needs to be changed there. The unique customer number would not need to change (if it is meaningless as we discussed above), so order records which only contained a customer number would not change when the customer name changed.

There is one situation in which a denormalized design (which violates the principle of "no derived or dependent data") might be appropriate. If the database is simply for lookup, and performance is a very high priority, then it might make sense.

Here's an example. A high-volume website might need to access data that was fairly static. The definitive version of the data might be stored externally to the web server in a true relational design. A denormalized copy (for speed of access) could be kept on the web server. This denormalized copy would typically be reconstructed on a very infrequent basis by exporting the entire definitive database.

Determining Validation Requirements for Data Fields

Your requirements will often contain sentences such as "A shipping carton can contain a maximum of twelve books." There are also implicit and often unstated requirements. For example, we would presume that a price cannot be negative, even if that was not explicitly stated.

Modern relational databases can enforce these conditions. If a program attempts to insert data violating the conditions, the database engine returns an error.

Go through the database design and the definition looking for any desirable validation on data fields. Sometimes validation for a field is dependent just on that field. Sometimes validation is dependent on security considerations. And sometimes validation is dependent on other fields. An employee's termination date, for example, should be later than the start date.

Building Queries or Stored Procedures

As the database is being designed, watch for operations which will be carried out regularly. Particular queries or actions may be needed which will be called from various programs and should act the same way in each program. The logic for such actions should be stored in the database.

Microsoft Access has limited capability for this kind of work. Only stored lookup queries and limited action queries are available. However, SQL Server and other server-based systems have extensive capability to place this functionality in the database. If you are working with SQL Server, become familiar with stored procedures and Transact SQL, and set up databases with these capabilities. This can dramatically simplify the actual program development.

Referential Integrity

Modern relational database systems allow you to specify that certain relationships must be in place before data can be inserted into the system. For example, if you are creating an order for a customer, the database system can require that the customer already be on file. It can also require that any products referenced in the order be on file.

Such a capability is called referential integrity. Enforcing these rules ensures that the data is consistent.

Most database engines give an option to enforce referential integrity, and the enforcement is the default in most systems except for Microsoft Access. It is a good idea to turn referential integrity on in almost all database designs.

An Example of Database Design

Suppose we have the following requirements for a system:

1. We need to track the courses taken by a group of students.
2. For students, we need to keep up with their name, address, phone number, and other demographic information.
3. Each course has a name, and a number of credit hours.
4. Each course may be held multiple times. A student may take a given course more than once. A particular instance of a course is called a session of the course.
5. A session has a start date and an end date.
6. We also need to track the trainers for the courses. Each session is taught by exactly one trainer, but a trainer can teach multiple sessions and courses.
7. For trainers, we need to know their name, address, and other demographic information.
8. For each session of a course taken by a student, we need to know if the student completed the course material.

Determine the Tables

To perform a design for a database layout, first we would need to determine the tables that are needed. In this case, we come up with the following list:

- Students
- Courses
- Sessions
- Trainers

Determine the Fields

Next, we would decide what fields need to be stored. For the Students table, we would have fields like:

- LastName
- FirstName
- Address
- Phone, etc.

For the Courses table, the requirements state that we need the name of the course and the number of hours. For Sessions, we need a start date, an end date, and the trainer for the session. For Trainers, we need Lastname, FirstName, etc. (much like the Students table).

Determine the Relationships

Next we need to look at the relationships. Each course can have several sessions, so there is a one-to-many relationship between courses and sessions. Likewise, each trainer can teach several sessions, so there is a one-to-many relationship between trainers and sessions

The complex relationship is the one between students and sessions. A given student can take many sessions, and a given session can have many students in it.

Note that we don't have a direct relationship between students and courses. A student takes a course by taking an individual session of that course. We can still use SQL to find out the courses taken by a student, even with no direct relationship.

The relationship between students and sessions is an example of the many-to-many relationships that we discussed earlier. To implement this relationship, we need an intermediate table. (This table is referred to in several different ways in different books about data design. I've seen it called a "relationship table," a "cross-reference table," or a "junction table.") Each record in this table holds a student-session pair. Such a record indicates that a particular student took a particular session.

Let's call this table "Sessions Taken." There is a one-to-many relationship between the records in the Students table and the "Sessions Taken" table. Likewise, there is a one-to-many relationship between the Sessions table and the "Sessions Taken" table. Put together, the result is a many-to-many relationship.

Each record in the "Sessions Taken" table will therefore need a StudentID field and a SessionID field. Also, because of requirement 8 above, the record needs a field to indicate if the student completed the session.

At this point, a picture of our database design might look something like the one shown in Figure 20–1. This screen was done with Microsoft Access, but screens in any data design tool would be similar.

Determine the Indexes

Most of the fields used in the relationships above are primary keys for some table. Following our practice of making primary keys meaningless, they all should be assigned a counter, identity, GUID, or some other field which ensures uniqueness, but has nothing to do with the actual data.

(In the real world example from which this was taken, the Courses field actually used a primary key that was an alpha code for the course — basically a course name abbreviation. The list of courses was relatively short, and use of this code was already standard for the users. In this case, the advantages of meaningless keys were not sufficient to replace the existing codes. Keep this kind of situation in mind, and don't be dogmatic about using meaningless keys.)

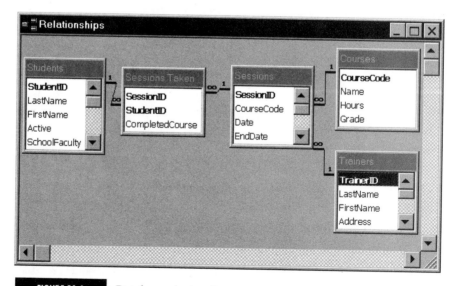

FIGURE 20-1 Database design for a many-to-many relationship.

Other indexes would depend on access and reporting needs. Typically, indexing by the name fields would be appropriate. It's a good bet that the sessions will need to be accessed by date, so placing an index on date in the Sessions table would be a good idea.

If you are using SQL Server 7, you can actually let the system determine the best supplementary indexes. There is a wizard which will do a lot of the work for you. This can be of great benefit on a complex system. Check the SQL Server 7.0 documentation for information on how to do that.

Normalizing the Data

The data design above is in pretty good shape with regard to normalization. With practice, you will usually design in appropriate normal forms when you create your tables and fields. However, it's a good idea to check your normalization just to make sure you haven't missed anything.

Validation and Stored Procedures

The final steps would be validation on the fields, and any necessary stored procedures.

Validations for the above data might include:

- Properly formatted and complete phone numbers
- Non-negative numbers for credit hours for a course
- End date for a session after the start date

Stored procedures might be needed for such functions as:

- Registering a student for a session
- Updating all the students in a session when the session is completed

Using ADO for Database Access

With Visual Studio 6, the ActiveX Data Objects (ADO) model was enhanced to version 2.0, and it has lately been enhanced to 2.1. You should consider using ADO in all of your data-related projects from this point forward.

Microsoft recommends specifically that you do *not* use Remote Data Objects (RDO) for new projects. The original Data Access Objects (DAO) model is okay for projects which will only use the Microsoft Access Jet engine. However, with a slimmed-down version of SQL Server 7.0 for the desktop on the way, the Jet engine will diminish in importance. So if you are only acquainted with Jet, it would be a good idea to start switching to ADO. The switch is not too difficult — the object models are very similar.

Suggestions for Further Reading

Using Visual Basic 5 by Loren D. Eidahl contains a good section on data design and database programming in general. It is Section VI of the book.

A more comprehensive treatment is *Database Design for Mere Mortals: A Hands-On Guide to Relational Database Design* by Micheal J. Hernandez. Even though it covers a lot of ground, it is down to earth and relatively easy to read.

User Interface Design and Usability Testing

No part of the design has as much potential for generating controversy as the user interface. Users who would never think of arguing with you about system design get very emotional about design of the user interface.

There's a powerful myth that causes a lot of these problems. Users believe that just because they use Windows ™ software, they therefore know how to design a graphical user interface. This is as silly as a typical television viewer believing they can produce a hit television show.

Of course, with a video camera, a typical television viewer could produce a show. It just would probably not be something other people wanted to watch. There is a creative aspect and a craftsmanship aspect to such efforts.

It's the same with user interfaces. To be an effective user interface designer, you must first master the craft. That means your are responsible for such areas as:

- Knowing Windows UI standards
- Knowing what controls are used for what purposes
- Working on different kinds of user interface platforms, such as VB forms and browsers
- Understanding the needs of different classes of users, from novice to advanced
- Understanding how help systems and other user assistance mechanisms tie into user interfaces
- Observing many different kinds of Windows software to know what's acceptable and unacceptable

However, as with any activity involving a creative component, just being a good craftsman will not necessarily produce superior results. Some developers hate user interface design, and in some cases it is because they just don't have the visual sense of what makes up a great user interface.

If you are in that category, then at least learn the basics so you don't produce garbage when you do a user interface. But I would hope that most Visual Basic developers aspire to do better than that. You should want to produce an excellent user interface because it adds to the value of the system you are developing.

There's another, more selfish reason to become good at UI design. The better your user interface is, the better your users will accomplish their tasks and the less they will have to bother you. Your efforts to put great functionality into your product goes for naught if the user can't find and use that functionality.

Make no mistake — user interface design is tough. Witness how often it is done poorly. Even commercial software is not immune — much of it was obviously designed by someone with no clue of how a real user thinks.

Examples of Poor Interfaces

Alan Cooper, sometimes called the father of Visual Basic, has a good book on interface design called *About Face*. In it, he criticizes software vendors who get a piece of information from the user and then throw it away when the operation is over. For example, most fax programs ask you for the phone number to use for faxing. Then, when the fax is done, that number is simply thrown away. The user must explicitly remember to save the number to a phone number directory to keep it from being lost.

This is silly. Computers are a lot better at remembering things than people. If you give them a piece of information, they generally should not throw it away without checking to see if you don't want it any more.

About Face is better at pointing out things that developers do wrong than presenting the solutions to these problems. But it will force you to do some thinking about the people who have to use your designs.

Another wonderful book to help you think about designing things for real people is *The Design of Everyday Things* by Donald A. Norman. This book covers general design principles in the everyday world, not just in the computer industry.

There are several common mistakes this book dissects in detail. One is not to sacrifice usability to make something pretty. We see this in Windows™ products in the form of rows of identical buttons on the screen. In the real world, an aircraft manufacturer had rows of identical switches, with the landing lights and the landing gear switches right next to each other.

After several crashes where the pilots turned on landing lights instead of lowering landing gear, the design was changed.

We don't usually find out so dramatically when our designs are bad, but the point is that the purpose of each item on a user interface should be clearly distinguishable.

General Principles for Good User Interface Design

Most experienced developers are aware of the basics of good UI design, but here's a quick summary.

Keep It Clean

The cleaner, the better. Cluttered screens are the bane of good interface design. Here are some more detailed suggestions for reducing clutter.

USE CONTEXT SWITCHERS

If there are too many elements to present cleanly on a single screen, use a context-switching design. The most commonly used design is a tabbed interface, but other alternatives include a selection bar like the ones in Quicken and Microsoft Outlook.

Context switchers are definitely needed in many circumstances. But they can be misused. Tabbed interfaces are especially susceptible. There is a more detailed section below on some of the problems with tabbed interfaces.

FEW LAYERS AT THE TOP

Avoid too many layers at the top of your screens. Even Microsoft products often get this one wrong. Stacking menus, toolbars, rulers, and folder tabs can deeply daze a user with too many options. Visible elements such as these should carefully focus on the most common tasks. Leave less common tasks to menu options only, or allow the user to add them to toolbars if they desire. But keep the default, installed state of the screen simple and clean.

BE CAUTIOUS WITH FRAMES

Stay away from having too many frames. You may need one or two per screen to group some screen elements. But if you have more than two, start asking if you really need them.

Use white space instead of frames to break things up. This may require moving some screen elements to another screen, or in some cases coming up with a completely different design. But do anything you can to stay away from crowded, incomprehensible screens.

Don't forget that a frame can be invisible. If one is needed, for example, to group option buttons, but is not needed visually, then set the border to none.

Make the Interface Responsive

It's a cardinal sin in user interface design to allow a user to press a button and then put up an error message saying "That option not available" or some such. It's your responsibility as the developer to disable screen elements which should not be available at a given time. If you have such an element (which shouldn't be enabled in the first place) display an error message when pressed, it is unnecessary, annoying, and insulting to the user.

The way I take care of this is to have a general routine for each form which checks to see what elements are permitted right now. I often call it "ControlAvailabilityCheck." It then enables or disables controls as necessary. I call that routine in just about every click event in the form.

This routine centralizes the logic needed to check on controls. Some developers place the enable/disable logic all over the form, in various events, but this is error-prone, hard to debug, and hard to maintain.

User Color Sparingly

Use color sparingly. Appropriate use of color can dramatically improve an interface, but it's easy to overdo.

Avoid bright colors for backgrounds. Use Windows system colors for all routine functions.

There are situations where color can be used effectively, such as red flags to indicate items that need attention. Just don't go wild and use color all over the place. A small amount of color captures the user's attention. Too much color, and it loses its impact.

And make sure that the user's ability to use the interface properly doesn't depend on the ability to perceive colors as you perceive them.

For web-based applications, you can be somewhat more generous with color. But there are plenty of ugly websites that demonstrate the use of too much color.

Tailor the Interface to the User

Users come in a broad spectrum, from totally inexperienced to technically proficient. Part of the definition process covered earlier in this book was to find out what kinds of users you must support. Then design an interface appropriate to those users.

If you are top-heavy on clerical folks and data entry operators, make sure keyboard shortcuts and minimizing keystrokes is high on your priority list. If your users will only see the product once a month, the interface should "take them by the hand" and lead them through typical operations.

Support the broadest range of potential users that is practical. This may take the form of having both "standard" and "expert" menus. In extreme cases, you may need two completely separate user interfaces — one for advanced users and one for more casual users. In this case, the interface for casual users is often wizard-based.

Use Tool Tips

I'm always surprised at the number of developers who leave tool tips out of finished products. Perhaps they had an excuse with earlier versions of Visual Basic, when support for tool tips was not automatic. That excuse is no longer available. Most controls have a ToolTipText property which makes it very easy to add tool tips to most screen elements.

Tool tips provide you with the capability to give a more precise explanation of the purpose of a control than will often fit on the screen. If the screen element is an icon, such as those in a toolbar, a tool tip should be considered essential, since the icon has no verbal label. For other controls, captions are usually short to conserve screen space, so the tool tip text should be a little longer and more helpful. Don't just repeat captions in the tool tip. That's insulting.

Don't Stack Up Dialog Boxes

Keep down the number of "layers" in your user interfaces. Don't have dialog boxes calling more dialog boxes, etc. This becomes confusing for the user to navigate. The general principle is that you want to be modeless whenever possible. Modal dialog boxes definitely have their place, but use them sparingly.

Rather than having a dialog box call another dialog box, a trick Microsoft uses a lot is to make the dialog box expand with an "Advanced" button. Then you can hide less frequently used options without having to layer on another dialog if those options are needed. This is incredibly easy to do in Visual Basic. Just design the screen in the advanced form, with the advanced controls at the bottom. Then make the default size of the form short enough so that the advanced controls do not show. The "Advanced" button can then just change the height of the form.

Use Right-Click Menus

Right-click pop-up menus are supposed to be for common, context-sensitive actions. Commercial software vendors do a pretty good job of using them. Advanced users will really appreciate this ease of access to common functions.

It is surprisingly easy to create a right-click menu in Visual Basic. In the help files, check the PopUpMenu method of forms for syntax and an example of how to do it.

Don't depend on such a feature as the only way to accomplish something essential because inexperienced users may never find the pop-up menu. And keep pop-up menus down to six or eight choices for maximum usability.

Copy Good Ideas

Companies like Microsoft spend literally million of dollars doing design of interfaces and testing usability. You might as well benefit from their work. Use the best commercial software as templates and as sources of ideas.

For web applications, you have the whole world to choose from. Try to find sites that accomplish similar tasks to your site. Save those HTML pages and use them as sources for cutting and pasting to work on prototypes.

You also have an option with web pages to look "under the hood." If you see a clever technique in a web page, you can view the HTML source to see the syntax that accomplishes that technique. Wholesale copying of such source code would be piracy, of course, but you don't need to copy outright. Just use the example as a guide to point you in the right direction.

Development of a Good Interface

Developing a good user interface is not like other development tasks. It is much more iterative, and more work gets thrown away.

If you are working on a code module, you can usually determine all by yourself if a particular design is effective. If it accomplishes its intended purpose, and nobody sees the design except you, then no problems arise.

But everybody sees the user interface, and judgements on its quality are quite subjective. You have to please a lot more people. That changes the approach you should use.

Prototypes

If you are writing a utility with a list box and a few option buttons, then you won't need a prototype. But any complex interface will be designed better if prototypes are done before developing the finished product.

What Exactly is a Prototype?

Many Visual Basic developers believe a prototype is no more than an early version of their program. That is a huge misunderstanding.

A user interface prototype should restrict itself to simulating the operation of the user interface. There should be no significant code underneath which accomplishes real "production" work. For example, I often don't load list boxes from a database in a prototype, even though I know the final product will need to do that. I just use the List property in the property box to pop in a few items, or write a few lines of code to add bogus items to the list box on the fly.

If you are investing so much effort in a prototype that you are reluctant to throw it away, you are putting too much into it. We will talk more about that later. One way to avoid that is to make your early prototypes out of paper.

Using Paper for Early Prototypes

It sounds silly to many Visual Basic developers to use paper to prototype a user interface. Isn't that what Visual Basic does best?

Yes it is. But user interface design is as much about psychology as it is about technology.

When users see something on paper, they clearly understand that it is not finished. Not just intellectually, but emotionally, they know that they can change it or criticize it as much as they want.

User interfaces shown on the screen do not carry the same psychological associations. The design on the screen looks to them like a finished product. Emotionally, many users also regard a design on the screen as representing a lot of work. This makes them reluctant to criticize such designs as openly.

With a paper prototype, a user might say "This just doesn't work. Let's throw it out and try a new concept." The emotional feeling is that throwing away paper is no big deal. With a design on the screen, the same user might be more likely to say, "This needs improving. Can we switch this part around with this part?" They know that moving things around is not much work, but the idea of throwing out an idea and starting from scratch does not come as easily when looking at a screen.

This is true even though paper prototypes may take as long or longer to construct as screen designs. In fact, a common way to do paper prototypes is to use VB to create the screens and then just print them out.

TIPS FOR PAPER PROTOTYPES

For paper prototypes, you create separate pieces of paper representing different screen elements. These might be separate screens, or just a piece of a screen, such as a popped-down combo box. These separate elements can then be "juggled" into different design arrangements. You can present possible designs to the user by showing different paper designs and how they accomplish tasks.

While going through a session with the user, you "pretend" to be the computer. When they make a selection, you show them how the screen would change because of their action. That may mean switching to a different piece of paper representing a different screen, or just placing another piece of paper on top of the one already in front of them. 3M Post-It-Notes™ work well, too. You can use them to simulate various controls in paper prototyping, such as list boxes and drop-downs.

Keep highlighter pens and different colors of pens handy to mark up the paper prototypes. It's also a good idea to have more than one copy of your screen elements so you can mark separate copies up in separate ways.

I find that paper prototyping works best with just one user at a time, or at most two. It gets clumsy if several users are involved simultaneously.

For smaller projects, paper prototyping may not be worth the effort. But I suggest you try it and see if it works for you.

The Need for Multiple Prototypes

When prototyping (on paper or on the screen), try every way of accomplishing a function that you can think of. Ask everyone who could possibly tell you a different way. This will give you the raw material to create a good final design.

Do not blindly accept the first way you think of, even if it looks pretty good.

Once you have developed one way of accomplishing a given function, put it aside and start fresh with the question, "Is there another way to accomplish the same result?" Keep doing this until you can't think of any other ways. If you can only think of one way, you've placed your mind in a straightjacket, so go to someone else and get them to do it.

I often go through four or five iterations of design for really complex user interfaces. Lots of good ideas get thrown away.

After you have several approaches, create prototypes for each. Start showing these prototypes around. Get reaction from various actors. Is many cases, the ultimate answer combines features from the different prototypes.

It's very important for good user interface design that you don't stop when you've found one way of accomplishing the program's purposes. A far better way may be out there if you look for it.

Iterate the Prototype

Most developers understand the importance of iterating their prototypes. The interface must be validated with users, and then their changes must be incorporated into the design.

Ask advice constantly during this prototyping stage. Ask just about anyone who might have some information to contribute — other developers, users, your spouse, your dog... well, maybe not your dog, but do ask for lots of feedback, especially when you are early in the process.

Those giving feedback should understand that all their recommendations will not necessarily be adopted. I recommend that you mention that before getting anyone's advice.

Throw Away Your Prototype!

Most Visual Basic developers would never throw away a prototype. They prefer to convert it to the finished product. But there are many good reasons to throw away prototypes. You should start every prototype with the understanding that it will be thrown away when you've found the final user interface design that works well.

If you know you are going to throw the prototype away, you'll be more free to explore options and fudge things that you don't have the time to do right. You can hack the code all you want to save time, knowing that the hacked code will never get into the production system. You can do things you would never do in production code, such as using public variables for properties, and leaving the controls with the default Visual Basic names.

A prototype which is then developed into the final product is of inferior quality anyway; any prototype has detritus that builds up during prototype refinement. As things get changed, some of the code associated with abandoned screen elements gets left in the system because you don't want to take the time to sort out what you need and what you don't. It is like cholesterol in your bloodstream — it clogs up the system. Get rid of it by throwing away the prototype and starting fresh as soon as you know what the basic UI design will be.

If while creating the prototype you had to develop a particularly fussy function or object, and the code in it is of production quality, then you can copy just that piece over to the new system. But don't do wholesale copying. Start fresh.

Almost any program can be better written the second time. Usually, better designs and methods suggest themselves the second time. The result is cleaner, more bug free, and more maintainable — and it even saves development time in the end.

An Example from a Real Project

A few years back, I had to design a user interface for a report generator. The part of the program that allowed the user to specify the columns on the report proved to be a design challenge.

Earlier programs in the product line had an interface for choosing columns that looked like Figure 21–1.

That screen was designed with a philosophy used by too many Visual Basic developers — keep putting controls on the screen until you think you have handled everything that the user needs to tell you. It also had other difficulties. The option buttons actually varied dynamically depending on which choice was highlighted in the right list box above. You can probably find additional weaknesses.

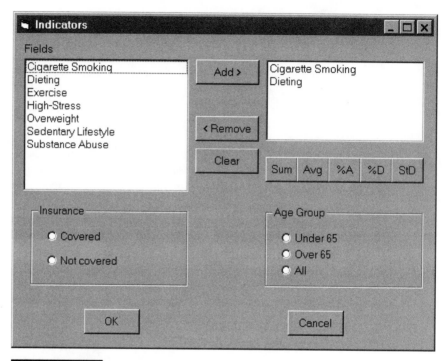

FIGURE 21–1   Existing column selection screen.

Perhaps the biggest flaw in this screen was that it was for choosing report columns, yet there was nothing about the screen that suggested a column metaphor. When first looking at this screen, the user had no clue what the screen is supposed to do.

To extend this interface for the new product would require dumping even more controls onto a confusing screen. So I began prototyping, trying to find an interface that would make specifying the columns easy.

My first attempt was cute, but pretty laughable. It looked like Figure 21–2.

The theory was that the users would slide the rows of "blocks" back and forth to get the combination they wanted (by lining up the blocks in the shaded area), and then add a column. They could select a column for manipulation in the lower box.

Reviewers liked the "preview box" at the bottom, but the rest of this design was rightly rejected. Even though it could have been made to work, it was just not understandable to the average user.

Next was a variation on the above design that looked like Figure 21–3.

This was straightforward, and again would have done the job. But it still did not make much sense to users.

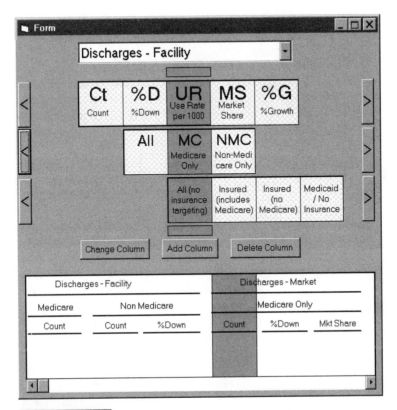

FIGURE 21–2   An attempt at a new column selection screen.

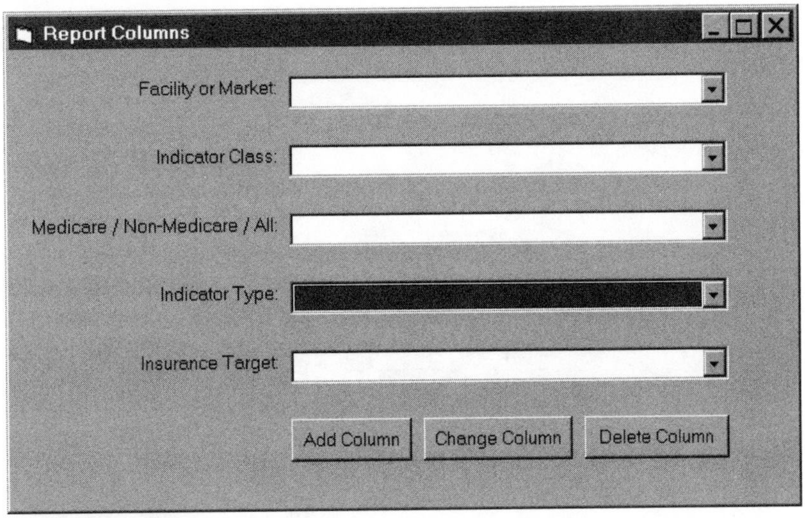

FIGURE 21–3   Another attempt at a new column selection screen.

Back to the drawing board. This time, the "preview box" idea from earlier was taken, and expanded upon. That yielded a design for column selection which looked roughly like Figure 21–4.

Finally, we had something that the users understood. This idea evolved into the final design, after incorporating some additional functionality.

Notice how wildly different these designs are. That is what you should strive for. The more radically different concepts you try, the more likely one will be close to ideal.

The Role of Users

We've previously discussed the role of users in the creation of a user interface design. They have two very important roles:

Validation — Ensuring that the design is complete and appropriate to the purpose

Usability — Discovering if the design is easy enough to learn and use

Validation

The validation phase is accomplished by showing interfaces to users and then doing direct questioning about the utility and completeness of the interface. This can be done early in the process with prototype interfaces that are virtually nonfunctional, or even on paper.

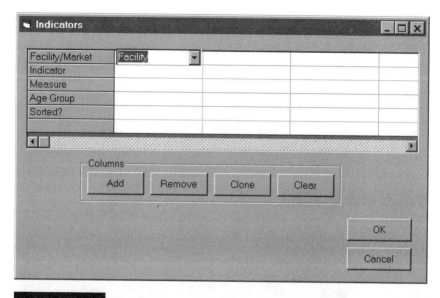

FIGURE 21–4   The first step towards a workable design for column selection.

The primary purpose here is to check that the interface will indeed accomplish what it needs to accomplish. While it's always important to ask about ease-of-use issues, that should only happen after ascertaining that the interface can do what it is supposed to. If the interface doesn't serve its purpose, then its ease-of-use is academic.

Basic Usability

This phase of UI design is almost never done properly except in large software development companies. But it's not that tough — it's just that few developers understand why it needs to be done and how to go about it.

There are labs that test usability. They have sophisticated setups with video cameras and one-way mirrors. There is no doubt that they can help you with a comprehensive test of usability if you have the bucks and the time to use their services.

But you don't have to have a fancy usability lab to test usability of your UI design. You just need the ability to keep your mouth shut.

After you've constructed a prototype which you feel is complete (has all the functions it needs) and looks like a pretty good design to you, you are ready to do usability testing. Choose a person who very much represents a typical user. It's best if they have not seen any of the prototypes up to this point. Ask for an hour or so of their time. Then go through three basic phases with them:

- Initial exposure to the interface (to elicit initial, even visceral, responses to the UI)
- Investigative questioning (often with task-based questions)
- Explanation and discussion (for final user comments and recommendations)

Initial Exposure to the Interface

First, put them in front of your prototype and tell them to try to use it. That's all. Don't give them any detailed instruction. If they are unfamiliar with this category of application, then you can give a short, general description of the purpose of the program, and perhaps lay out a few general goals for them to accomplish. But if they are familiar with this type of software, you may not want to give them any suggestions at all about what the interface is supposed to do. Just sit back and watch and take notes.

The user will fumble around and try things. Some parts of the interface will immediately do what they expect (those are the good parts). Some parts will become evident to them after a while (those are the OK parts). And some parts will either require explanation or never make any sense (those are the bad parts).

During this phase, resist offering explanation even if asked for it. As soon as you start explaining how things are supposed to work, you are contaminating their reactions to the interface. Just make sure you're either recording their responses or taking very accurate notes. You'll refer to them later in the development process.

This is harder than it sounds. You will have a natural tendency to explain (and defend) why you made the interface the way you did. If possible, you may want a colleague who did not work directly on the interface to facilitate the session. That allows you to take the role of a completely silent observer.

During this phase, if you wonder why a user did something, write the question down for later. But don't ask it now.

Use of a video camera during this phase is optional. It is helpful in two ways:

- Reviewing what the user did (supplementing your memory)
- Convincing skeptical people who did not see the session that the interface needs adjustment

Investigative Questioning

After the user is finished, then you can start asking questions. Do this *before* explaining how the interface is supposed to work. Get as much information from the user as possible before explaining anything.

You may have written down questions during the first phase which you can ask now. What you are trying to do at this point is find out *why* a particular part of the interface was confusing or vague to the user. Start with the parts of the interface they had the greatest difficulty with.

In many cases, the user will not be able to give a coherent answer as to why they had trouble. Don't press them too hard — you'll make them feel dumb.

If the user did not try some significant tasks, you can pose those tasks and let them do some work with the interface. If you need to do this, make it the first thing you do during this phase.

The information gathered during this phase is helpful, but not as important as the information gathered during the previous phase. In the first phase, you found out where the problem areas are. That's the most critical information — you can often figure out on your own why it didn't work well, with hindsight.

Explanation and Discussion

This phase is as much for the user as it is for you. They deserve a complete explanation of how things were supposed to work. You were not supposed to do that up until this point.

But you can sometimes be surprised by what you find out during this phase. Sometimes an explanation of what you were trying to do will elicit a suggestion from the user on how to do it better.

A One-On-One Experience

Keep the number of observers of these usability sessions down to a minimum, with one-on-one being ideal (if you have the discipline to keep quiet). The more people that are involved, the greater the possibility of contamination by outside influences. Unlike most other design activities, don't bring in the whole development team. And take special care to keep the sponsors away. They are more likely than anyone else to contaminate the testing.

Tabbed Interfaces — Pros and Cons

Tabbed interfaces seemed to mushroom throughout the industry a few years ago. You see them everywhere. If you use Microsoft products, you are practically inundated with them.

I consider tabbed interfaces overused. They are a quick and dirty solution to the problem of overcrowding, so they often get used by default. In many cases, a rethinking of the entire design to significantly reduce the number of controls will work better.

No doubt about it, tabbed interfaces can make things simple for the developer. But interfaces are not for the developer — they are for the user. And usability testing gives mixed results for tabbed dialogs. Some of the problems with tabbed interfaces, from a users perspective, include:

Inadequate Classification

Have you ever gone to a tabbed dialog with a dozen tabs, and then searched in vain for the tab that contained a particular option you wanted? Headings for tabs are necessarily short. They are often too short to give an accurate idea of what's on the tab.

Using tabs for a quick and dirty solution to cluttered screens often leads to tabs with poorly classified options and inadequate descriptions. If you must use tabs, at least use logical grouping and descriptive tab headings.

Confusion On Levels of Operation

Suppose a set of tabs has a button that says Apply. Does the button work on all tabs simultaneously? Or just the one that's visible? The user should not have to think about such distinctions.

Hidden Changes —
"Out of Sight, Out of Mind"

Once changes are made to a tab and another tab is made active, the user no longer sees those changes. The interface sort of expects the user to remember everything that has happened on all the tabs. Again, the memory job is supposed to be with the computer, not the user. They have a thousand distractions, and it's easy for them to forget what they did.

If a user has made some changes on a tabbed dialog and switched to a different tab, those changes have usually not been applied. If they then get distracted for a few minutes and come back to the screen, they may naturally hit Cancel to get rid of the dialog box. But that means they just lost their changes, unless the developer takes great pains to warn them.

So when should tabbed interfaces be used? Functions that are used infrequently are good candidates. A less-than-optimal design doesn't cause as many problems for something users don't need very often.

I also use tabbed interfaces for complex data entry screens, especially if the fields for the record can be easily divided into fields used very commonly and fields used less commonly. But such screens must be carefully designed to minimize the problems outlined above.

The Move to Browser-Based Interfaces

There are many situations in which a browser-based interface may be preferable to a traditional Visual Basic forms interface. Systems with a browser interface require no special installation on the client, and browsers will automatically update any support files which are needed. And browsers are familiar to a broad range of users.

Doing such software means writing your system on a server using Active Server Pages, Visual Basic web classes, or other web-oriented software tools. If you are not already familiar with such tools, you should make it a priority to become experienced with them.

Once you have done a system or two using a browser-based interface, you will be in a better position to judge whether an interface should be done in traditional Visual Basic fashion, or with a browser as the front end. You will also learn a lot about design of interfaces for browsers. There are some significant new challenges. You don't have as many controls to choose from, for example. And you definitely should understand n-tier architectures to do a serious browser-based system.

When you make the move to browser-based interfaces, take some time to research the differences from classic Windows and Visual Basic interfaces. That should save you time and give you better results during the actual user interface design stage of a project.

Suggestions for Further Reading

We have already mentioned *About Face* by Alan Cooper and *The Design of Everyday Things* by Donald Norman. Here are some additional resources.

Visual Interface Design for Windows by Virginia Howlett provides a great introduction to user interfaces in the Microsoft world. Fundamentals are well covered, but the book is also reasonably comprehensive on user interface topics. While it's fun to read Alan Cooper's diatribes, this book is much more practical.

A good website to check out for user interface information of all types is *www.uie.com*. This is the website for User Interface Engineering, a consulting firm specializing in user interface issues.

TWENTY - TWO

Designing Objects

Up to this point, we have not discussed much about how objects are designed. The part which introduced and defined objects in Visual Basic specified in detail the design of the objects discussed. Naturally, in your own project, you will have no such guidelines, so one of your most significant tasks is to design the objects that will be needed in your application.

Before doing system-wide object design, you *must* have a decent understanding of what objects are good for. You can gain that understanding by designing isolated objects for particular purposes. Let's look at that process first.

Designing Individual Objects

Once you know that you need an object, and you understand its basic purpose, the starting point in designing the object is almost always to design the interface. That is, what properties and methods is the object supposed to have?

The importance of the interface is hard to overstate. An object can have all kinds of internal changes later, and the calling code can stay the same (we saw many examples of this in the section on objects). But if you have to tamper with the interface after other code modules are already using the object, then every single location where an object is called will have to be checked and changed as necessary.

Start on Paper

When you are getting started with design of individual objects, the initial design should be done on paper or in a word processor (not in the class builder or with other tools). You should not proceed to object design tools until you can do a fair job of designing an object manually.

A simple, effective way to start an object design is with a format that looks like the one shown in Figure 22–1.

Properties are generally easier to list first. However, you will think of methods as you work on properties, and it's fine to write them down as soon as you think of them. And while considering some methods, you will realize that there are properties that are needed to support the methods.

No matter how much you write down, there are likely to be changes as you produce the actual code. Don't make your design a straightjacket.

Remember that during development of the object, you are usually testing with a temporary "testbed" interface. So you can make some changes to the interface as necessary without incurring problems with production code elsewhere. But if you start making major changes as soon as you start writing code, you probably didn't spend enough time on design. Step back and try some more designing.

Get Help On Your Early Efforts

Your first object designs are sure to be somewhat lacking in true object-oriented thinking. That's okay — later designs will be much better on that score. To help through the first ones, though, it's best to have an experienced object developer critique your efforts. It's a lot easier to do that if you write your design down and have that critiqued first. Then have the final code critiqued as well.

Object Name:

Purpose of object:

Object Properties:

Property	Type	Validation	Purpose

Object Methods:

Method	Arguments	Purpose	

FIGURE 22-1   Object design worksheet.

Some General Principles

METHODS SHOULD HAVE FEW ARGUMENTS — UNLESS THEY ARE REMOTE

In general, object philosophy is to keep down the number of arguments that methods use. Most methods should have no arguments. A few may need one. Very few should need two or more. Remember that the purpose of properties is to make the setting of values obvious and explicit. If a method needs four inputs, it is generally better to create four properties containing the inputs than to have the method require four arguments.

However, there are performance implications for objects which are remote from the calling code. Every time Windows needs to resolve an object reference, there is overhead. So it is sometimes desirable to have a method contain several arguments to reduce the number of calls to a remote object.

PROPERTIES SHOULD HAVE COMPLETE VALIDATION

It's very easy to get in the bad habit of just allowing the class builder or other tool to create shell object code which implements your properties. But the class builder cannot know how to constrain the values of properties. While type-checking provides some level of validation, Property Let procedures should also have logic to test the incoming values in any appropriate way. Remember to specify validation on properties during design.

USING ROUTINES INSIDE AND OUTSIDE THE OBJECT

A class module may have other routines besides methods and properties. It may have private methods (private subroutines, really), and it may have its own functions. Don't think every subroutine has to be a public method. If nothing outside the object needs to use the subroutine, by all means make it private.

It's sometimes acceptable for objects to call routines in common libraries, but remember that every external module that an object needs to function reduces its independence. If an object has many outside dependencies, it becomes non-reusable for practical purposes.

A major omission in VB is the ability to store related objects together. Always note in module headers when there are relationships among objects.

Analyzing Requirements for Objects

Once you understand how to design and use individual objects, you are ready to start designing whole object-based systems.

As always, start with the definition documents. Then, as with data design, identify nouns which represent entities. Many of these will become objects in your system. Some of the objects will actually be wrappers for the database records for the same entity. That is, you may have a Customers table and a Customer object which wraps a customer record. The wrapper can handle internal storage and validation of the customer information during processing.

Here's a short example. Suppose we have some a functional specification with a section which looks like this:

> A patient may be scheduled to take a number of tests. Some tests must come before other certain other tests, and some tests may occur in any order. The system must keep up with the status of all tests for a particular patient, and these status states can be any of the following: (etc.)

From this we could anticipate that we will probably need a "patient" object, and a "test" object. We might want the patient object to contain a collection of test objects. Similarly, any noun in the specification might need to be an object in the system.

Don't neglect nouns which are computer constructs (as opposed to things in the real world). In our report generation example, the column object was critical to making the approach work. The column object was only vaguely related to a real-world object (namely a column on a printed report).

Other Object Candidates

Nouns in the specification are not the only candidates for objects. Sometimes transactions between other objects need to be objects in and of themselves. And some objects are subclasses of a generic object, which needs to be designed first.

SYSTEM OBJECTS

There may also be what I call "system objects" in your design. These are objects which are implemented just to make construction of the system easier. They may not readily match up with objects you can touch in the real world. But their ability to encapsulate functionality makes them very valuable.

The best example of such an object in this book was the data maintenance object. It was covered in detail in Chapter 17, "Object Workshop — Programming the Data Maintenance Object." It does not represent a "thing" in the real world. It is just an encapsulation of commonly used logic, implemented with an object structure.

I believe that these types of objects are neglected in many discussions of object design and implementation. They can be incredibly useful and speed development of software. But it's a significant challenge to figure out when to create one.

If you reach the point where you have implemented some of these "system" objects, you can be sure you have turned the corner and are a true object-oriented developer.

Relationships Among Objects

The most common relationship for objects to have is for one object to hold a collection of another object. This is conceptually similar to the one-to-many relationship discussed in Chapter 20, "Data Design."

Other relationships include the superclass-subclass relationship, and a collaboration relationship. For example, the data maintenance exercise had a form object which collaborated with a data maintenance object to get the job done. The data maintenance object encapsulated functionality needed by a typical form. This is similar to a one-to-one data entity relationship.

Documenting Object Designs

After listing the objects needed by your system, you need to pin down the interrelationships. If you have several interrelated objects, you will typically need to draw a diagram that shows their relationships. Object design tools can help with this, and are discussed later in the chapter. But there are many alternatives for doing this work.

The "Butcher Paper" Method

I was involved in one complex, team-based project where we tried an interesting approach to object design. The system contained about a dozen major objects, and over two dozen minor ones. We knew we would have to iterate many times to get a good design. We used a very low-tech solution — butcher paper.

For those youngsters who have never seen a real butcher shop, butcher paper is white paper about two feet wide that comes in continuous rolls. We covered the walls in the team office with this paper, and began designing objects on it. For each object, we would map out the interface and the relationships to other objects. Having all the object designs visible at once was a huge help during team discussions.

We used a format similar to the one presented earlier in this chapter, where each object had a name, a purpose, and a list of properties and methods. We drew relationships with connecting lines, with the type of relationship written on the line. If an object needed to be related to an object across the room, we would indicate the relationship with a "proxy" — a symbol representing the object across the room.

When a change needed to be made to an object, we would just scratch out obsolete information and add new information. When a particular object got difficult to read, we would take down the strip of butcher paper it was on, transcribe the object to another sheet, and place the new sheet back on the wall.

Our object design took close to a month. We debated object functions and interfaces until we had a design everyone on the team knew would work well. Only then did we write any code whatsoever to create the objects.

The key ingredient for this approach to work is a room where the paper can stay on the walls for an extended period of time. If you have such a room, the butcher-paper method can work very well.

CRC Cards

A similar technique to the butcher paper method is to use index cards instead. These are sometimes called CRC cards. CRC stands for Class, Responsibility, and Collaboration.

There are many variations on how the card is laid out. Some layouts ignore the object interface entirely (leaving that to a later stage in design). Others include it, and I prefer this approach.

The "original" layout for CRC cards (which left off the interface) looked like Figure 22–2. A typical CRC card that includes the interface might look like Figure 22–3. You'll want to use 4x6 cards because 3x5 is really too small.

In a team-based environment, CRC cards are usually produced by the team as a whole in interactive design discussions. The initial version of the card might not contain the properties and methods. These can be left to the individual team members who will be responsible for creating the objects. However, when the object interfaces are designed, the team needs to get together again to validate the design.

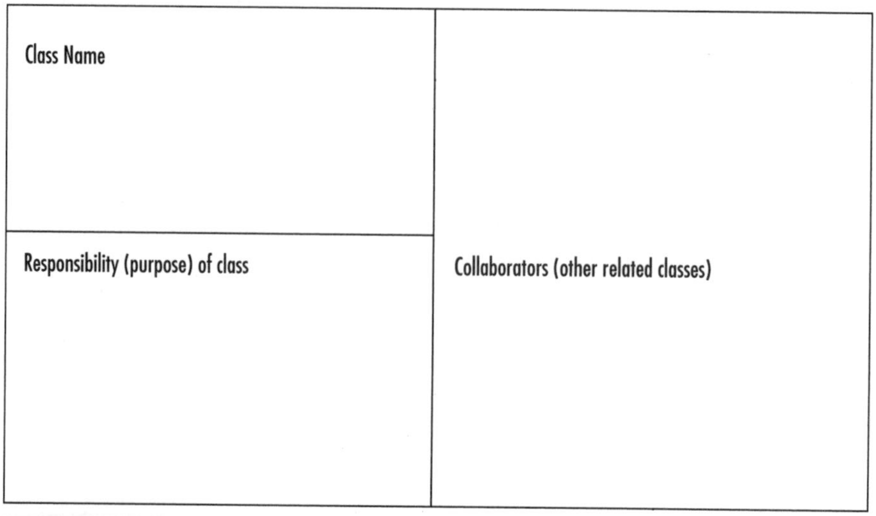

Class Name	
Responsibility (purpose) of class	Collaborators (other related classes)

FIGURE 22–2 Original design of CRC cards.

Class Name	Responsibility (purpose) of class
Properties / methods of class	Collaborators (other related classes)

FIGURE 22–3 Typical CRC card.

One of the main advantages of CRC cards is that object designs can be laid out on a table with related objects grouped together. As different groups and relationships are examined, the cards can be shuffled around to suit the current discussion.

CRC cards facilitate good discussions during design. They allow teams to quickly map out the parts of the design that are easy to pin down, and then start adding the parts that are more difficult.

One key point about CRC cards is that they help a team arrive at a good design through various paths. That is, design with CRC cards is not necessarily top-down, or bottom-up, or anything else. The team starts where they are most comfortable and iterate to a complete design.

CRC cards are also helpful during presentations of a potential design to other groups. They allow the design to be discussed a piece at a time. The basic parts are laid down and explained, and the additional parts of the design are easier to understand as they are presented because there is a conceptual context already in place.

GETTING TACTILE

You might think that with the availability of modern design tools (which we talk more about below), manual methods such as CRC cards are no longer useful. That's definitely not true. It overlooks the tactile nature of a card, which you can pick up and manipulate.

For example, when people are talking about the relationship between two objects, they can grab the relevant cards and use them (non-verbally) during the discussion to emphasize how they will work. And when it becomes obvious that a particular object that was initially thought to be needed is not needed, the card holding the object can be crumpled and thrown out. This kind of tactile interaction can be much better for team-based design than working with a computer screen where only one person is "driving").

UML Design Tools

A more standardized and formal way of representing object designs has been introduced recently called Universal Modeling Language, or UML. Though the manual methods above continue to be useful, UML provides a way to standardize notation used in computerized design tools.

A Short Introduction to UML

As object-based design has become more common, there has been an attempt to standardize the descriptions of object designs. These standardized descriptions are collectively called Unified Modeling Language, commonly abbreviated UML. The initial definition of UML was done by Grady Booch, Ivar Jacobsen, and James Rumbaugh, all pioneers in object-oriented technologies.

UML is not a method for doing object design. It is a language that is useful for several object design methods. But you will generally find that it is more useful if you are using classic object design techniques such as use cases.

Types of UML Diagrams

The most commonly used UML diagram is the one used to define a class. It bears a resemblance to other graphic techniques for class definition. It contains the class name at the top, followed by a listing of the properties and methods.

However, the notation used to show properties and methods is standardized. For example, a property is shown like this:

```
PropertyName:DataType = InitialValue
```

For example, in our settings object, we might have a MaxFiles property. This could be an integer with a default value of 500. In that case, we would represent it as:

```
MaxFiles:Integer = 500
```

Methods are shown like this:

```
MethodName(argument list):ReturnDataType
```

These are combined with the class name to get diagrams that look like Figure 22–4.

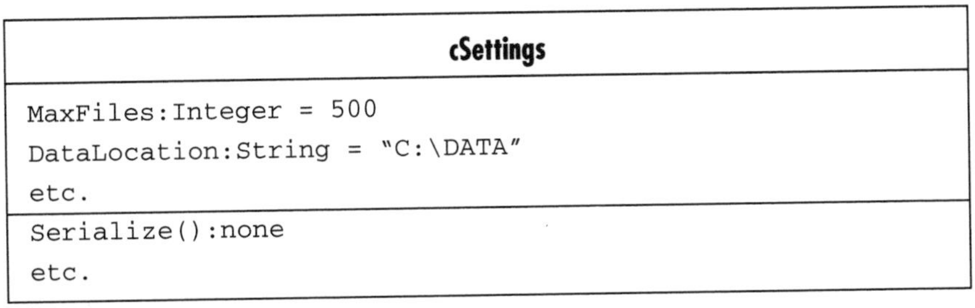

cSettings
MaxFiles:Integer = 500
DataLocation:String = "C:\DATA"
etc.
Serialize():none
etc.

FIGURE 22–4   Class diagram for cSettings.

Other diagrams show multiple classes and their relationships. The relationship is indicated with a number or range of numbers. The symbol "*" is used for "many. " For example, if a collection class named cHouses contained zero or more instances of cHouse, then the relationship line would have a "1" next to the cHouses box, and a "*" next to the cHouse box, like Figure 22–5.

In such relationship diagrams, the properties and methods may or may not be present. It depends on the stage of design you are at.

Other types of UML diagrams cover other aspects of design. Use cases can be represented with a standard notation that contains Actors and a System, with Use Cases inside the system. Figure 22–6 shows a simple example.

There are a number of other types of object diagrams, including:

- Activity diagrams
- State chart diagrams
- Class hierarchies
- Collaboration diagrams
- Package diagrams
- Sequence diagrams
- Deployment diagrams

Each has specific notation to represent common elements of design.

To learn about these other diagram types, take a look at a good beginning book on UML, such as *UML Distilled* by Martin Fowler.

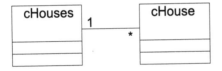

FIGURE 22–5   Class relationship diagram.

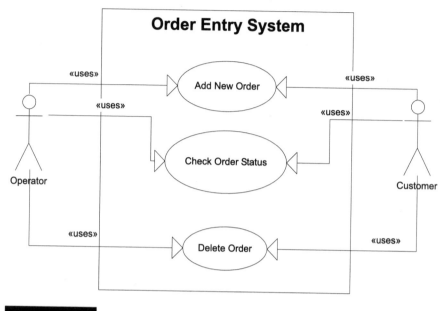

Order Entry System

«uses»	«uses»
Add New Order	
«uses»	«uses»
Check Order Status	
Operator	Customer
«uses»	«uses»
Delete Order	

FIGURE 22-6   A use case in UML.

Using a UML Diagramming Tool

UML diagrams can be done by hand, but fortunately there are tools which make the process a lot easier. Rational Software™ is one vendor of these tools. A simplified version of Rational's tool is included with Visual Studio 6.

Another vendor is Visio Corporation™. A trial version of Visio Enterprise is included on the enclosed CD-ROM.

Visio Enterprise creates UML diagrams with their familiar "stencil-connector" user interface. Stencils are included for all the UML elements, and intelligent connectors allow you to specify connector attributes such as the type of relationship.

Playing around with such a tool is a good way to become more familiar with UML. The documentation included with Visio offers a good overview of the different UML diagram types, and how to create them.

REPLACING THE CLASS BUILDER

One of the major advantages of using a UML tool is that you can get the shell code for your classes automatically generated. Once you have specified the properties and methods, most UML tools will then create classes with the tedious routine code already written. This is similar to what the class builder does in VB, but the resulting source code is far superior. If you use industrial-strength tools for this kind of work, you'll never go back to the class builder again.

Some of these tools, including Visio, have the ability to read existing classes (from source code) and create UML diagrams based on them. This allows you to document existing systems, and to construct an object model of an existing system as a starting point for the design of new versions.

USING THE MICROSOFT REPOSITORY

Most of the tools for UML design in the Microsoft environment use the Microsoft Repository to store object models. This is not strictly necessary — you can store the models in their own files. But it provides a good way to keep all the object designs together and consistent.

The first version of the Microsoft Repository, which came with Visual Studio 97, was pretty lame, and I don't recommend using it. The latest version is 2.0, and it comes with Visual Studio 6 (Enterprise version). It works pretty well, and I'd recommend that you give it a try.

Design Patterns

If you've been in this business long enough, you start to notice a lot of commonality among the problems you are solving. Similar situations come up again and again, with similar problems to be solved. Usually, an overall generic design works pretty well for a broad class of these problems. Knowing about that generic design can save you a lot of time when a specific situation comes up that can use it.

For example, it is often necessary to ensure that a class only has one instance in a project, and to provide a global point of access to it. There's no need for you to wrack your brain solving this problem when you can simply look up the solution.

Generic designs that solve such common situations are called "design patterns." The best known book on design patterns is *Design Patterns* by Erich Gamma, Richard Helm, Ralph Johnson, and John Vlissides. It is several years old, and talks about implementation in terms of Smalltalk and C++, but it is still useful as a compilation of useful design patterns.

Any time you have a problem to be solved that probably has applicability in lots of different systems, take a little research time to check out solutions which are already available, instead of investing all the time yourself to come up with a solution from scratch.

Common Mistakes in Object Design

As you begin switching to object-oriented design, you may be tempted to try some things that will cause problems in developing your applications. Let's look at some common examples of such mistakes.

"Everything's An Object"

When developers "get the religion" on objects, they may go too far and decide that everything has to be an object. That means wrapping functions and subroutines in objects, and swearing never to write another BAS module.

This is silly. Objects are just another tool to help you do better software development. Just because you have a new tool does not mean your old tools are worthless. I love my power drill, but when I need to pound in a nail, I don't turn the drill around and pound with its handle. I use a hammer, because that's the right tool for the job. Similarly, if I need to reformat a string field from many places in my application, a function may be just the right tool for the job.

Too Many Collections

Collections are extremely powerful, but they can have an impact on performance. So they should be used when needed, not just for the heck of it.

For example, if you have a customer file with several thousand records in it, you might be tempted to place each customer record in a Customer object, and then have a collection of these objects. There are even situations where that would be a good idea. But most of the time, it would just slow down your app (and make more work for you) while providing no great benefit.

Often recordsets can be used just the way they are. After all, they are already a collection, of a sort, especially if the database has some good validation on the fields. If you are just dumping records into a list box or grid, or onto a report, use the recordset itself.

When working with a recordset that can benefit from an object wrapper, I usually just instantiate an object for the current record. Then when I change records, I throw away the old object and create a new one. If this is being done for a program collecting user input, this approach is fast enough that the delay is not noticed. But if you put fifty thousand customers into a collection when loading a form, I guarantee the users will notice it — and they won't like the delay.

Restricting Attention to Data Objects

Using the suggestions above for analysis, the first objects you are likely to decide you need are objects related to data. That is, if you have a Customer table, you may very well need a Customer object to handle interaction with customer data.

We've already covered one concern with such objects above with the warning not to create huge collections of such objects. Another pitfall is that these objects are easy to identify, so they may end up constituting the entire object design.

If you do this, you'll be losing some of the nice capabilities of objects. We've previously discussed "system objects" which are basically objects that represent entities or processes which are internal to the system. These objects are just as important to a real object-based system as the data objects. Don't neglect them in your design. They are harder to find, and sometimes you don't realize you need one until the development stage. But make sure you use them whenever appropriate.

Trying Too Hard to Model the Real World

Here's another variation on the same problem. One of the appealing characteristics of object-based development is that many of the characteristics of a software object do in fact "model" analogous characteristics of some real world object. An automobile object can have a Color property, and that corresponds to the fact that automobiles in the real world also have a color.

However, that should not blind us to the weaknesses of the correspondence. Some cars are not a single color. Colors can have different shades and can fade. The object property Color cannot possibly capture all of the real-world possibilities for the color of an automobile. We simply hope the object property captures enough of the real-world possibilities to fulfill its role in a software system.

There are other weaknesses to this approach of matching objects to the real world. A library book object can certainly have a "CheckOut" method for the convenience of our software system design. But library books can't check themselves out. That can only be done by people. And our object design would probably not work well if we placed the CheckOut method with the person object instead of the library book object.

I am not impressed with object methodologies in which all or almost all of the objects model something physical. There are too many limitations to the modeling. Besides, objects are also a way of packaging logic, and can serve a broader array of functions than just resembling items in the real world.

Suggestions for Further Reading

We have already mentioned the book *UML Distilled* by Martin Fowler, which contains a good introduction to UML notation.

In *Visual Basic 6 Object-Oriented Programming* by Gene Swartzfager, et al. (Coriolis Technology Press), Chapter 2 contains a good detailed example of dissecting a specification for appropriate objects.

We previously mentioned the original design patterns book, *Design Patterns*, by Erich Gamma, et al. I'm not aware of a book on design patterns specifically for Visual Basic. There is one for Java with only about one-fourth of the material being code-specific. It is *Applying UML and Patterns* by Craig Larman. I recommend it both for more UML information and for its presentation of design patterns.

Additional Design Topics

This chapter wraps up our discussion of the design phase with comments on several miscellaneous design topics.

Special Considerations for Commercial Software

The majority of development projects using Visual Basic are done in the corporate world. This environment has plenty of challenges, and the pressure can be intense. But Visual Basic is also used a lot for commercial software development. This includes any situation where software is being produced to be resold in quantity. Such development steps up the pressure another notch.

I've spent most of my career in the commercial software arena. Here are some suggestions based on that experience for commercial software development projects.

Error Handling and Activity Logging

All quality software written in VB should have good error handling, but in a commercial system, it is absolutely essential. Having a system constantly crash with an obscure VB runtime error is just not acceptable when a product has a large, distributed user base. Though you can never anticipate and handle all the errors that can occur, a good error trapping strategy will go a long way towards the ideal.

As an experienced VB developer, you are probably familiar with basic error handling concepts, but here's a short review. In code with proper error trapping, every routine in the user interface except the most trivial, and almost all functions and subroutines, have error trapping. This typically involves a line at the top that looks like this:

```
On Error Goto ErrorHandler:
```

and a section at the bottom of the routine that looks something like this:

```
Exit Sub        ' or Exit Function or whatever

ErrorHandler:
If Err = nnn Then     ' might need a Select Case if many
                      ' errors are handled individually

    ' do some action which handles the specific error …
    Exit Sub
End If

ErrorLogMessage "Error in routine ThisRoutine: " _
    & Err & " - " & Err.Desc, Err, esSeverityFatal

End Sub
```

Notice that this type of error handling may not be appropriate for routines in a object, because you typically want the calling routine to handle object errors.

At the end of the code above is a line which logs the error. For commercial software, this logging process is important. Typically, the routine which logs the error messages also puts a message to the user in a message box if the severity level makes this appropriate.

There are lots of ways to log errors. The simplest way is to just append error messages to a text file. Some projects store log messages in a database. With Windows NT, you can use the built-in event log.

For commercial software, it is almost always advisable to design in some kind of logging capability.

ACTIVITY LOGGING ROUTINES

Most log files keep putting log messages at the bottom, and never erase any messages. This makes it tedious to wade through lots of messages to find the one you need.

About ten years ago, I produced my first set of activity logging routines based on a "wrap-around" structure. That means that the log does not grow indefinitely in size, but wraps around when full to keep reusing the same disk space.

These original routines in QuickBASIC were later converted to VB, and have seen minor enhancements over the years, such as getting the location of the log file out of an INI file. The name of the module holding these routines is LOGSUBS.BAS. Another module for access to INI files is also needed, and it is named INIFiles.Bas. These files are included on the enclosed CD. They are with a project in a directory called /Examples/VB5/ActivityLogging.

The main routine from a developer's point of view is LogIt. This routine accepts a message to be logged, along with an error number (typically a VB error) and a two-character severity code. The log record created includes this information, plus the time, date, and the EXE name generating the error.

LogIt is pretty smart. It gets the location of the log file out of an INI file. The default name is LOGFILE.LOG, and its default location is the application's path. These defaults may be overridden by placing an entry in an INI file to specify a different location for the log file. The name of this INI file is ERRORLOG.INI (and it should be in the Windows system directory). The name can be changed by changing a value of a constant in the Declarations section of the module LOGSUBS.BAS. You may also wish to switch to using the Windows registry instead of a private INI file.

If the log file does not exist, Logit will created one. The INI file can have an entry for the size of the log, but if it is not present, the log file will be set to 1000 records.

Note that several programs can share the same log because they can get the location out of the INI file.

The activity logging routines use VB's fixed-length random access capabilities. That means there is no need for the Microsoft Access Jet engine or any other database. This also means that logging is very fast, and uses comparatively small resource amounts. Even for resource-intensive programs, there's no reason not to use these logging routines.

VIEWING LOG RECORDS

The log can be viewed with any text editor because each fixed-length record has a carriage return/line feed on the end of it. You have to be careful though, because the first line in the file will contain some binary information.

It is easy to write a log browser, and a simple one is included on the CD. It uses a routine called GetLogMessage to read log records. The comments in that routine contain information on how to use it. You can enhance the included browser by giving it some searching and selecting capabilities. That will enable users to narrow down the log to just the messages they are interested in.

LOGGING ROUTINE ACTIVITIES

Activity logging can be used for far more than just errors. Log records could be generated:

- At the start and end of the program
- When data records are added, deleted, or changed
- When system information is changed
- When a user logs in to your program
- When you need some debugging information (such as the command line)

These types of log messages are easy to add to your programs. For commercial software, they can be enormously helpful during support. Any experienced technical support person can tell you how tough it is to find out what a user did that caused an error. With activity logging, the information available for technical support is dramatically improved.

Installation and Packaging

Many corporate software systems have only rudimentary installation programs. If there is a problem with installation, there is typically someone around who can troubleshoot.

Commercial systems must have far better installation programs. That has several implications for the analysis, design, and development phases.

In analysis, it is especially important to pin down all the platforms on which the system will be supported. Testing (both of the software and the installation program) will have to be done on each platform.

During estimation, appropriate time must be budgeted for creation and testing of the installation program. Large software firms often have dedicated developers who do nothing but work on installation programs.

In design, there may be options which might make development easier, but will make installation much tougher. Someone on the design team should have experience with installation programs to catch such problems before the development phase begins.

For commercial systems, creation of that "gold CD" is a huge milestone in the project. It is a tangible moment when the development team has essentially finished their work on the product.

A Higher Bar for User Interface Design

With the large number of users of a typical commercial package, user interface considerations are elevated in commercial software development. The comments in Chapter 21, "User Interface Design and Usability" are especially important to commercial developers. More effort in brainstorming, prototyping, and designing the user interface is important. And a commercial development project should always include usability testing.

Commercial packages are also more likely to need multiple user interfaces for different classes of users. The most common combination is a standard interface which does everything, and a wizard interface which does common functions and is painless to use. Systems may also need a browser-based interface.

N-Tier Architectures

The need for multiple user interfaces is just one factor which is encouraging n-tier, object-based design for modern Visual Basic projects. It is significantly harder to support two or more completely separate user interfaces with old-fashioned structured software development.

This leads to a recommendation for system design for any project. It's a good idea to pretend that you will need multiple user interfaces, even if that need is not in the requirements. Pretending that you many need to "plug-in" an alternate user interface will just about force you to do a layered, n-tier structure.

We looked at that kind of structure briefly in Chapter 15, "More About Objects." Figure 15-10 presented a simple n-tier structure. As we discussed there, there is communications only between adjacent layers. Each layer typically is made up of a group of related objects, and the object interfaces are used for communication.

Do not get the misconception that an n-tier design is only possible in a distributed system (with servers and clients). Even on a single machine, an n-tier design is possible, and usually desirable. However, n-tier design is practically mandatory on a distributed platform.

This book does not cover n-tier design in detail, but it does prepare you for n-tier design in an important way — by helping you to embrace objects.

The Component Object Model (COM)

There is another prerequisite for getting started with n-tier design and development, and that is an understanding of Microsoft's Component Object Model, referred to as COM.

As a Visual Basic developer, you are actually surrounded by COM, whether you know it or not. The internal workings of VB and most other modern Windows packages are based on COM.

As with so many other system-level technologies, Visual Basic hides the details. When you are learning VB, you don't have to worry about COM just as you don't have to worry about the Windows API.

But if your development becomes sufficiently advanced, you do need to learn about what is going on under the hood. You may have already reached a point where you needed to get to the Windows API directly. You will almost certainly get to the same point concerning COM in the future.

That's because everything in Windows is becoming component-based. Components are basically software building blocks, and modern software systems are almost all built from components. The days of monolithic EXE files are just about gone.

Component-based design has many advantages, some of which spring from the object-oriented capabilities of COM. A huge additional advantage is that component-based design allows pieces of an application to be updated without affecting the rest of the application.

For a component, COM is basically a convention or standard that defines how other components can interact with it. That is, COM is a standard (at the binary level) for specifying the external object interface of a component. COM is also a standard means for locating a component when it is needed.

Distributed COM, or DCOM, extends COM to the network by extending the standard method used to locate a component. DCOM will locate a component anywhere on the network, whereas COM is restricted to a single physical machine.

Before getting serious about n-tier design, it is recommended that you invest some time becoming more knowledgeable about COM. An excellent introductory book is *VB COM: A Visual Basic Programmer's Introduction to COM* by Thomas Lewis.

Microsoft Transaction Server

If you get really serious about developing distributed, n-tier systems, you will also need to learn about Microsoft Transaction Server (MTS). MTS lets you create objects that pretend to be for a single user, and then MTS runs those objects in an environment where they can serve multiple users. This is particularly relevant to objects that manipulate data.

There are some special requirements for objects that run under MTS, particularly in how the objects handle their internal states. But if you understand COM, MTS is not a major stretch from there. In fact, COM and MTS are being unified in the next major version of these technologies from Microsoft, which will be called COM+.

VB COM: A Visual Basic Programmer's Introduction to COM by Thomas Lewis, which we discussed above, also has a good introduction to MTS.

Designing Routines

Design does not just apply to architectures. Thinking through a problem and creating a design to solve it can go all the way down to the level of writing a single routine.

As with an object, one of the first design tasks for a routine is designing its interface. What arguments will it need? What information will it furnish to the calling code?

Then comes the actual logic in the routine. I almost always design a routine's logic flow before writing it (unless the routine is very small).

Some people like to flowchart. Flowcharting is excellent for overall systems, and good for complex routines, but there are other methods. One is using Program Design Language (PDL).

I first read about PDL in *Code Complete* by Steve McConnell. With PDL, you "write" the routine in English. It is recommended that you stay away from computer-language-specific phraseology — a routine design written in PDL should be readable by almost any technically-informed person.

A single line of PDL can describe either a large or small chunk of functionality. Start by writing about large chunks. Then refine that by writing more PDL to break down the large chunks. When you get to the point where you realize it would be simpler to write code than to do any more detail, then you can actually start writing the routine in computer language.

When the PDL version of the routine is done, it can be saved for documentation, and it can also be imported into your code editor to use as a starting point for the routine. It should be marked as a comment block. Then code is inserted between lines of PDL, using the PDL as running commentary on the routine's code. This is a near painless way to do better documentation of your code.

I recommend that you try PDL if you have never done it. It is not to everyone's taste, but I find it very useful. *Code Complete* by Steve McConnell features a complete discussion, including good and bad examples of PDL.

Methodologies and Best Practices

Proper analysis and design are just part of the complete software development process. As we saw at the beginning of the book, design phases into development, and then comes testing, implementation, and follow-up documentation.

Just how does analysis and design fit best into the overall process? There are a lot of opinions about that. And there have been many trends and fads over the years to try to find the "best" process for developing software.

Of course, there really isn't a way that is best for all circumstances. A process that works well on a single-person, three-week project isn't necessarily very much like what is needed for a five-person project which consumes two calendar years.

But there are some practices which seem to fit into most good development processes. We will look at some of the most important of these.

Structure vs. Flexibility

It's not enough just to know good practices and consistently apply them (though that will take you a long way). It's also important to know when particular practices should be applied at all. As we mentioned above, circumstances vary, so the practices you use on individual projects should vary too.

A structured approach to software development uses standardized tools and techniques, and well-defined processes to move through the phases. A structured process typically has built-in feedback mechanisms and progress measurements.

Structure helps a project by giving solid, consistent goals, and by making sure members of a development team are not working at cross-purposes. Most Visual Basic projects suffer from not having enough structure. The culture of the Visual Basic developer community seems to encourage a loose, unstructured approach, and this often gets carried to excess.

On the other hand, too much structure can be a detriment. For example, status reports can be helpful, particularly on large projects. But filling out pointless status reports which nobody reads is a sure way to demoralize developers, besides the obvious waste of time. The appropriate amount of structure varies greatly with the size and nature of the project.

If you are leading a typical Visual Basic project, you'll probably want to try more structure. But it's a good idea to review the amount of structure imposed on development efforts at regular intervals. Poll the development team to see if elements of the structure have become constraining or stifling. If parts of your process are not delivering benefits to balance the costs, then change them or dump them.

Good Development Practices

An Appropriate Definition/Analysis Phase

The first part of this book dealt with this subject in detail, so we won't repeat everything here. It is enough to emphasize that the definition/analysis phase usually should take around twenty percent of the calendar time for the entire project (plus or minus, depending on circumstances).

Developer Involvement in Setting Deadlines

We've talked about this one in the first part of the book also. We can sum it up by saying that any deadline that is set without developer involvement is more of a wish than a goal.

A "Go/No Go" Decision Point

Far too many development efforts are carried too far because of inertia. Often, what looked like a great idea became a not-so-great idea when the details came out, but the project was already underway, and developers just kept plugging away at it.

A good development effort should have a decision point at which a conscious effort is made to decide if the system should really be developed. This is typically sometime around the time the functional specification is done, and a realistic estimate is generated. The estimate provides a rough guide to the cost of the project, and the analysis often leads to a better understanding of the benefits.

It's a good idea to have someone involved in the process play the role of Devil's Advocate. This person should try to come up with all the reasons why the project should not go forward. If there aren't any good ones — great, get to work. But if the project looks to have costs which outweigh the benefits, it's better to find that out before the costs are already incurred.

Developers sometimes do something at this stage that I consider unprofessional. A developer may decide that it's a great idea to do a project, and minimize the costs, or outright slant the estimate to get the project started. Then the project is likely to proceed to the end, even if it exceeds the estimate.

It is not the developer's job to decide the business case for a project. Some management person has that responsibility. It is the responsibility of developers to give the best estimates they can give, and leave the go/no-go decision to the managers.

Iterative Design

Any good design process should iterate until a stable point is reached. The first stab at a design is almost guaranteed to be inadequate. Critique the first version of a design, and make changes as necessary. Then critique again, and change again if necessary. When the changes start to drop to the insignificant level, it's time to start real development.

Source Control

On any project with more than one programmer, a source control system is essential to coordinating the work. Typically, the system works like this:

1. When a module is created, it is stored in the source database, which is on a shared network drive.

2. When a programmer needs to make changes to the module, the module is "checked out" from the source database.

3. When the changes are made, the module is "checked in" by the programmer who checked it out.

4. The source database maintains a record of all changes made, and stores all previous versions of the source.

5. Only one programmer can have a module checked out at any one time.

6. If a module is used in more than one Visual Basic project, it is "shared" among the projects so that only one copy exists (and can be checked out) in the source database.

7. Programmers periodically refresh all their modules to get the latest changes checked in by other programmers.

The most popular software for doing source control in Visual Basic is SourceSafe, which comes with the Enterprise version of Visual Studio. In SourceSafe, the source database is represented in a folderized structure similar to Explorer.

USING SOURCESAFE WITHIN VISUAL BASIC

SourceSafe can be installed as a Visual Basic add-in. In that configuration, managing modules within SourceSafe can be done right in Visual Basic. When new modules are saved, the programmer will immediately be asked if the module should be placed under source control.

The alternative is using stand-alone SourceSafe. This works, but there is one thing that programmers must be careful never to do. Modules should never be checked out while the programmer is in the act of changing them. That's because the copy being changed may not necessarily be the latest version in the source control system — it could be an obsolete version. If a programmer starts working on such an obsolete module in VB (so that the module is in memory) and then checks out the module in stand-alone Source-Safe, it is possible that changes made by other programmers to the module will be lost when the obsolete version with some changes is checked in.

SOURCESAFE ADMINISTRATION

One person must have responsibility for administering SourceSafe. That includes setting up new log-in accounts for developers, arranging to back up the source database, and managing the organization of the projects stored in the source database. Access to individual projects can be set for individual developers, and various rights (such as the right to establish a new project or rename an existing one) must be administered.

Depending on the administrator's preferences and the circumstances of a particular installation, security may be weak or strong. For smaller projects, it is typically better to have minimal security, with a log-in password for each developer or other team member that gives access to all projects.

WHAT GOES UNDER SOURCE CONTROL?

Developers usually understand that all the code goes under source control. But in fact, any file connected to the development project is a candidate to be managed through the source control system. This includes:

- Requirements documents and functional specs
- Technical specs
- Graphical images
- Help files
- Prototypes
- Compiled components (internal or third-party)

WHEN TO USE SOURCE CONTROL

If possible, always. Even if you are working alone, source control will help:

- Keep up with old versions
- Prevent inadvertent changes
- Share code among projects
- Make it easy to add another developer

I have been surprised many times to find a multiperson project in which source control was not being used. In every one of those projects, a persistent problem was losing programming changes. That happened because two developers would be working on a module at the same time, and the second one to copy his version onto the common disk would wipe out the changes made by the first one.

A Mechanism for Gauging and Measuring Progress

If you have developed software for very long, you are familiar with the following scenario. Let's call the system we are developing System X. At first the development of System X seems to show visible progress. Developers are coding modules and there are screens being developed. The person running the project gets status reports that indicate that jobs are proceeding from "0% complete" to "20% complete," and then on up the scale to "80% complete."

Then something starts going wrong. The percentages stop increasing on the status reports. They all seem to get stuck around 90%. The weeks go by, and sponsors start to get worried. They start making more frequent inquiries about when things will be done. The developers all say "just a few more days now" or some such response.

Eventually all of the status reports keep saying that various components are "almost" done week after week. But they never seem to actually get done. And when you ask to look at actual work, the developers usually respond, "Well, it doesn't compile cleanly right now because I'm still working on some pieces."

It's hard to say what the root cause of such a problem is, because there are many candidates, with poor analysis and design being the most likely suspect. But there is a way to find out that the problems exist much earlier in the process. All that is required is a way to really find out what the state of a project is at any given time. And the elements that are needed to do this are regular builds of the product, and product drops.

REGULAR BUILDS

A "build" is a complete compile of the current state of a software project. It should have no compile errors, though it may have known defects (and is sure to have unknown defects). The resulting EXE should have all currently working functionality accessible.

In a project of any size, the software should be "built" very regularly. Microsoft builds daily, but they can afford to have people who have no other responsibility. In a typical environment a build should be done once or twice a week.

The project is typically built from modules checked into a source control system (and if you are doing multiperson development without source control, I have to question your sanity). That implies that developers should take care to check in modules that compile cleanly.

Doing something that prevents a clean compile is called "breaking the build." This could be checking in a module with a syntax error, creating a new module and forgetting to place it under source control, or changing the interface to an object or routine but forgetting to fix all the places that call the object or routine. One of the purposes of regular builds is to find these problems as soon as possible, and to incidentally encourage developers not to cause them in the first place.

Builds have many good effects. Builds prevent problems from being hidden, and facilitate communication among developers. Builds keep all developers on a project "in synch" with the latest versions of various modules, which also helps prevent problems that arise when developers work with obsolete versions of system modules. Builds also give a tangible sense of accomplishment to development teams who are on track.

WHAT IS A PRODUCT DROP?

A product drop is a presentation of a build of the current state of product, warts and all. It is shown to any interested parties. This typically includes marketing, other IT professionals, and user representatives, as well as regular development team members.

It should be regular, approximately once a week, or every two weeks at the most. There should be no special preparation for it. Team members show the current state of product elements that they are personally responsible for.

Critique of any element is allowed. The users can bash the user interface, and anyone that will interact with the product (someone with a database it needs, for example) can highlight any technical issues that have not been adequately addressed. Praise is also appropriate if it is deserved.

Product drops remove the fog from development efforts. They strip away the excuses, deceptive status reports, and other things used to rationalize lack of progress. The clarity they bring is a great asset towards having a successful development process.

During drops team members should strive to not be defensive. If there is a misunderstanding in the audience, they should address it, but they should not be ashamed of problems that come up or elements that require change.

Post-Production Documentation

After the system is done, one of the best things that can be done to increase the long term value of the system is to do post-production documentation. This basically documents how the code actually works (instead of how it was supposed to work, which was in the technical spececification documents).

I call the post-production documentation a "care-and-feeding" document, because it is specifically written to assist programmers who come along later and need to change the system. It should include the following:

■ Update of functional and technical specs to reflect changes during the development process.

■ A description of major modules and routines in the system, including what they do and how they are accessed.

■ Documentation of all methods and properties of major objects.

■ Cookbook instructions for changes which are virtually certain to be done in the future (for example, adding a new type of transaction). The instructions should highlight the places that will require change and the general nature of the changes that will be needed.

This should not be a long effort — two or three days should be sufficient. Investing those two or three days can make a dramatic long-term difference in the extensibility of the system.

As with all the other documents we have discussed, the care-and-feeding document is not related to user documentation. It is for development staff only.

A Celebration

Celebrate your successes. Development efforts are intense. They require dedication, creativity, teamwork, and many other elements to be successful. When the success comes, observe and savor it.

Methodologies

In trying to capture many of the practices mentioned above, many organizations have developed formal descriptions of their software development process. This description usually includes standards and practices which the process is supposed to observe. Such a description is sometimes called a methodology.

The Microsoft Software Development Methodology

One of the most commonly used methodologies is from Microsoft and is called the Microsoft Solutions Framework™ (or MSF, for short). It is derived from practices developed during real development efforts inside Microsoft.

You can actually take classes from Microsoft on using the MSF. To find out details about that, check their website at *http://www.microsoft.com/msf/*.

The MSF addresses many of the most common problems that arise during development efforts, such as:

- Products get "stuck in the pipeline."

- There is a lack of ownership of products — no one feels responsible for their success.

- People focus on tasks to be done instead of how to get products finished.

- There is an over-the-wall mentality.

- There is a general lack of development discipline — deadlines don't mean anything.

These problems often stem from the same source. Software development efforts are usually structured along standard corporate lines, and often by people who don't know that much about how software is really developed. It may be impossible to make significant structural change. But you should at least understand what the possibilities are.

All of these problems can be overcome. The MSF is one structure that can help do that.

Fundamentals of the MSF

The Microsoft MSF is built around the team concept. A development team is a small group of individuals whose mission is to get a product done. The fundamental elements of the concept are:

- The team consists of peers, not a manager and a staff.

- The team is totally focused on the product — they spend 90%+ of their time on it.

- The team is focused on a fixed ship date, which they participate in setting.

- Planning and scheduling are milestone-driven.

- The functional spec is a contract between the project team and its customers.

- The team is constantly producing deliverables — specifications at first, and later evolving versions of the product.

Traditional Methods

To understand more about MSF, it is helpful to compare it to "traditional" approaches. A very common one used in large projects is sometimes called the "waterfall" approach. In this method, there are separate people who work on:

- Requirements
- Design
- Development
- Testing

When a group finishes their part, they pass the results "down the line" to the next group. Rarely are inadequate efforts "kicked back" for more work. When a group is finished with their part, they go on to something else.

In such an environment, a development project is usually seen as a distinct process, with a beginning, a middle, and an end. It is usually pictured as a straight line.

The MSF Process Model

The basic development process is depicted in MSF as a circle, as shown in Figure 24–1.

There are basically four phases to the process: (1) the initial conceptual phase, (2) the planning phase, (3) the development phase, and (4) the quality assurance phase. As far as is practical, the entire team is involved in all four phases.

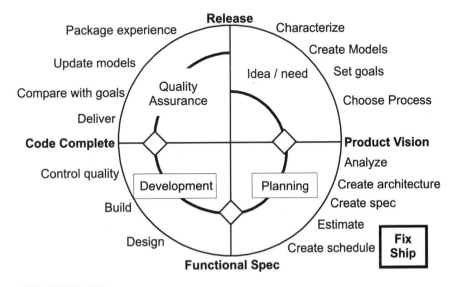

FIGURE 24–1 The Microsoft Solutions Framework process model. (Reprinted with permission of Microsoft® Corporation.)

THE DEVELOPMENT TEAM

The team consists of the following roles:

- Product manager
- Program manager
- Analyst(s)
- Developer(s)
- Quality assurance
- Training
- Users

The team has a leader, but none of the roles above is singled out for that job. The team begins with no leader until one develops into the role naturally. The most typical leader is the lead developer.

The **product manager** is the primary interface to marketing and other business elements such as finance. In some cases, the product manager can be the team leader, if the person in the role has sufficient respect from the technical team members.

The **program manager** is a very different role, and is almost never that of a leader. The program manager is more of an "auditor" who maintains the task list, nags everybody about their part, and keeps the schedule. This person should be detail-oriented.

The **analyst** role may be played by the product manager and/or one or more of the developers.

Developers encompass anyone who designs or writes code. Typically there is a senior or lead developer, but this person is not usually the manager of the programmers in the bureaucratic sense (though this person may guide the programmers' day-to-day activities).

Quality assurance has the testing function. Their involvement from the beginning serves to make them better understand the what and why of their testing. Being a full team member from the beginning makes testers far more effective.

Users and trainers may be involved, but they may also be called in at various phases and not be full members of the team. It depends a lot on the size of the effort.

Some of the Philosophy

Members of an MSF team do not break themselves down in the standard way. They don't consider their job to be just programming, or just testing, or just manual writing, or whatever. They consider their job to be "shipping the product." The enables team members to assume responsibilities they would never be allowed to undertake under more bureaucratic systems. And it enables tasks or jobs to find willing recipients. Highly bureaucratic systems can suffer greatly from centralized decision making, resulting in various holdups and substandard results. The MSF decentralizes decisions, and makes it more likely that someone will "step up to the plate" to make sure something happens.

Team members also make commitments to one another, and this furnishes much of the motivation to do a good job. No one wants to let down another team member. And if someone is not doing their job, the team is far more likely than an individual manager to work on getting that person back on track. It is surprising how much the team approach encourages and demands accountability.

The Culture of the MSF

A full-fledged methodology such as Microsoft's will not work unless the culture of the organization allows it. Unfortunately, most organizations just don't have the culture to do things this way. But you can take whatever elements you can from the MSF to make the development effort more effective. These would typically include:

THE TEAM-BASED APPROACH • Getting testers and developers on board as early as possible in the process pays big dividends. Even if the team consists only of those members, it will still be more effective than isolated developers.

UP-FRONT DESIGN • You're probably tired of hearing about this, but it can't be stressed often enough.

REGULAR BUILDS AND PRODUCT DROPS • These have many, many good effects. They serve as a motivator. They are an early warning system for problems. They allow users or any other interested parties to see progress (or lack thereof) and also to familiarize themselves with the product gradually. They especially help to keep the team "in synch."

DEVELOPER INVOLVEMENT IN SETTING DEADLINES • Arbitrary deadlines are just about useless for producing good software. Only raw recruits are motivated to meet impossible deadlines imposed by someone who doesn't have a clue about the scale of the work. On the other hand, a self-imposed deadline produces intense motivation to meet it. And it will typically give a much more honest picture of when things will be ready to the rest of the organization.

Some Final Comments on the MSF

The MSF was developed for an environment that produces software for resale. It is very hard to beat for those environments, because it provides the best balance I know of between speed and quality.

However, the typical corporate shop has somewhat different needs. A delay of three months in rolling out a corporate system does not mean nearly as much as a three-month delay in getting a competitive product to market. And the culture of a typical corporation is not oriented around software development.

Other Methodologies

There are lots of other methodologies besides MSF. Most of the major consulting firms (for instance, Ernst and Young) have them. Most of theirs are more formalized. I admit to some bias against highly formal methodologies, but they obviously can be successful in the right circumstances. Certainly any methodology which requires some design and accountability is far better than nothing at all.

However, beware of the "methodology evangelist" who thinks that a particular methodology will cure all the ills in a software development process. Someone who is evangelistic about the "Hammer Methodology" probably thinks everything looks like a nail, and someone else who loves the "Power Drill Methodology" thinks everything needs a hole in it.

Two average development projects are likely to be more different than they are alike. Rigid methodologies can sometimes create as many problems as they solve if they are applied to the wrong project. Better to know many methods and approaches, and choose the ones that apply to the problem at hand.

Getting a Methodology Started

Converting an entire organization to any methodology is tough. In a large organization, the methodology will often get compromised to death. And a radical approach such as the MSF is often not palatable to corporate managers.

Your best bet for using the advantages of a good methodology is in small projects where you are a major player. Get the appropriate team players on board and go as far as you can with it. If it starts to make a big difference in product development times and product quality, you will probably be allowed to keep doing things your way.

Processes Don't Build Software — People Build Software

Some organizations seize on software development methodologies the same way a drowning person grabs a life preserver. Everything starts to revolve around "the process." Sometimes there are people involved who start being more concerned about the process than the end result.

But a process is just a beginning. If you have the perfect methodology and follow it precisely, but the developers in it are untalented, undisciplined, or unmotivated, the project will almost certainly fail. On the other hand, if the development team contains superior developers, even a poor process may lead to a success.

There's no doubt that a good process or methodology can increase the odds of success. But solid developers are the foundation. Without them, the process is pointless.

Always remember that processes and methodologies are supposed to help members of a development team, not get in their way. *The process has no reason to exist except to help the development team succeed.* If the process is not accomplishing this prime purpose, it needs to be modified or replaced.

Thinking Outside the Box

There are many aspects to good design. Hard work and structured effort are required. But there's also a creative component.

One of the problems with many formal definition/design processes is that they consider most of the work in software development to be fundamentally mechanical. There's no denying that some drudge work is required, but a good designer must be able to step back and get outside the mechanical details.

Locking onto the First Design

There's a tendency among some developers to use the first solution they come up with. As soon as the solution is thought of, their brain locks onto it, and stops considering alternative approaches. This can lead to poor design. The first solution to appear is very often not the best solution. Sometimes a completely different solution is dramatically better. Sometimes several potential solutions can be combined to get the best result. But you must have the creativity to come up with those alternative approaches.

Stimulating Creativity

When I was in graduate school, I learned one of my most valuable lessons in an advanced math class. I would work on a problem for hours and get no solutions. I'd give up and go to bed. Then, about the time I started to fall asleep, I'd suddenly wake up with the solution in my head.

There is a part of our brains that does analysis and pattern matching unconsciously. It will work on problems that you have concentrated on, and if you give it a chance, it will present solutions to you. Getting that part of the brain to do its thing is what most people mean when they talk about stimulating creativity.

There are as many ways of stimulating creativity as there are people. But they all have in common the ability to step back from the task at hand and consider other ramifications. Here are a few of the many things that may help set the right mental state to do that:

- Take a walk outside.
- Go visit a zoo or a junkyard.
- Go to a library, pick out a book at random, and read a few pages.
- Put on some music and concentrate on the music for a while (this is best done with headphones).
- Doodle.
- Take a nap.

There are also many things you can ask yourself to help you step outside the structure you have already established on a problem. For example, you can:

- Ask yourself how another person would look at the problem.
- Ask yourself "What if we couldn't do it the way we are expecting to. What other way could work?"
- Discuss the problem with someone completely disconnected from the project. (Sometimes the solution becomes obvious in the process of explaining the problem to them.)

A book which will give more ideas in this area is *A Whack on the Side of the Head* by Roger von Oech.

An Example of Literally "Thinking Outside the Box"

I once had to design a wizard for a reporting application. But this was no ordinary wizard. There were over thirty screens that could potentially be in the wizard. A typical report only needed six or seven, but there was no way to predict which six or seven it would be.

The first attempt to build the wizard used totally separate forms for each wizard screen, with buttons on each screen for Next, Back, Finish, and Cancel. But the forms had lots of duplicated logic, and the performance was not very good. It was also difficult to manage which forms needed to be shown for a given run, and very hard to know if all the information needed had been entered.

The next attempt used a tab control, with every wizard screen on a different tab. The Next and Back buttons were used to go from tab to tab. This got everything onto one form, which allowed more control. The problem here was that again the performance was poor, but now the resource requirements were very heavy because all of the controls needed for all of the wizard screens had to be loaded every time.

This version was also buggy. I spent over a week attempting to make it work by fixing bugs and getting around performance problems. But nothing worked. The tab control simply wasn't designed to support so many tabs and controls.

Then I took a day off and looked at alternatives. (I should have done this earlier.) I asked others for suggestions, and considered the most outlandish possibilities I could think of.

After a day or so, an idea came up to use Multiple Document Interface (MDI) forms, and for the wizard screens to be MDI child forms. This final design used MDI forms in a way totally outside what they are intended for. Here's how it worked:

The MDI parent was set to a certain size and made non-resizable. It had no menu, and we even changed the border to be more like a dialog box. This required some API calls from within Visual Basic.

The MDI parent had the standard wizard buttons along the bottom, and the buttons caused various child forms to appear and disappear.

Then the individual child forms were made to display one at a time. But their position was set to place their border *just outside* the border of the client area of the MDI parent. That is, when the MDI child was displayed, the user could not see its border, and therefore could not resize it. Figure 25–1 shows how this worked.

This design had some tremendous advantages:

- The individual wizard screens were separate forms, so they could be nicely encapsulated.
- The wizard screens needed for a particular run were placed into an ordered collection. When the wizard was finished, the collection was processed to collect the information entered on the individual forms.

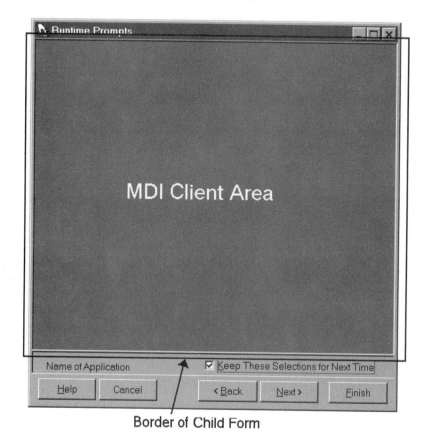

Border of Child Form

FIGURE 25–1   Using MDI forms to construct a wizard.

The wizard screens had properties and methods to allow this. (This is an example of polymorphism.) One of the properties was a Complete property. Every time the user did anything, the Complete properties of all the wizard screens were checked. If they all indicated that they were Complete, then the Finish button was enabled. If any were not complete, then the Finish button was disabled.

Using this design, the entire wizard program was produced in about four days. It was stable, had great performance, and was easily extended. Many of the wizard screens created turned out to be reusable for other projects, and the wizard engine (the MDI form) was completely generic, so it was adopted as a standard for all products in the product line.

This example taught me a valuable lesson — do not force a design that just doesn't work. Instead, go back and find one that does work.

Use All of Your Brain

The above shows an example of the results you can get from taking the time to re-evaluate a design. Don't just beat your head against the wall — try to find a door.

The key is using all of your brain, not just that coding engine that you use most of the day. The techniques covered in this chapter can give the rest of your brain a chance to contribute creative insights to your development project.

You can use these techniques at any phase of design. But always remember to use them when you are at an impasse.

Conclusion

This book has attempted to give you practical advice on defining, designing, and building software in Visual Basic. We have discussed many concepts and techniques, and I hope you will find many of them useful.

There are a few final ideas that should be emphasized as you start applying what you've learned.

Processes Don't Build Software — People Build Software

We discussed this in Chapter 24, "Methodologies and Best Practices," but it bears re-emphasizing. There is no doubt that methodologies and design processes can help you build software faster and better. But processes and methodologies do not build software — people do. The design process does not replace developers. It is meant to help them succeed. Design processes are never a substitute for talent and dedication among the developers.

Dealing with Bad Developers

Because of the tremendous shortage of software development talent, there are many people doing development who lack the capabilities to do it well. Some simply lack the training, and that's fixable. Others just don't have the fundamental talent.

I'm sure lots of human resource managers would disagree with me, but I believe firmly that the fundamental ability to develop software is fairly uncommon, and a particular person either has it or doesn't have it. It's not possible to make someone a good software developer if they don't have that fundamental ability. No process will do it. No training course will do it. No management technique will do it.

If you have members of your team who cannot produce results, even after appropriate training and instruction, you will have a very difficult time applying the concepts in this book. An untalented (or unskilled) developer will still, most likely, build bad software, no matter what processes are in place.

Worse, these folks contaminate the process for others. It is disheartening to other developers to know that no matter how well they do, there are others on the team who cannot get the job done.

You must be ruthless, if necessary, to get bad developers off of your team. It may help you to know that you are not doing them a favor by pretending that they are in the right career. The sooner they find out the truth and make any adjustments necessary, the better off they will be.

Spotting Good Developers

Finding and hiring good developers for your team is one of the most difficult things in the entire industry. The acute shortage has given good developers no shortage of opportunities.

But if you have a good development process in place, you have a powerful tool for attracting good developers. These folks don't want to labor under arbitrary deadlines or see huge portions of their work thrown away.

Make sure that you mention product builds and product drops when talking to a potential developer. Also let them know that they will participate in definition and estimation. Good developers will be excited to hear these things. Bad developers will realize that their poor performance will not be tolerated, and they will look elsewhere.

Here's one final hint on recruiting good developers. When talking to candidates, ask them for sample code which they have personally written. Looking at a half dozen pages of sample code will tell you more about a developer's real capabilities than any resume.

Be Flexible

The final point to make was mentioned early in the book, but it needs to be emphasized. Keep your development process flexible!

Software development projects can vary greatly. Commercial software development is not the same as corporate software development. Large projects are handled very differently from small projects. A team of developers will do things differently from a single developer.

If a particular part of a definition or design process does not make sense for a particular project, then don't do it! Don't spend two months doing object design for a utility which is only going to be used by two people. Don't develop a fifty-page document for a program which can written in an afternoon.

Be suspicious of any attempts to place a lot of bureaucratic overhead into the software development process. Make sure any process you adapt has the flexibility to allow you to jettison parts which don't make sense for a particular project.

The Framework Concept

To emphasize that a definition/design process should have flexibility, some people like to use the word "framework." This implies a set of tools which are intended to help you, rather than a set of rules you have to follow. When setting up your own design process, you may want to make use of this term.

Don't Stop Learning

As our industry moves into the Internet age, all of the concepts in this book become open to challenge. The best practices from ten years ago look pretty silly in many respects today. Likewise, the practices discussed here will be refined and changed over the years.

And remember that this book has used the 80/20 rule to be as concise as possible. The goal in this book was never to be exhaustive — it was just to get you started. Many resources for further reading have been discussed in this book, and studying these will help you continue to become a better definer and designer of software.

You'll also need to work on your "soft skills," the ones that don't involve writing code or even designing systems. You must be able to listen. You must learn to write well enough that others can understand what you say. You must learn the discipline to avoid writing code until you understand a system in depth.

And, perhaps most importantly, you must learn to be straightforward to everyone in the development process. That means learning to say no, and to tell people things they do not want to hear. Miscommunication is the bane of software development, and you must strive to eliminate it from your projects.

It's tough, but the effort is well worth it. You'll experience greater satisfaction from more successful projects, and you'll likely be more successful in your career.

I hope this book has been helpful in starting you down a good path. It's up to you to keep traveling. Good luck and happy developing!

Sample Code References for the Object Workshop

This appendix contains code references for the detailed exercise in the chapter entitled "Object Workshop — Programming the Data Maintenance Object." These code references are to help you through the exercise if you get stuck on a particular step. Most steps involving code refer to one of the references below.

Note that the references are not necessarily in the order that you will need them. This is intentional.

Code Reference #1

```
Private mcolFields As Collection
```

Code Reference #2

```
Public Function AddField(sFieldName As String) As cField
' This method instantiates a new field, gives it a name, and
' adds it to the fields collection. The function returns a
' reference to the field object so that more properties
' can be set.

' Instantiate a new field
Dim objField As cField
Set objField = New cField

' Set its name and add it to the fields collection
objField.Name = sFieldName
```

```
mcolFields.Add objField, sFieldName

' Return a reference to the field
Set AddField = objField

End Function
```

Code Reference #3

```
Public Sub AddBookmark()
' This method instantiates a new bookmark, gives it a name, and
' adds it to the bookmarks collection.

' Instantiate a new field
Dim objBookmark As cBookmark
Set objBookmark = New cBookmark
Dim sBookmarkName As String

' Set its name and add it to the bookmarks collection
sBookmarkName = mrsRecordSet.Fields(msBookmarkField)
objBookmark.Name = sBookmarkName
objBookmark.BookmarkValue = mrsRecordSet.Bookmark

On Error Resume Next
mcolBookmarks.Add objBookmark, sBookmarkName
On Error GoTo 0
End Sub
```

Note the presence of the On Error around the collection Add method. This just takes care of trying to add a bookmark twice. In that case, the bookmark is not added, and the error is ignored.

Code Reference #4

```
Public Sub NewRecord()

mrsRecordSet.AddNew

ClearForm
Dim objField As cField

For Each objField In mcolFields
  If Not objField.UseLastValue Then
    objField.Clear
  End If
Next objField

RefreshForm

End Sub
```

Code Reference #5

```
Public Sub ClearForm()
' This method places the null values for fields into the
' corresponding controls on the form.

Dim objField As cField
Dim ctlControl As Control

For Each objField In mcolFields

  Set ctlControl = objField.Control

  ctlControl.Text = objField.Default

Next objField

End Sub
```

Code Reference #6

```
Public Sub RefreshForm()
' This method places the current values of the fields into
' the corresponding controls on the form.

Dim objField As cField
Dim ctlControl As Control

For Each objField In mcolFields
  Set ctlControl = objField.Control

  If Not IsNull(objField.Value) Then
    ctlControl.Text = objField.Value
  Else
    ctlControl.Text = ""
  End If

Next objField

End Sub
```

Code Reference #7

```
Public Sub MoveNext()

mrsRecordSet.MoveNext
If mrsRecordSet.EOF Then
  mrsRecordSet.MoveLast
End If
```

```
LoadFieldValues
RefreshForm

End Sub
```

Code Reference #8

```
Public Sub LoadFieldValues()
Dim objField As cField

For Each objField In mcolFields
  objField.Value = mrsRecordSet.Fields(objField.Name)
Next objField

mrsRecordSet.Edit

End Sub
```

Code Reference #9

```
Public Sub UpdateRecord()

MoveControlValuesToFields
MoveFieldValuesToRecordBuffer

mrsRecordSet.Update
mrsRecordSet.Bookmark = mrsRecordSet.LastModified

End Sub
```

Code Reference #10

```
Private Sub MoveControlValuesToFields()
Dim objField As cField
Dim ctlControl As Control

For Each objField In mcolFields
  Set ctlControl = objField.Control
  objField.Value = ctlControl.Text

Next objField
End Sub
```

Code Reference #11

```
Private Sub MoveFieldValuesToRecordBuffer()
Dim objField As cField
```

```
For Each objField In mcolFields
  mrsRecordSet.Fields(objField.Name).Value = objField.Value
Next objField

End Sub
```

Code Reference #12

```
Public Sub ListBookmarks(cboBoxToUse As Control)

' Clear the list or combo box and fill it with
' current bookmarks
cboBoxToUse.Clear

Dim objBookmark As cBookmark
For Each objBookmark In mcolBookmarks
  cboBoxToUse.AddItem objBookmark.Name
Next objBookmark

End Sub
```

Code Reference #13

```
Public Sub GoToBookmark(nIndex As Integer)

mrsRecordSet.Bookmark = mcolBookmarks(nIndex + 1).Bookmark-
    Value

LoadFieldValues
RefreshForm

End Sub
```

Code Reference #14

```
Set mcolFields = New Collection
```

Bibliography
and References

This appendix contains a list of the various books and articles that were used in the production of this book. Many of them are referred to in the body of the book as recommendations for further reading.

Axelrod, R., *The Evolution of Cooperation*. BasicBooks, Harper Collins Publishers, 1984, pp. 1-69, ISBN 0-465-02121-2

Coad, P., and E. Yourdon, *Object-Oriented Analysis*, 2nd ed. Englewood Cliffs, NJ: Yourdon Press, 1991, ISBN 0-13-629981-4

Cooper, A., *About Face: The Essentials of User Interface Design*. IDG Books Worldwide, 1995, ISBN 1-56884-322-4

Eidahl, L. D., et al., *Platinum Edition Using Visual Basic 5*. Indianapolis, IN: Que Corporation, 1990, ISBN 0-78971-412-4

Fowler, M., and K. Scott, Chapters 3-11, *UML Distilled: Applying the Standard Object Modeling Language*. Reading, MA: Addison Wesley Longman, Inc., 1997, ISBN0-201-32563-2

Gamma, E., R. Helm, R. Johnson, and J. Vlissides, *Design Patterns: Elements of Reusable Object-Oriented Software*. Reading, MA: Addison-Wesley Publishing Company, 1995, ISBN 0-201-63361-2

Gause, D. C., and B. Lawrence, "User-Driven Design: Incorporating Users into the Requirements and Design Phase," *Software Testing and Quality Engineering*, 1, no. 1, 1999, pp. 23-28.

Hernandez, M. J., *Database Design for Mere Mortals: A Hands-on Guide to Relational Database Design*. Addison-Wesley Publishing Co., 1997, ISBN 0-20169-471-9

Howlett, V., *Visual Interface Design for Windows : Effective User Interfaces for Windows 95, Windows Nt, and Windows 3.1*. New York, NY: John Wiley & Sons, 1996, ISBN 0471134198

Jackson, M., *Software Requirements and Specification: A Lexicon of Practice, Principles and Prejudices*. New York, NY: AMC Press Books, 1995, ISBN 0-201-87712-0

Kurata, D., *Doing Objects in Microsoft Visual Basic 5.0*. Emeryville, CA: Ziff-Davis Press, 1997, ISBN 1-56276-444-6

Larman, C., *Applying UML and Patterns: An Introduction to Object-Oriented Analysis and Design*. Upper Saddle River, NJ: Prentice Hall PTR, 1998, ISBN 0-13-748880-7

Lewis, T., *VB COM: A Visual Basic Programmer's Introduction to COM*. Olton, Birmingham, Great Britain: Wrox Press, Ltd., 1999, ISBN 1-861002-13-0

Luce, R. D., and H. Raiffa, *Games and Decisions: Introduction and Critical Survey*. New York, NY: John Wiley and Sons, Inc., 1957.

Martin, J., and J. J. Odell, *Object-Oriented Methods: A Foundation*. Englewood Cliffs, NJ: PTR Prentice Hall, 1995, ISBN 0-13-630856-2

McCarthy, J., *Dynamics of Software Development*. Redmond, WA: Microsoft Press, 1995, ISBN 1-55615-823-8

McConnell, S., *Code Complete: A Practical Handbook of Software Construction*. Redmond, WA: Microsoft Press, 1993, ISBN 1-55615-484-4

Norman, D. A., *The Design of Everyday Things*, rev. ed. Currency/Doubleday, 1990, ISBN 0-38526-774-6

Schneider, G. & Winters, J, *Applying Use Cases*. Reading, MA: Addison Wesley Longman, Inc, 1998, ISBN 0-201-30981-5

Sekula, J. M., & Sheridan, P. W., *Iterative UML Development Using Visual Basic 5.0*. Plano, TX: Wordware Publishing, Inc., 1999, ISBN 1-55622-638-1

Swartzfager, G., R. Chandak, P. Chandak, and S. Alvarez, *Visual Basic 6 Object-Oriented Programming Gold Book: Professional Skill Builder*. Albany, NY: Coriolis Technology Press, 1999, ISBN 1-57610-255-6

Venners, B., "Introduction to Design Techniques," *JavaWorld* [On-line serial], vol. & no. not available, February 1998, 10 pages. File:http//www.java-world.com./javaworld/jw-02-1998/jw-02-techniques.html

vonOech, R., *A Whack on the Side of the Head: How You Can Be More Creative*, rev. ed. New York, NY: Warner Books, Inc., 1990, ISBN0-446-39-158-1

Walther, S., *Active Server Pages Unleashed*. Sams, 1997, ISBN 1-57521-351-6

Web Snapshot CD #4, Volume One [computer software]. Redmond, WA: Microsoft Corporation, 1998.

INDEX

Keep Up-to-Date with
PH PTR Online!

We strive to stay on the cutting-edge of what's happening in professional computer science and engineering. Here's a bit of what you'll find when you stop by **www.phptr.com**:

Special interest areas offering our latest books, book series, software, features of the month, related links and other useful information to help you get the job done.

Deals, deals, deals! Come to our promotions section for the latest bargains offered to you exclusively from our retailers.

Need to find a bookstore? Chances are, there's a bookseller near you that carries a broad selection of PTR titles. Locate a Magnet bookstore near you at www.phptr.com.

What's New at PH PTR? We don't just publish books for the professional community, we're a part of it. Check out our convention schedule, join an author chat, get the latest reviews and press releases on topics of interest to you.

Subscribe Today! **Join PH PTR's monthly email newsletter!**

Want to be kept up-to-date on your area of interest? Choose a targeted category on our website, and we'll keep you informed of the latest PH PTR products, author events, reviews and conferences in your interest area.

Visit our mailroom to subscribe today! **http://www.phptr.com/mail_lists**

LICENSE AGREEMENT AND LIMITED WARRANTY

READ THE FOLLOWING TERMS AND CONDITIONS CAREFULLY BEFORE OPENING THIS CD PACKAGE. THIS LEGAL DOCUMENT IS AN AGREEMENT BETWEEN YOU AND PRENTICE-HALL, INC. (THE "COMPANY"). BY OPENING THIS SEALED CD PACKAGE, YOU ARE AGREEING TO BE BOUND BY THESE TERMS AND CONDITIONS. IF YOU DO NOT AGREE WITH THESE TERMS AND CONDITIONS, DO NOT OPEN THE CD PACKAGE. PROMPTLY RETURN THE UNOPENED CD PACKAGE AND ALL ACCOMPANYING ITEMS TO THE PLACE YOU OBTAINED THEM FOR A FULL REFUND OF ANY SUMS YOU HAVE PAID.

1.   **GRANT OF LICENSE:** In consideration of your purchase of this book, and your agreement to abide by the terms and conditions of this Agreement, the Company grants to you a nonexclusive right to use and display the copy of the enclosed software program (hereinafter the "SOFTWARE") on a single computer (i.e., with a single CPU) at a single location so long as you comply with the terms of this Agreement. The Company reserves all rights not expressly granted to you under this Agreement.

2.   **OWNERSHIP OF SOFTWARE:** You own only the magnetic or physical media (the enclosed CD) on which the SOFTWARE is recorded or fixed, but the Company and the software developers retain all the rights, title, and ownership to the SOFTWARE recorded on the original CD copy(ies) and all subsequent copies of the SOFTWARE, regardless of the form or media on which the original or other copies may exist. This license is not a sale of the original SOFTWARE or any copy to you.

3.   **COPY RESTRICTIONS:** This SOFTWARE and the accompanying printed materials and user manual (the "Documentation") are the subject of copyright. The individual programs on the CD are copyrighted by the authors of each program. Some of the programs on the CD include separate licensing agreements. If you intend to use one of these programs, you must read and follow its accompanying license agreement. You may <u>not</u> copy the Documentation or the SOFTWARE, except that you may make a single copy of the SOFTWARE for backup or archival purposes only. You may be held legally responsible for any copying or copyright infringement which is caused or encouraged by your failure to abide by the terms of this restriction.

4.   **USE RESTRICTIONS:** You may <u>not</u> network the SOFTWARE or otherwise use it on more than one computer or computer terminal at the same time. You may physically transfer the SOFTWARE from one computer to another provided that the SOFTWARE is used on only one computer at a time. You may <u>not</u> distribute copies of the SOFTWARE or Documentation to others. You may <u>not</u> reverse engineer, disassemble, decompile, modify, adapt, translate, or create derivative works based on the SOFTWARE or the Documentation without the prior written consent of the Company.

5.   **TRANSFER RESTRICTIONS:** The enclosed SOFTWARE is licensed only to you and may <u>not</u> be transferred to any one else without the prior written consent of the Company. Any unauthorized transfer of the SOFTWARE shall result in the immediate termination of this Agreement.

6.   **TERMINATION:** This license is effective until terminated. This license will terminate automatically without notice from the Company and become null and void if you fail to comply with any provisions or limitations of this license. Upon termination, you shall destroy the Documentation and all copies of the SOFTWARE. All provisions of this Agreement as to warranties, limitation of liability, remedies or damages, and our ownership rights shall survive termination.

7.   **MISCELLANEOUS:** This Agreement shall be construed in accordance with the laws of the United States of America and the State of New York and shall benefit the Company, its affiliates, and assignees.

8.   **LIMITED WARRANTY AND DISCLAIMER OF WARRANTY:** The Company warrants that the SOFTWARE, when properly used in accordance with the Documentation, will operate in substantial conformity with the description of the SOFTWARE set forth in the Documentation. The Company does not warrant that the SOFTWARE will meet your requirements or that the operation

of the SOFTWARE will be uninterrupted or error-free. The Company warrants that the media on which the SOFTWARE is delivered shall be free from defects in materials and workmanship under normal use for a period of thirty (30) days from the date of your purchase. Your only remedy and the Company's only obligation under these limited warranties is, at the Company's option, return of the warranted item for a refund of any amounts paid by you or replacement of the item. Any replacement of SOFTWARE or media under the warranties shall not extend the original warranty period. The limited warranty set forth above shall not apply to any SOFTWARE which the Company determines in good faith has been subject to misuse, neglect, improper installation, repair, alteration, or damage by you. EXCEPT FOR THE EXPRESSED WARRANTIES SET FORTH ABOVE, THE COMPANY DISCLAIMS ALL WARRANTIES, EXPRESS OR IMPLIED, INCLUDING WITHOUT LIMITATION, THE IMPLIED WARRANTIES OF MERCHANTABILITY AND FITNESS FOR A PARTICULAR PURPOSE. EXCEPT FOR THE EXPRESS WARRANTY SET FORTH ABOVE, THE COMPANY DOES NOT WARRANT, GUARANTEE, OR MAKE ANY REPRESENTATION REGARDING THE USE OR THE RESULTS OF THE USE OF THE SOFTWARE IN TERMS OF ITS CORRECTNESS, ACCURACY, RELIABILITY, CURRENTNESS, OR OTHERWISE.

IN NO EVENT, SHALL THE COMPANY OR ITS EMPLOYEES, AGENTS, SUPPLIERS, OR CONTRACTORS BE LIABLE FOR ANY INCIDENTAL, INDIRECT, SPECIAL, OR CONSEQUENTIAL DAMAGES ARISING OUT OF OR IN CONNECTION WITH THE LICENSE GRANTED UNDER THIS AGREEMENT, OR FOR LOSS OF USE, LOSS OF DATA, LOSS OF INCOME OR PROFIT, OR OTHER LOSSES, SUSTAINED AS A RESULT OF INJURY TO ANY PERSON, OR LOSS OF OR DAMAGE TO PROPERTY, OR CLAIMS OF THIRD PARTIES, EVEN IF THE COMPANY OR AN AUTHORIZED REPRESENTATIVE OF THE COMPANY HAS BEEN ADVISED OF THE POSSIBILITY OF SUCH DAMAGES. IN NO EVENT SHALL LIABILITY OF THE COMPANY FOR DAMAGES WITH RESPECT TO THE SOFTWARE EXCEED THE AMOUNTS ACTUALLY PAID BY YOU, IF ANY, FOR THE SOFTWARE.

SOME JURISDICTIONS DO NOT ALLOW THE LIMITATION OF IMPLIED WARRANTIES OR LIABILITY FOR INCIDENTAL, INDIRECT, SPECIAL, OR CONSEQUENTIAL DAMAGES, SO THE ABOVE LIMITATIONS MAY NOT ALWAYS APPLY. THE WARRANTIES IN THIS AGREEMENT GIVE YOU SPECIFIC LEGAL RIGHTS AND YOU MAY ALSO HAVE OTHER RIGHTS WHICH VARY IN ACCORDANCE WITH LOCAL LAW.

ACKNOWLEDGMENT

YOU ACKNOWLEDGE THAT YOU HAVE READ THIS AGREEMENT, UNDERSTAND IT, AND AGREE TO BE BOUND BY ITS TERMS AND CONDITIONS. YOU ALSO AGREE THAT THIS AGREEMENT IS THE COMPLETE AND EXCLUSIVE STATEMENT OF THE AGREEMENT BETWEEN YOU AND THE COMPANY AND SUPERSEDES ALL PROPOSALS OR PRIOR AGREEMENTS, ORAL, OR WRITTEN, AND ANY OTHER COMMUNICATIONS BETWEEN YOU AND THE COMPANY OR ANY REPRESENTATIVE OF THE COMPANY RELATING TO THE SUBJECT MATTER OF THIS AGREEMENT.

Should you have any questions concerning this Agreement or if you wish to contact the Company for any reason, please contact in writing at the address below.

Robin Short

Prentice Hall PTR

One Lake Street

Upper Saddle River, New Jersey 07458

About the CD

This CD contains the source code for all the examples in this book. It also contains:

- Microsoft Word 97 templates for use creation of specification documents
- 60-day trial versions of Visio Enterprise 5.0 and Visio Professional 5.0 from Visio Corporation

Please review the license terms and disclaimers in the file LICENSE.TEXT on the disk before using any of the source code.

Using the Source Code and Templates

To use the source code, copy the appropriate directories to an appropriate location on your hard disk. No installation program is provided for source code or templates.

The source code examples are all in the \Examples directory of the CD. Almost all examples are available in both Visual Basic 5 and Visual Basic 6 format. The VB5 format examples are in \Examples\VB5, and the VB6 format examples are in \Examples\VB6.

The Microsoft Word 97 templates are in the \Templates directory of the CD. They should be copied to the location on your system that Microsoft Word uses for templates (such as "C:\Program Files\Microsoft Office\Templates"). Then these templates will be available when the File New menu option is selected in Word.

A sample database used by several examples is Biblio.mdb, which comes with Visual Basic. If you need a copy of this database, it is at \Examples\Biblio.mdb.

For more information about using the examples on the CD, check the entry in the book index for "enclosed CD."

Installing Visio Trial Versions

To install Visio Enterprise, run the program \Visio\Enterprise\Setup.exe program on the CD. License terms and additional instructions will be presented by the setup program. To install Visio Professional, run the program \Visio\Professional\Setup.exe program on the CD. License terms and additional instructions will be presented by the setup program.

There is also a setup program for all included Visio software. It is \Visio\Setup.exe. However, this program will not run on all versions of Windows.

Platform Requirements

The source code examples will run on any system which runs Visual Basic 5.0 or Visual Basic 6.0. The templates will work on any system with Microsoft Word 97 installed.

The recommended requirements for the trial version of Visio Enterprise are:

- Microsoft Windows 95, Windows 98, or Windows NT 4.0
- Intel Pentium processor or greater
- 32 MB of RAM and up to 130 MB of free hard disk space for a typical application
- CD-ROM drive for installation only